A Cop's Guide to Occult Investigations

A Cop's Guide to Occult Investigations

Understanding Satanism, Santeria, Wicca, and Other Alternative Religions

Tony M. Kail

PALADIN PRESS
BOULDER, COLORADO

A Cop's Guide to Occult Investigations:
Understanding Satanism, Santeria, Wicca, and Other Alternative Religions
by Tony M. Kail

Copyright © 2003 by Tony M. Kail

ISBN 1-58160-425-4
Printed in the United States of America

Published by Paladin Press, a division of
Paladin Enterprises, Inc.
Gunbarrel Tech Center
7077 Winchester Circle
Boulder, Colorado 80301 USA
+1.303.443.7250

Direct inquiries and/or orders to the above address.

Visit our Web site at: www.paladin-press.com

ACKNOWLEDGMENTS

This book would never have been possible without the help of the following people. I sincerely apologize if I have somehow missed you:

God; Jackie, daughter of Oshun; Steve Nawojczyk; Jack Roper; Choya; Mary Jo Schneller; Greg Reid; Detective Chuck Goode, Edmond Oklahoma Police Department; Lt. John Lambert, Jackson Tennessee Police Department; Alan Peterson; Jeff Fox; Tony Smith, Los Angeles Probation; Agent Todd Adams, Federal Bureau of Investigation; Captain Andy Garrett, Nashville Metro Police Department

Jasmine and Botanica Yemaya/Chango; Captain John Craig, Madison County Sheriff's Department; Greycat; John Gonce; Luanne McNab; Lisa the social worker; Cindy Medlin, Madison County Juvenile Department; Agent Steve Paris, Bureau of Alcohol, Tobacco, and Firearms (BATF); Steve Wortham, BATF; Tennessee Gang Investigator's Association; Daystar; High Priestess Christy; Greg; Paul Myers at Nashville State Technical College; Militia Watchdog

Rafael Martinez, cultural anthropologist; Detective Jeff Fitzgerald, Madison County Sheriff's Department; Sheriff David Woolfork; Gayland Hurst; Lady Weaver; Circle Ravenfain; Tish and Goddess and the Moon; Ebbo Spiritual Goods; Lady Emmachia; Brock with Coven Tangled Moon; Dr. Milliard Bass, forensic specialist; Velvet the Swampwitch; Maria from Brazil; Johnny and Egil; Clan Elder Rune; Steve Hassan

Nuri, daughter of Yemaya; Reverend Robert; Leon and Brenda; Ann Williams, Exchange Club Child Abuse Center; Trey Hooper (the one who started it and has no idea!); Rhonda and Ben; Ginny Fouts; Curt Voiles, New Mexico Department of Safety; Kerri and Our Lady of the Streets (much respect for you and those that reach out to the streets!); the deacon and witch that laughed; Summerland Grove; SPIRAL

M.R. Sellars and Rowan; Stephanie in Oklahoma; Tata Doc; Lydia Cabrera; Fernando Ortiz; Tommy and Needful Things; Carter Smith; Marcos Quinones, New York Police Department; Dawn Perlmutter, Institute for Study of Ritual Violence; Lt. Curtis Baxter, Humboldt Police Department; John and Jaquie Devries (thank you for taking time and opening my mind to new worldviews; Barry Watt; Denise Tordoff.

To my wife, friends, and family: Thank you for your patience and support.

This book is dedicated to
those victims of abusive religious groups
who have suffered while sincerely seeking a spiritual path.

TABLE OF CONTENTS

PREFACE

So it is said that if you know others and know yourself,
You will not be imperiled in a hundred battles;
If you do not know others but know yourself,
You win one and lose one;
If you do not know others and do not know yourself,
You will be imperiled in every single battle.
—Sun Tzu, *The Art of War*

This manual offers an analysis of occult religions in America. The aim is not to judge the validity of any of the religions presented here but to provide a cultural understanding of the vast array of religious faiths that officers may encounter in hopes of ensuring the safety of the officer and protecting the officer and the department from any liability.

Some readers may be uncomfortable reading about the beliefs and practices of these religions; many assume that any nontraditional group or subculture is involved in criminal or malevolent activities. Data, however, suggest that the majority of initiates into these religions observe and obey the laws and regulations of the land.

In researching these belief systems, I have found that it is typically the deviants in our society who misuse religion for their own selfish purposes. For this reason, one should not judge any religion by its adherents. In order for readers to form an unbiased opinion of these groups, the religions discussed in this text will be approached from a criminological, anthropological, and sociological viewpoint.

Officers may question why they should even give time and energy to reading about such groups.

In light of the heavy caseload that today's officer faces, why should such focus on nontraditional groups be taken? The truth is that if officers can attain a working knowledge of the dynamics of these groups and their activities, they will be better prepared to deal with cases involving these groups. Demystifying these obscure movements can assist officers in moving on to criminal-related matters as opposed to spending time trying to decipher the numerous conspiratorial schools of thought that have been accepted as the standard by many of today's professionals.

There are a number of reasons that members of law enforcement need to examine this subject:

1. Knowing how to effectively communicate with people involved in the occult will assist the officer in taking reports and questioning suspects, as well as help the officer avoid possible hostile situations with followers of these paths. Law enforcement professionals must accept that nontraditional approaches to religion, medicine, and philosophy are becoming part of Western society. This embracing of the nontraditional includes many Americans becoming involved in so-called occult religions. Because of this popularity, officers will continue to see bizarre altars and shrines, some of them containing contraband, when answering calls.

2. The flow of legal and illegal immigrants into the United States has brought many alien religions, practices, and rituals with it. Many of these religions practice animal sacrifice. Law enforcement officers must be educated on the practices of these groups as well as understanding the constitutional rights that protect many of these followers.

3. Many occult groups that are aligning themselves with racist and extremist groups encourage hatred and even violence against government authority, which is usually represented by law enforcement officials. Officers' safety depends on knowing the practices of all segments of society.

Religious scholar Houston Smith once noted that a fellow scholar was pondering how followers of a certain Egyptian religion could use a cow to represent their "god." The scholar just couldn't understand how something as mundane as a cow could be elevated in such a way. Smith's response was, "Well, it meant something to those people."

As you begin to enter the world of magico-religious belief systems, you may ask yourself the same question: "How in the world could someone believe in that?" The same conclusion that Houston Smith arrived at applies here. It means something to someone.

Author's note: This guide was written from an outsider's perspective. I did not participate in any of the activities or join any of these groups; I relied only on observation and what informants chose to share.

When reading this text, please keep in mind that cultural interpretations may differ according to the individual church, lodge, coven, house, or temple. The information obtained during this study was limited to a small cross-section of religious culture. Officers may find that the beliefs, symbols, and meanings they encounter differ from group to group.

Some of the photographs in this book are grainy or slightly out of focus. The photos were taken over the years during actual ceremonies and investigations and therefore could not be recreated.

INTRODUCTION

For this science, said the crowd,
there is nothing impossible,
it commands the elements,
knows the language of the stars,
when it speaks the moon falls blood red from heaven,
the dead rise in their graves and utter ominous words.
—Eliphas Levi, 1865
Transcendental Magic

THE OCCULT

T he word occult is defined by most dictionaries with the words "secretive" or "hidden." The term has become a label for phenomena that society considers paranormal or mysterious; everything from ESP to ghost sightings is attributed to an alternative spiritual realm. This manual is not meant to be a litmus test to determine the reality of the occult realm, or to be a scientific examination of it. It is meant to be a guide to help officers understand the concepts and philosophies of the occult and the groups that follow it.

A typical occult group uses the concept of "magick," even if they do not use the term. The concept of impersonal or personal energy that can be manipulated to produce tangible results is called by many

Top: Example of a "working" found in a cemetery in Miami. The bones represent the intended target of the spell.

Bottom: Candles may be used in homeopathic magick spells. The candles can represent the target of the intended spell.

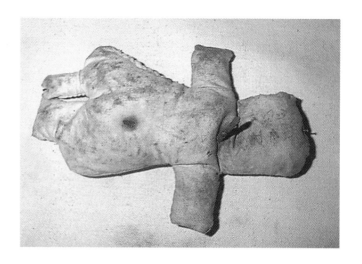

This doll was found nailed to a ceiba tree. The ceiba is an important tree in the working of Afro-Caribbean magick. The name of the victim was written on the back of the doll.

names: the Voudon religions may call it *ache*, while the neo-Pagan religions may call it "earth energies." However, its purpose is that of magick, which is the glue that binds these belief systems. (The spelling "magick," as opposed to "magic," is used to differentiate between stage illusions performed by theater magicians and a real change in the environment.)

Magick can be obtained from deities, natural sources, or even from within. It is typically seen as an impersonal force that can be used for positive or negative purposes. Some groups classify magick by color to show its intent: white magick is used to heal sickness, grow crops, and create love; red or gray magick is used to heal or kill, with its course relying totally on the person invoking it; black magick is destructive, selfish, and can harm others. Most occult scholars do not subscribe to an intent-based explanation of magick but simply view it as a neutral concept.

Occult historians categorize magick as one of two types, thaumaturgy or theurgy. Thaumaturgy, also called lower magick, is the use of magick to influence everyday events, such as those involving love, work, and family. Theurgy is the use of magick to connect with a deity or spiritual being.

SPELLS

A spell, or a "working," is a ritual that sends magick out to perform a specific function. Many use the concept of sympathetic magick in their ceremonies; this is described by some occult historians in a philosophy that embraces the concept of, "As is above, so is below." This translates to "whatever you do in the physical realm will happen in the spiritual realm." One

anthropologist calls this belief the Law of Similarity; it is also called homeopathic magick. In popular media, this magick is seen in the form of the voodoo doll, where the physical pushing of a pin into a doll causes the spiritual pain to manifest itself in the intended victim. An occultist may perform any type of ritual to affect the spiritual realm.

In the course of investigating an occult-related criminal group or act, officers might find dolls, candles, drawings, or other artifacts that may resemble an intended victim. These items are used to make the spiritual world act on the physical realm.

The use of someone's hair, clothing, fingernails, or personal possessions in a spell to affect that person is called contagious magick. It is believed that any object that has been in contact with another object will always be in contact.

WHAT IS A CEREMONY?

A ceremony is a religious performance that is used to honor or call upon the spiritual realm. Ceremonies many times include an invocation, which is a "calling out" to deities or spirits. They often require the use of ritual tools and implements that are considered sacred and have the ability to affect the spiritual world. Ceremonies may have restrictions on who performs them, when they are performed, and exactly how to perform them. Some traditional religious ceremonies require such taboo subjects as blood, sex, and animal sacrifice.

It is human nature to have different interpretations of religious philosophies and beliefs; this presents an investigating officer with the job of deciding what is considered normative and what is considered deviant in a group's or individual's action related to a religious practice. The investigating officer may be faced with an act that seems totally illogical but is very logical and symbolic to followers.

An example of this was found in a criminal case involving a suspect who was accused of murder. Several leads in the case suggested that the suspect might be involved in a very malevolent black-magick group, and the criminal act itself could have been a part of his involvement with this group. When the suspect was apprehended, he claimed to officers that he was not in a black-magick group but was involved in white magick with a neo-Pagan group.

When investigators looked into the neo-Pagan community to find evidence of the crime and any possible accomplices, they discovered that elements of the crime scene, as well as some ritualistic tools and literature found on the suspect, were inconsistent with the beliefs and trappings of a normative neo-Pagan group. Having this information ahead of time could have saved the investigators time and resources as they looked into the wrong end of the religious community.

A situation like this can create other problems. Many noncriminal occult groups have faced persecution for what others have committed in the name of occult religions. This creates an environment in which officers can find themselves possibly in violation of civil rights.

There have also been cases in which an occult group that follows normative practices in rituals and activities has been involved in unrelated criminal activities. In these cases, it is important that the religion and the crime be kept separate. The religion should be brought into the investigation only if there is credible evidence that it is related to the criminal act.

It is important that officers know the difference between normative and deviant practices exercised by these groups.

NORMATIVE PRACTICES

Normative practices by an occult group can be assessed through the following:

1. An examination of historical documentation of the group's origins, activities, and practices
2. Interviews with practitioners and ex-practitioners
3. Analysis of the group's literature and sacred texts
4. Observation of normative rituals and ceremonies
5. Analysis of group activity from law enforcement reports, media reports, and opposing viewpoints

To gain a well-rounded perspective, it is important that all of these channels of research are pursued. Unless proper research has been done, it is easy to develop a viewpoint that is either sympathetic or contrary to the group.

Most practitioners of these religions do not use their religions for criminal means; they are sincere believers who hold their deities, ceremonies, and ritual implements sacred. This manual is designed to give officers a working knowledge of the more popular occult-based belief systems that are in practice in the United States, and the criminal acts committed by those that use these belief systems for selfish means.

WHAT IS OCCULT CRIME?

The concept of occult crime is very controversial. A research study by the State of California Office of Criminal Justice Planning found that "scholars continue to scramble for an acceptable definition of this phenomena." One publication concluded that "the real problem is that everyone has a valid perspective, but the valid perspectives are all too often based on fears, emotion, spiritual beliefs and hearsay."[1]

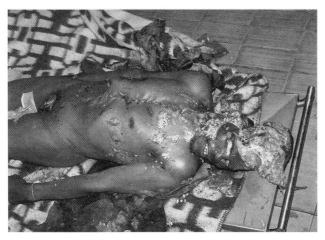

The victim of an African ritual homicide. Sections of the victim's body were taken as implements to be used in ceremonies.

Cruelty to animals may result from juveniles who become involved in self-styled occultism. Criminal acts may be required by the group for a new member to gain membership.

Skeptics say there is no agreed upon definition of occult crime. One text criticizes focusing on occult religions and states, "The fact is that far more crime and child abuse has been committed by zealots in the name of God, Jesus and Mohammed than has ever been committed in the name of Satan."[2]

Another viewpoint teaches that an occult crime is "any criminal activity that is part of a religious practice, is inspired by a person's religious beliefs, or is committed under the color of religion."[3]

The problem with these approaches is that they focus on a particular religion. The truth is that crime can be committed within any religious framework. However, this text will focus on those acts that are committed using or misusing a magico-religious (occult) belief system.

Members of deviant occult religions commit crimes for any number of reasons. One of the reasons is for recruitment or initiation purposes. This is seen mostly in juvenile occult groups, where the leadership will require new members to commit crimes such as grave robbing, vandalism, or animal cruelty to attain membership.

Another criminal act may be in the form of domestic terrorism to bring attention to the group's philosophies and goals. Charles Manson and his Family committed the infamous Tate-

LaBianca murders in order to start Helter Skelter, their name for an all-out race war.

Crimes may also be committed in hopes of appeasing the group's deity. Some homicides have been attributed to sacrificing to a deity; however, the most popular form of this crime is animal sacrifice. (Some states have provisions for animal sacrifice for religious purposes.)

In 2003 a self-described Satanist in Woodbridge, Virginia, was sentenced to 48 years in prison after pleading guilty to four counts of raping a young girl over the course of two years, beginning when she was 10 years old. Russell John Smith claimed that most of the sex acts were part of his Satanic rituals, according to a story by the Associated Press.

Criminal acts may also be committed by an occult group to finance their activities. Most noncriminal occult groups publish newsletters, perform magickal services, and sell ritual implements to finance group activities. Criminal occult organizations have been found participating in narcotics distribution, trafficking in human remains, prostitution, and other illegal activities to fund group activities.

ORGANIZED CRIME AND OCCULT GROUPS

Law enforcement officials have reported find-

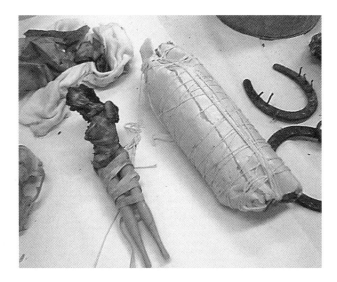

An example of a malevolent working against a subject. The doll is bound physically with electrical tape in the hope that the actual subject will be magickally bound.

ing criminal groups forming relationships with occult groups. These relationships can empower criminals. Agents with the Drug Enforcement Administration (DEA) in Florida have found several relationships between drug dealers and Afro-Caribbean religious groups. A dealer using the trappings of Santeria can certainly influence members of the Cuban community, where this religion is seen as a powerful and effective force.

Criminals can use the trappings and beliefs of occult religions to play on people's superstitions. I personally assisted in a case involving a small-time drug dealer who, because of his apparent ties to a Satanist group, was feared by other dealers on the streets.

An occult group may be used as a distribution point for criminal groups. In 1993, Bureau of Alcohol, Tobacco, and Firearms (BATF) agent Julie Torres infiltrated a Santeria group that was selling illegal firearms for a criminal operation.

A drug dealer may find a group of regular buyers in an occult group that uses drugs as a means to contact the spiritual realm.

An occult group may provide services for a criminal group. Voudon groups in Miami, Dallas, and Washington have reportedly been providing rituals designed to protect shipments of narcotics.

Some agencies have reported finding ritual implements in drug labs to give magickal protec-

tion from law enforcement. The drug dealers behind the 1989 Matamoros murders in Mexico, who used Voudon religions as protection from the law, were busted when one of them drove through a roadblock, believing himself to be invisible to authorities.

Some criminal organizations may use occult beliefs and traditions to structure an otherwise unstructured criminal enterprise. The addition of religious beliefs not only binds criminals to personal faith and faithfulness to the group but also creates an open door for manipulation by group leadership. To many in the occult world, magickal retribution and punishment is far worse than physical torture and death. This belief can be exploited by those criminals who have a working knowledge of the occult.

LAW ENFORCEMENT AND THE OCCULT

There are many reasons for an officer to develop a working knowledge of occult religions. One is to help steer an investigation in the right direction.

Let's say that officers working a crime scene in an area with a Santeria community discover a sacrifice site. By examining the artifacts at the scene, they are able to determine that their suspect is a devotee of the *orisha* (deity) Chango. If officers know what Chango calls for in his offerings, they might learn more about the subject. Officers who wanted to stake out this suspect might be able to predict his whereabouts by knowing that followers of Chango attend special rites on December 4. They will also know that the suspect is probably wearing an *eleke* (necklace) of red and white beads in patterns of six.

It is also comforting for officers to be able to make sense of the sometimes bizarre practices of occult religions. Knowing that the goat carcass found in a local cemetery is merely an offering to win the favor of a god can save a police department time and effort that might have been wasted hunting for a violent animal killer.

Finally, an officer who displays a knowledge and acceptance of a practitioner's belief system may meet with more cooperation than an officer who either knows nothing or shows uneasiness or contempt. This can lead to developing sources within the community that may be able to assist in future investigations.

ENDNOTES

1. "Occult Crime: A Law Enforcement Primer." *California Office of Criminal Justice Planning: Research Update*, *State of California*, Vol. 1 (6), Winter 1989–1990.

2. Kenneth V. Lanning, "Satanic, Occult, Ritualistic Crime: A Law Enforcement Perspective." *The Police Chief*, October 1989.

3. William Edward Lee Dubois, *Occult Crime: Detection, Investigation, and Verification* (San Miguel Press, 1992).

WICCA

We are an old people, we are a new people,
We are the same people, stronger than before.
—Pagan hymn

Sheriff's deputies receive a call from a man regarding a group of alleged Satanists. The caller states that his "weird" neighbors are holding strange ceremonies behind his home that include animal sacrifice, drumming, and possible abuse of children.

Local authorities and a state police officer who happens to be in the area respond. As the squad cars pull up to the scene, officers see several men, women, and children dressed in robes. Forming a circle, the ominous-looking group stands in front of a bonfire. A table that appears to be set up as an altar sits at the north end of the circle. In one motion, all officers open their doors and draw down on the group. "Everyone freeze!" one deputy yells. The people in the robed group stop their movement.

Top: Officers may be called to the scene of a ritual in progress. While the initial trappings of a Wiccan ceremony may appear malevolent in nature to the outsider, the rituals of true Wiccans do not include any kind of criminal activity.

Bottom: Officers may respond to calls involving loud drumming, singing, or chanting. These elements are used to raise spiritual energy known as the cone of power. This power is used as a catalyst for the intended working.

An officer calls out, "Who is the leader here?"

A woman dressed in a green robe steps forward and lowers her hood. "Sir, this is my property. What's the problem?"

The supervising officer speaks up: "We had a call that there were animals being killed here and that someone was harming children." As he speaks, he steps toward the group. The state officer walks into the group and looks at the altar. He looks at a blade lying on the altar and looks up at the robed man behind it. "What are you doing out here?" the officer asks.

"We are Wiccans. This is our seasonal celebration," the man replies. The state officer examines the altar and the ritual area, then returns to the group of deputies. "Guys, it looks to me that these people are not doing anything outside of drumming too loudly. I've had training on these groups—they are legal in what they are doing. They are not into criminal activity. They don't kill animals." Being the only one in the group who shows any kind of knowledge applicable to the bizarre scene, the other officers nod and back down.

The local sheriff arrives on the scene. "Just what is going on out here?" he cries out. The state officer pulls him to the side. "These people are strange, but they are practicing their religion. They aren't breaking the law. I told them to quiet down. They're on their private property."

The sheriff looks at the group and makes an expression of disgust. "Just what are you people doing out here? With your children watching you? Have you got no decency?"

The landowner steps forth. "Sir, this is our church. Don't you take your kids to church?" The sheriff looks at the woman and remarks, "This ain't no church, and this ain't no religion. And you ain't gonna practice it in my damn county!"

Unfortunately, this true encounter ended with a group of lawyers being called on the department to seek restitution for harassment against religious practices. Was the sheriff right in his assumption that because this was not his religion of preference, it shouldn't be practiced? What would be the best way to handle this situation? This chapter explains just what the religion of Wicca is and how to respond to practitioners in a professional manner.

WITCHCRAFT IN AMERICA

The smell of burning incense hangs in the air, and the flickering of candles catches my eye. A tall, robed figure with a long, gray beard holds open his arms and beckons to the group of onlookers: "We welcome everyone here to the celebration of Beltane. I invite anyone who would like to join our circle to come forth." Several men and women dressed in robes of various colors stand and join their hands to form a circle around the bearded priest. The priest picks up a gold-colored lamp and walks around the circle, spreading the scent of sandalwood and jasmine.

The group begins to sing a melodious chant: "We all come from the Goddess, and to her we shall return. Like a drop of rain, flowing to the ocean." They begin to walk clockwise. As the singing and walking speeds up, the priest slams his large wooden staff to the floor. The crack of the wood against the hard floor silences the crowd. An eerie feeling of energy flows across my face as the doors to the spiritual realm begin to open. The priest's voice changes to an authoritative call to the gods. "Cernunnos, Pan, Herne, Horned One, manifest, make yourself known. Join us in this circle."

This elaborate ritual took place in a secluded area of a state park and lasted for more than an hour. The participants in this religious rite were from different locations all over the southern United States. They had gathered to practice a religion known by many simply as "the Old Ways," the religion of Wicca.

The term "witchcraft" has many negative images associated with it. Hollywood has influenced American culture to view witchcraft as being filled with secret pacts with the devil, black cats, and evil curses. However, modern-day witchcraft has nothing to do with Satan or the devil. Practitioners generally shun anything having to do with the devil or negative spells.

PAGANISM

The term Pagan has many different definitions. Those who were not part of a traditional church were once considered Pagan, which made them social outcasts. In regard to magickal religions, the term Pagan comes from the word *pagani*, which means "country dwellers," since in the early days of Christianity the conservative rural inhabitants continued to follow the ancient religions. (Along the same lines, a "heathen" was "one who lives on the heath.")

The early practitioners of Paganism believed in spirits of nature and in magick. Magick was simply the ability to harness the power of nature and channel it into something productive. Like electricity, the energies of the elements could be used to heal, control weather, and make crops grow. Early Pagans also believed that animals, humans, and plants were all connected to each other. These beliefs, combined with the behaviors of hunter-gatherer cultures, became the basis for Paganism.

Practitioners of this belief system were driven underground during the Catholic Inquisition. Followers were bound to secrecy about their allegiance to the gods and goddesses of nature for fear of being tortured and killed. This chapter will focus on Wicca, but there are several other Pagan religions, including Druidism and neo-Shamanism.

Druidism

Followers of religions based on one of the Celtic pantheons generally call themselves Druids and their religion Druidism. There are a number of groups in the United States, including ADF (Ar n' Draioght Fein) and Keltria.

Neo-Shamanism

This form of shamanism may recognize a large number of pantheons including many held by American Indians. Shamanism is marked by its ecstatic qualities of drumming, dancing, and trance. Drug use in rituals is not common but cannot be completely ruled out. Shamanism denotes a methodology and isn't itself a religious belief.

WICCA

Many years later, a new generation began to pick up on the ancient tenets of Paganism and earth religions. The term *neo-Paganism* became used to describe those who chose to recreate and revive the old ways. The religion of Wicca was born out of this movement.

Wicca is taken from an Old English word that means "wise one." The central focus of Wicca is worship of the Goddess and the Horned God. The religion focuses on the use of magick, the change of the seasons, and healing.

The Goddess

The primary deity of Wicca is the Goddess. The Goddess is seen by most Wiccans as a literal spiritual being, though some groups believe that the Goddess is merely a symbol of the female element in nature. The Goddess has been represented by a number of female deities in many different world cultures. In Egypt she was known as Isis, in Greek culture she was known as Diana, and she is seen in many different forms throughout the religions of the world.

Modern concepts about the Goddess typically teach that she has three aspects, or stages of life, which correspond to the changing phases of the moon. (The Goddess herself is often represented by the moon.) Her phases of life are seen in the forms of maiden, mother, and crone. The maiden is the young innocent girl in waiting; the mother is a pregnant, nurturing woman; the crone is an old, wise woman who is a respected elder in society. The Goddess is sometimes portrayed in ritual dramas and is even manifested in the high priestess in a ritual called "Drawing Down the Moon."

The Horned God

The Horned God is typically symbolic of the "lord of the hunt." In early Pagan cultures, men would draw images and dress in a fashion that would call upon spirits of the hunt before hunting for food for their village. The Horned God is representative of the male element, denoted by the horns. The horns *do not represent Satan.* Many historians believe we get the image of a horned "devil" from this early Pagan image. The Horned God has been represented in many different world cultures as Pan, Cernunnos, Herne, and several other male deities. The Horned God can also be called upon, prayed to, and can be manifested in rituals in which he is called.

History of Wicca

In the 1920s an archaeologist named Margaret Murray created a stir by publishing *The Witch Cult in Western Europe* and *The God of the Witches.* Her writings spoke of an ancient European religion that was part of a surviving lineage of folk magicians. Years later, much of her research was disputed by historians and anthropologists.

In 1951 the English Witchcraft Act of 1735 was replaced with the Fraudulent Mediums Act. This opened the door for the public and legal practice of witchcraft. In 1949 an Englishman named Gerald Gardner published a book called

High Magic's Aid. This book of fiction encouraged many to pursue the ways of witchcraft. Gardner also wrote *Witchcraft Today* (1954), which became an instant classic. Gardner was the creator of what is known today as Gardnerian Wicca. It is his interpretation of a religion he claims to have discovered in active practice in England.

Gardner was initiated by an English witch named Old Dorothy Clutterbuck. It was her teachings that became the basis for Gardnerian Wicca.

Her teachings were passed on to him through the *Book of Shadows.* This book of spells and ceremonies was supposed to have been passed down and added to through several generations of witches. From this branch there are several traditions that have splintered from its original form. Gardnerian Wicca (also known as British Traditional Wicca) is probably the most practiced form of Wicca in the United States.

The debate over the origins of the Wiccan religion continues as many scholars seek to find if the religion is an ancient practice that has been revived or if it is a new invention. Some scholars believe that it has secretly survived underground and has emerged into a newer, open-minded society.

Traditions

There are several traditions or interpretations of Wicca. The following are some of the more popular forms of Wicca found in North America.

- **Alexandrian Wicca**—This tradition was founded by Alex Sanders, whom the press called the "King of the Witches." Rituals in Alexandrian Wicca are very complicated and bear a similarity to what is known as ceremonial magick (also known as ritual magick), which uses Judeo-Christian symbols and terms for the purpose of summoning angels, demons, and spirits.
- **Blue Star Wicca**—This tradition came out of Philadelphia, Pennsylvania. In 1975 a group was formed called "Coven of the Blue Star." The tradition

was started by a peace activist who was very instrumental in the Vietnam Veterans against the War. The focus is on worship of Pagan deities instead of active spellwork. There is an initiation tattooing as well as standard worship songs and group officers. There are three stages of initiation: dedicant, neophyte, and elder.

- **Dianic Wicca**—This tradition is popular in the lesbian and feminist communities. Its focus is on women's issues and the power of the Goddess found in women.
- **Eclectic Wicca**—This is a path that is open to many faiths. Followers take deities, rituals, and philosophies from different religious traditions. The practitioner is not bound to a particular dogma or rule.
- **Frost's School of Wicca**—This branch of Wicca is studied primarily through correspondence courses. The creators of this course are Gavin and Yvonne Frost, the authors of *The Witch's Magical Handbook*. Many in the Wiccan community feel that the Frosts cater to a "get rich quick through witchcraft" crowd.
- **Gardnerian Wicca**—Gerald Gardner was an English occultist who asserted his branch of witchcraft came from an ancient lineage of European witches. Gardnerian Wicca is usually denoted by ritual nudity, called being "skyclad." There is a three-degree system of initiation.
- **Georgian Wicca**—This tradition was started in Bakersfield, California, in 1971 by George Patterson. The tradition takes elements from Gardnerian and Alexandrian traditions and from the texts of Edward Fitch's *Grimoire of the Shadows*. Membership in Georgian Wicca is very obscure.
- **Hereditary Wicca**—Many American witches have traced their lineage back to generational witches. Spells and rituals have been passed down to them orally and through texts. While a Wiccan may belong to a "fam trad"

(family tradition), they may belong to a current tradition to identify with other believers.

- **Mohsian Tradition**—Started in the 1960s as "Eclectic American Tradition." Draws inspiration from Gardnerian Wicca, European shamanism, and Celtic influences. Public groups are active in Arizona and California.
- **Strega Tradition**—Italian witchcraft, known as Strega, has traditionally been followed by generational practitioners. However, there has been a new interest in the subject by those Americans unaffiliated with any kind of Italian tradition. Strega is concerned with the legend surrounding the witchcraft classic, *Aradia: Gospel of the Witches*, which teaches that the Goddess Diana and her consort Lucifer are deities to be revered.

WICCAN BELIEFS

Since there is no solitary source of dogma or theology for Wiccans, principles of belief can be analyzed from a few of the major texts that are considered guidelines for principles of Wiccan belief.

One of the first sources that will give outsiders an insight into the beliefs and rituals of Wicca is the complete Wiccan Rede. The word *rede* is Anglo-Saxon for "wise counsel." The rede is usually read in its shortened form. The basic philosophy of "An ye harm none, do what thou wilt" is usually quoted as the Wiccan golden rule. The complete rede gives instruction as to how to conduct rituals. The following is one version of the rede in its entire form:

The Wiccan Rede
Bide the Wiccan Laws we must,
In Perfect Love and perfect Trust
Live and Let Live,
Fairly take and fairly give,
Cast the circle thrice about,
To keep the evil spirits out
To bind the spell every time
Let the spell be spake in rhyme

Soft of eye and light of touch
Speak little, listen much
Deosil go by the waxing moon
Chanting out the Witches' rune
Widdershins go by the waning moon
Chanting out the baneful tune
When the Lady's moon is new
Kiss the hand to her, times two
When the moon tides at her peak
Then your hearts desire seek
Heed the North wind's mighty gale
Lock the door, and drop the sail
When the wind comes from the South
Love will kiss thee on the Mouth,
When wind blows from the west
Departed souls will have no rest
When the wind blows from the east
Expect the new and set the feast
Nine woods in the cauldron go
Burn them fast and burn them slow
Elder be the Lady's tree
Burn it not or cursed you'll be
When the wheel begins to turn
Then the Beltane fires burn.
When the Wheel has turned to Yule,
Light the log and the Horned One rules,
Heed ye flower, Bush and Tree,
By the Lady, blessed Be
Where the rippling waters go,
Cast a stone and truth you'll know
When ye have a true need
Hearken not to other greed
With a fool no seasons spend,
Lest ye be counted as his friend
Merry meet and merry part,
Bright the cheeks and warm the heart
Mind the threefold law you should
Three times bad and three times good
When misfortune is enow
Wear the blue star on thy brow
True in Love ever be,
Lest thy lovers false to thee
Eight Words the Wicca Rede fulfill:
An ye Harm None, Do What Ye will.

The Charge of the Goddess
The Charge of the Goddess is a text that was given to folk writer Charles Leland by a *strega*, an Italian witch. It is printed in *Aradia: Gospel of the Witches*. The content of the Charge gives several recommendations for worship and ritual surrounding the Goddess:

> Listen to the words of the Great Mother; she who of old was also called among men Artemis, Astarte, Athene, Dione, Melusine, Aphrodite, Cerridwen, Dana, Arianrhod, Isis, Bride, and by many other names.
>
> Whenever ye have need of anything, once in the month, and better it be when the moon is full, then shall ye assemble in some secret place and adore the spirit of me, who am Queen of all witches. There shall ye assemble, ye who are fain to learn all sorcery, yet have not won its deepest secrets; to these will I teach things that are yet unknown. And ye shall be free from slavery; and as a sign that ye be free, ye shall be naked in your rites; and ye shall dance, sing, feast, make music and love, all in my praise. For mine is the ecstasy of the spirit, and mine also is joy on earth; for my law is love unto all beings. Keep pure your highest ideal; strive ever towards it; let naught stop you or turn you aside. For mine is the secret door that opens the door of Youth, and mine is the cup of the wine of life, and the Cauldron of Cerridwen, which is the holy grail of immortality. I am the gracious Goddess, who gives the heart of joy unto the heart of man. Upon earth, I give the knowledge of the spirit eternal; and beyond death, I give peace and freedom, and reunion with those who have gone before. Nor do I demand sacrifice; for behold, I am the Mother of all living, and my love is poured out upon the earth.

Principles of Wiccan Belief
Another document that many modern-day Wiccans draw from is a paper entitled *Principles of Wiccan Belief,* which was adopted in 1974 by the Council of American Witches. It is used in

establishing many current circles and covens throughout the United States. The principles are as follows:

We practice rites to attune ourselves with the natural rhythm of life forces marked by the phases of the Moon and the seasonal Quarters and Cross-Quarters.

We recognize that our intelligence gives us a unique responsibility toward our environment. We seek to live in harmony with Nature, in ecological balance, offering fulfillment to life and consciousness within an evolutionary concept.

We acknowledge a depth of power far greater than is apparent to the average person. Because it is far greater than ordinary, it is sometimes called "supernatural," but we see it as lying within that which is naturally potential to us all.

We conceive of the Creative Power in the Universe as manifesting through polarity—as masculine and feminine—and that this same Creative Power lives in all people and functions through the interaction of the masculine and feminine. We value neither above the other, knowing each to be supportive of the other. We value sexuality as pleasure, as the symbol and embodiment of Life, and as one of the sources of energies used in magickal practice and religious worship.

We recognize both outer and inner or psychological worlds—sometimes known as the Spiritual World, The Collective Unconscious, The Inner Planes, etc.—and we see in their interaction of these two dimensions the basis for paranormal phenomena and magickal exercises. We neglect neither dimension for the other, seeing both as necessary for our fulfillment.

We do not recognize any authoritarian hierarchy, but do honor those who teach, respect those who share their greater knowledge and wisdom, and acknowledge those who have courageously given of themselves in leadership.

We see religion, magick and wisdom-in-living as being united in the way one views the world and lives within it—a world-view and philosophy-of-life which we identify as Witchcraft, the Wiccan Way.

Calling oneself "Witch" does not make a Witch, but neither does heredity itself, or the collecting of titles, degrees and initiations. A Witch seeks to control the forces within him/herself that make life possible in order to live wisely and well, without harm to others and in harmony with Nature.

We acknowledge that it is the affirmation and fulfillment of life in a continuance of evolution and development of consciousness that gives meaning to the Universe we know and to our personal role within it.

Our only animosity toward Christianity or toward any other religion or philosophy-of-life is to the extent that its institutions have claimed to be "the one true, right and only way" and have sought to deny freedom to others, and to suppress other ways of religious practices and belief.

As American Witches, we are not threatened by debates on the history of the Craft, the origins of various terms, the legitimacy of various aspects of various traditions. We are concerned only with our present and our future.

We do not accept the concept of "absolute evil" nor do we worship any entity known as Satan or the Devil, as defined by the Christian tradition. We do not seek power through the suffering of others, nor do we accept the concept that personal benefits can only be derived through denial to another.

We seek within Nature for that which is contributory to our health and well-being.

Several other documents are sources for rituals and ideologies surrounding modern-day

A coven is traditionally led by the high priest and high priestess. Officers encountering Wiccan rituals should address the leadership of the group for effective communication and assessment of the situation.

The high priest consecrates the ritual area.

A high priestess stirs the fire of the cauldron. The cauldron has a deep philosophical meaning in neo-Pagan religions—it represents the cauldron of rebirth and can also represent the Goddess.

Wicca. Many of these writings are kept in secret, such as the *Gardnerian Book of Shadows*.

GROUP STRUCTURE

The traditional group of Wiccans is known as a coven; alternate names such as circle, grove, or order may be used. The traditional leader of the coven is the high priestess. Because the female gender is held in a higher regard, the female clergy is considered to be more powerful. The priestess may have been initiated, or she may be self-appointed into the position. A respected priestess will have an enormous amount of training and knowledge under her belt in order to be bestowed with the title. She is in charge of most rituals and is the leader, teacher, and guide to the coven. If a member of law enforcement has questions about the operations of a coven, the high priestess is usually the spokesperson for the group. The male leadership of a coven is usually the high priest. He is seen as the earthly representative of the Horned God and leads rituals as well. He may also act as spokesperson for the coven. Some traditions alternate male and female leadership with the male taking over during the time of year the Horned God reigns in the religious mythology.

Covens may have several other offices. Some have officers that are craft makers for the group and some have members who act as summoners and carry out spiritual tasks for the group. Selected members may keep up with funds as a treasurer. A person responsible for communications outside the group may be called a tyler, or a "man in black."

Some groups have security personnel known as watchers. These are not to be confused with watchtowers, the spiritual beings that guard the directions. Watchers will be spiritually and physically prepared to watch and protect the ritual area. Some may carry radios, mace, and even firearms. Officers encountering watchers should be cautious about the presence of weapons and should always call for backup. Most watchers are very open and will not pose a threat to law enforcement; however, officers should never become lax in *any* setting while on patrol. It is advisable that your agency maintains a liaison with watchers and private security groups in order to avoid confrontations and to maintain an open line of communication. As well, it is a good idea for law enforcement to be notified when groups will be meeting in a public location or at a place that may generate calls by concerned citizens who see something unusual. This will cut down on wasting officers' time checking out harmless gatherings.

Police officers should also become familiar with the event and be able to protect the area from those who would seek to harm the practi-

The Wiccan altar. There are elements found on the altar that represent the God and the Goddess, the elements of nature, and ceremonial artifacts.

The artifacts on the Wiccan altar are considered sacred by practitioners. Officers should refrain from touching altar items unless they are needed as criminal evidence or for safety issues. Near the back and left of this altar is a statue of the Goddess.

tioners. Some neo-Pagan groups have been hesitant to initiate a relationship with law enforcement for fear of being misunderstood.

ALTARS AND RITUAL TOOLS

Officers responding to a call involving a ritual in progress may find some elements such as fire, knives, or even nudity that may at first appear to be malevolent in nature. A basic understanding of what goes on in a Wiccan ritual will assist the officer in assessment and tactical approach.

The Altar

The physical tools and implements an officer will see on the Wiccan altar all have spiritual connections and religious meaning. The typical Wiccan altar may be found on a wooden table. It may simply be a box covered with an altar cloth. It may be hidden under a bed or in a closet. The Wiccan altar is a place where the Wiccan communicates with the spiritual world.

Tools

There are several common tools that will be seen on the altar. The altar will usually have some type of object representing the Goddess and the Horned God. They may be represented by statues, dolls, or pictures of a male and a female. The Horned God may be represented by deer antlers, while the Goddess may be represented by an image of the moon.

The altar may include objects that represent one or more elements. Fire may be represented by a candle, dagger, or a red object. Water may be present as a bowl or chalice filled with water. Air can be represented with a feather, dagger, or a wooden wand (which may also be used to direct energy). Earth may be suggested with something green, such as money.

A chalice may be used to hold libations for rituals. A pentacle, the five-pointed star in a circle, may be found in wooden or glass form. Incense may also be found smoldering in a burner. Salt may be present in a bowl.

A common tool used in rituals and found on altars is the *athame* (pronounced ah-tha-may), the ritual knife used to direct spiritual energy. This knife is not used to cut human or animal flesh and may be a custom-made dagger complete with ornate handle or just a simple kitchen knife. However primitive the object may be, the use is the same. The athame may have strange characters carved or painted on the handle, which may be the owner's magickal name. It may be written in a number of magickal alphabets. (Alphabets will be discussed later.) There may also be a curved blade called the *boliene*. This is used to cut herbs and plants and traditionally has a white handle.

Rituals may take place outdoors, and the ritual space may be marked by physical items such a candles or rocks. This is a labyrinth that was constructed so that practitioners could walk in a spiral maze. This walk would build energy to be used in the following ritual.

A Wiccan altar.

The wand may be found on the altar and may be used as a replacement for the athame to cast the magickal or sacred circle.

The pentacle is usually a round plate with the five-pointed star carved or drawn on it and may be used to consecrate materials.

A bell may be used to dispel negative energies before a ritual and may also be used to banish spirits at the end of a ritual.

A censer may also be present. This is usually a lamp used to burn incense and create a magickal atmosphere. It may be carried around to create a sacred environment.

A scourge or cat-o'-nine-tails may be found on the altar. This is said to represent female dominance. It is usually made of a lightweight material so as not to cause harm.

A volume called the *Book of Shadows* may be found on an altar. The name comes from the time in history when witches faced death and hid their secrets and spells "in the shadows." The *Book of Shadows* may belong to an individual or may be owned by the group. It can be in a leather book, a three-ring binder, or even on a computer disk.

Candles, sometimes of different colors, shapes, or forms, may be found on the altar.

Cords may also be present that may be used in cord magick, which involves tying knots in a cord while expressing a wish, or may represent a level of initiation in a particular coven.

Scented oils may be found on the altar. These may be used to "dress" candles and ritual objects.

A small doll may be found on altars. This is called a *poppet*. It is used to represent someone and is typically used in healing rituals.

Tools may be "charged" in a common ritual that invests them with spiritual energy. Jewelry may also be charged. An officer touching a charged object will take away the spiritual presence on the object.

RITUALS AND CEREMONIES

Although rituals may change according to the tradition and the practitioner, some elements are considered nearly universal in Wiccan circles. Some of these are the following.

Correspondences

It is a common magickal belief that certain calendar dates, hours of the day, colors, scents, and planets are connected. Many Wiccans work all of these elements into rituals. Before any rituals are performed, a Wiccan may need to wait until all of these aspects have occurred. It is also believed that some days of the year have more power than others. Rituals may be specifically

Photos 1 and 2: A Wiccan coven performs a ritual in honor of the Mabon celebration.

Photo 3: Officers approaching ceremonies should allow those present in the circle to banish their ritual space before entering. This act may be construed as a threat because of the sweeping motion of the ritual blade.

Photo 4: The priestess invokes, or calls upon, her deity.

held on these days to give them more power. One high priestess explains the concept as "a type of linkage thought to exist between apparently unconnected objects and concepts."

A ritual area may contain items that are specifically colored to represent elemental correspondences. These colors are universal symbols of the elements. Some common color correspondences are these:

Air = blue, yellow
Fire = red
Water = green, blue
Earth = yellow, black, or brown

Preparation of the Ritual Area

The tools and altar may be set up in a specific location of a house or outdoor area. Many traditions place the altar to the east.

Consecration of Ritual Tools and Implements

The tools and ritual area may be cleaned with salt and water to purify them of negative energies. The ritual area may be swept with a broom to cleanse the space for the ceremony. The area may also be purified with salt and water. Some may take all the elements around the area to cleanse it while a chant or prayer may be performed over the tools to consecrate them. Ritual tools may be passed through the smoke of the censer to cleanse them. Then they may be passed through a candle flame, sprinkled with water, and rubbed with salt or dirt. This puts the tool through all of the elements. The American Indian custom of "smudging," the carrying around of burning herbs, is frequently used.

Grounding

Grounding is establishing a connection to the energies of the Earth. It is said to keep the body from being overstressed during the end of ritual. It returns excess energy to the Earth. The practitioner may place the athame on the ground to place the energy back into the Earth.

Casting the Circle

The Wiccan must open an area for spiritual work. This is accomplished by casting a circle. The Wiccan uses a finger, a dagger, a sword, or a wand to create a wall of spiritual energy. This wall is created by the Wiccan walking clockwise (called *deosil*) and pointing the object used to direct energy. The circle is not to be broken during the ritual because it is the sacred space in which the deities of Wicca manifest.

If the circle is to be broken, a doorway will be cut to let the practitioner walk outside the sacred space. This is cut open by the practitioner raising the athame and moving it counterclockwise (widdershins) and tracing a door.

Calling the Quarters

The directions of north, south, east, and west are protected by guardian spirits, which are sometimes called watchtowers. The four directions, or quarters, are called to witness the ritual. The Wiccan may draw, or "invoke," a pentagram in the air that represents the quarter and the element it represents. The practitioner may call on the guardians by addressing them in the following manner:

> Lords and Ladies of the Watchtower
> of the South, thou leaping salamanders
> and fiery ones, lion in passion and
> dragon in power, phoenix arising pure
> and whole from the flame, Notus, master
> of the South wind, be with us in
> passion and in truth, bring us the
> warmth of the hearthfire and the summer
> sun, and the clear sight of noonday.
> I do summon, stir and call you up—
> Come! Be welcome in this our rite.
> Blessed be.

These spirits are thanked and sent away at the end of the ritual.

Invocation of Deity

The deity is called and invited to appear in the circle. The god may be called by many names, such as Cernunnos, Pan, the Horned God, or Herne the Hunter. The Goddess may be called Diana, Hecate, Isis, or Cerridwen of the cauldron. An example of an invocation follows:

> Gracious Goddess,
> You who are the Queen of the Gods,
> The lamp of night,
> The Creator of all that is wild and free;
> Mother of woman and man;
> Lover of the Horned One, and
> Protector of all the Wicca:
> Descend, I pray,
> With Your Lunar ray of Power
> Upon my circle here!

Energy Raising

Energy is raised through singing, chanting, dancing, or drumming. Energy is contained within the magickal circle. This energy is then raised into a cone of power. The energy can then be channeled to a specific area of concentration to perform magick. The cone of power is directed jointly to a chosen purpose.

Spellwork

Spellwork is done with the energy raised. Spells are performed for healing, protection, spiritual peace, and other wishes. Destructive spells are prohibited by Wiccans because of the law of karma, which states that anything that you do will come back to you three times. This is also known as the Law of Threefold Return and the Threefold Law.

Cakes and Wine

The ingestion of wine and cakes will bring the Wiccan out of the ritual state of mind. This also binds the practitioners through the sharing of food. The food is typically consecrated by the high priestess and high priest. Alternative drink may be available for individuals who don't use alcohol.

Opening and Banishment of Circle

The circle must be banished after the

ritual. The Wiccan walks counterclockwise to take the energy away. This will open the ritual area and allow the Wiccan to leave the sacred space.

The closing of a circle is usually met with the cry "Merry meet, merry part, and merry meet again."

ESBATS AND SABBATS

Wiccans may gather at specific times to perform rituals and socialize. Wiccan traditions encourage gatherings during certain phases of the moon; these gatherings are called *esbats*. The word *esbat* is archaic French for "frolic." The moon is revered because of its representation of the Goddess, as well as its importance to nature. Public esbats may be advertised in metaphysical supply stores and on Internet Web sites.

Sabbats are considered the Wiccans' high holy days. Many of them correspond with changes in the seasons. Traditionally there are eight sabbats. The greater sabbats are Imbolc, Beltane, Lughnassad, and Samhain. The lesser sabbats are the summer and winter solstices and the autumnal and spring equinoxes. These holidays are usually pictured as a wheel that contains the seasons and turns as time passes.

Each sabbat has a specific ritual and symbolic meaning regarding the life and death of the gods.

Yule
Yule occurs around December 22, the winter solstice. Wiccans celebrate the longest night of the year, as well as the rebirth of the Sun God. This also is the death of the Holly King and the birth of the Oak King.

The yule log as holly and mistletoe are usually present in Wiccan celebration of Yule. A drama about the gods may be acted out at this celebration.

Imbolc
The holiday of Imbolc, which means "in the belly," occurs on February 2. This celebrates the first appearance of light. The Sun God stays up longer during this time. This cele-

bration is important to Brigid, the goddess of healing. The priestess may wear a crown of lights. This is usually a holly crown with candles on it.

Ostara
Ostara, or the spring equinox, is celebrated on March 21. This is the day of equal balance of day and night. Spring fertility is celebrated, as is Ostara, goddess of fertility. The Sun God starts to grow. The Christian celebration of Easter is taken from this holiday (rabbits and eggs may appear in rituals).

Beltane
The Sabbat of Beltane is celebrated on April 30. The holiday celebrates Baal. The fires of balefire used to burn on this date, which is where the term "bonfire" comes from. Maypoles are planted this day to symbolize the male phallus impregnating the earth. This holiday celebrates spring, nurturing, and fertility.

Litha
Litha is the celebration of midsummer's eve, or summer solstice. It is usually on June 21. It is the longest day and shortest night of the year with the Sun God at his peak. This is a celebration of transformation. The Oak King dies and the Holly King is born.

Lammas
Lammas is celebrated from July 31 through August 1. This is the time of harvest. The word "Lammas" comes from old English words that mean "loaf" and "mass." It is an ancient celebration of the first fruits of harvest coming in. The Celtic Sun God, Lugh, is also revered on this date, which gives the holiday its other name, Lughnassad. The Sun God begins to descend into the underworld.

Mabon
Mabon is celebrated around September 21. This is the autumnal equinox, which marks the sacrifice of the Sun God and a celebration of the balance between light and day. The autumn equinox marks the end of the harvest.

The high priestess may perform a ritual called Drawing Down the Moon. This ritual calls the Goddess down into the priestess. This act is described as a form of spiritual possession.

Samhain

Samhain (pronounced sow-in) is celebrated October 31. This is the celebration of the time of year when the veil between the worlds of the living and the dead are thinnest. Darkness is dominant. This is the New Year's Eve of the Celtic religions. The dead and the deities of transition and afterlife are honored.

TRADITIONAL CEREMONIES

There are a number of traditional ceremonies that Wiccans may perform. The ceremonies may vary according to the leaders and participants performing in them.

Wiccaning

The act of gaining protection from the Goddess and Horned God for a child is called a Wiccaning. This rite is not performed to dedicate a child to the path of Wicca, but to give protection. The child may be given a "witch name" during the ritual. The child may also be given a set of godparents to watch after him or her as well.

Initiation

Initiation into Wicca differs among groups. Many Wiccans may initiate or dedicate themselves to the God and Goddess if they practice alone. Some may have a priestess perform an initiation ceremony. The participant may go through a "rebirth" into the world of Wicca. Depending on the tradition, there may be a number of degrees that the initiate may attain. Each degree may consist of its own ceremony and test to show acceptability.

Handfasting

A handfasting is a Wiccan wedding. The man and woman are joined by hand to show dedication to themselves and the gods. The ceremony may be marked by the completion of a ritual called the Great Rite. The handfasting is legally binding if the priest or priestess is legally ordained.

The Great Rite

The Great Rite is a ritual that celebrates the coming together of the God and Goddess. It is a celebration of fertility. It is usually symbolically carried out, but it may actually be acted out with a male and female participant coming together sexually. In its symbolic form, witnesses may see the priest and priestess using the athame and a cup of wine to symbolize phallus and womb. A real version of the rite may consist of the female lying down with her arms and legs spread in the shape of a pentagram. The male comes before her and kneels and recites sacred passages that tell of the union. A sexual union is then formed between the two. The energy raised during the sexual act may be used to produce magick. The actual Great Rite is virtually always practiced in privacy, without an audience, and between an already established couple.

Drawing Down the Moon

The ritualistic act of Drawing Down the Moon is a ceremony in which the Goddess man-

ifests herself into the high priestess. The ceremony usually begins with an invocation to the Goddess to call her presence into the priestess. The priestess usually waits in heavy concentration till the Goddess chooses to speak through her. During this time she may espouse wisdom and instruction to her followers. The same ritual involving the Horned God is performed by the high priest in some circles.

LAW ENFORCEMENT AND WICCA

The relationship between Wiccan groups and law enforcement agencies has been strained through the years. Many agencies do not want these types of groups operating in their area, regardless of the lack of criminal activity. On the other hand, many agencies also utilize local Wiccans as informants in regard to criminal occult groups that give the Wiccan groups a bad name. It is imperative that officers know the difference between the criminal and noncriminal occult groups in their jurisdiction.

When interviewing Wiccans, take into consideration that many may automatically be on the defensive because of the fear of chastisement from the public; they may also have had negative experiences with the police in past encounters. It may be difficult to gain the trust of a member of one of these groups. Patience, time, courtesy, and understanding will yield positive results if applied correctly.

Approaching a Ritual

Officers may encounter a Wiccan ceremony in the course of answering an unrelated call, or they may be called to the scene because of the ritual itself. Many officers have been called to Wiccan gatherings because someone witnessed robed "devil worshippers" performing Satanic rites around a fire; this leads to officers arriving with a sense of an immediate threat. Upon arrival, officers may discover that the ominous-looking group is, in reality, totally harmless; however, additional backup is encouraged in case there actually is a problem.

The responding officer or officers should first assess any immediate threat or criminal activity. The Wiccans will probably be wondering what is going on and why the police were called; members may become hostile because of past dealings with law enforcement.

When encountering a Wiccan group during a ritual, realize that the group may need to close their circle before allowing you inside the perimeter. Be aware that sweeping actions with the ritual tools, including knives, may be to clear the area of energy. Exercise caution and common sense when encountering a group. In the absence of any obvious threatening behavior, officers should remain a short distance outside the ritual area.

One particular group invited an officer to enter the circle, making a door for him in the circle. He was told he could enter if he entered in "perfect love and perfect peace," which meant that he must remove his sidearm. He refused, explaining that he could not drop his duty weapon.

Participants in the circle may have knives or staffs. The arriving officer should stand ready and keep an eye on all hands, per officer safety

Top: This Wiccan altar was used as a hiding place for illegal narcotics.

Center: Artwork from a juvenile who knew just enough about Wicca to be dangerous. While he claimed affiliation with this peaceful religion, he threatened to blow up his school and harm a police officer.

Bottom: Animal bones may be found at some neo-Pagan sites to honor the dead and for their spiritual energy. However, these are usually from store-bought specimens or came from an animal that died naturally.

mandates; there is always the possibility that an individual may not follow the Wiccan laws and may participate in criminal activities. Officers are encouraged to communicate to the group the purpose of their visit, as well as ask what the officers can do to make them feel safe.

Most traditional Wiccan circles are very compliant with law enforcement in providing information and allowing officers to view the ritual area. If the officer feels threatened by the presence of ritual implements, he should ask to speak to the subjects away from the altar. If the situation makes the officer feel he should remove the ritual object from the altar, he should also keep in mind that he is tampering with a religious object and must have a good reason to back up his actions. As we will see among most magickal religions, ritual tools are considered sacred, and touching them will usually desecrate or pollute the object.

Absent any threat or unlawful conduct, officers should conduct themselves in a respectful manner just as they would upon receiving a call to a Christian church or synagogue.

Establishing a Relationship

An officer does not have to agree with the beliefs and tenets of Wicca to provide service and protection to these groups. *Constitutional protection is guaranteed to these groups* to openly and freely practice their religion. Refusing the religious rights of citizens can result in a trip to court.

Officers who are investigating possible wrongdoing by a coven should check for its affiliations with large sponsoring churches. Many covens are sponsored by neo-Pagan churches and religious organizations. This increases responsibility on the part of the coven

to perform in an ethical fashion. If an officer has a question about a particular group, he should check with the parent affiliate for any complaints on file. To establish contacts in the Wiccan community, officers could look for local Web sites, journals such as *Circle* or *Green Egg*, found in bookstores, or Universalist churches in the area.

If you wish to establish and keep communication open with members of the Wiccan community, never call them Satanists or devil worshippers. Show the same level of respect you would accord a traditional church, even if you personally disagree with their beliefs. Listen more than you talk to establish a good rapport.

Abuses of the Religion

Because of the growing popularity of Wicca, a number of teenagers are starting to become involved in this once-secret religion. This can put them at risk from adults seeking to entice and harm juveniles. Several cases have been recorded in which a perpetrator attempted to use the Wiccan religion to commit sexual acts on youths. In almost every case, the perpetrators were either unknown to, or rejected by, the traditional Wiccan community in the towns they lived in.

SANTERIA

Haiti is 70 percent Catholic,
30 percent Protestant,
And 100 percent Voodoo!
—African Proverb

HISTORY OF VOUDON RELIGIONS

I f we learn about the history and development of the Afro-Caribbean Voudon religions, it can tell us a lot about the behavior and movement of these groups in the United States. The religions we term "Afro-Caribbean" are those that have origins in Africa but evolved and mutated into other religions once their adherents were kidnapped into slavery. In the New World, these Africans were typically forced into adopting Christian practices. They blended these new ways with their old beliefs, and thus the religions of Santeria (Cuba), Candomble (Brazil), and Voodoo (Haiti) were born.

Many bits of Voudon culture have found their place in our mainstream culture. Pop songs such as Sublime's "Santeria" and David Byrne's "Papa

Top: A shrine for the orisha Oshun, the goddess of the rivers. The statue is that of Our Lady of Charity.

Bottom: Officers may discover offerings known as adimu left at various geographical areas. These bananas tied with red ribbon are given to Chango.

The work that goes into designing the dresses, crowns, and beads used in initiations is very elaborate and costly. This is a dress for an initiate of Oya, the goddess over the cemetery.

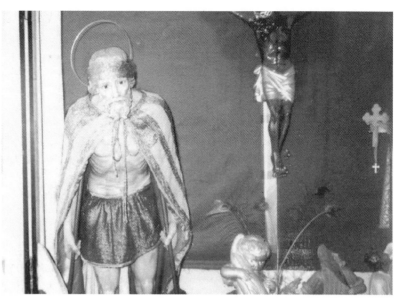

Some members of the religion spend exorbitant sums to build shrines to the orishas. Some statues can cost thousands of dollars. One crime scene in Florida contained statues with diamonds, rubies, and sapphires inside the statues of the saints.

Legba" have supernatural themes, and in the early '70s Marvel Comics even launched a short-lived comic book called *Brother Voodoo*. But just as the religions affect our culture, our culture has affected those religions, and many Voudon religions evolved into something entirely different once they hit American shores. However, there are a few groups in the United States that have kept their religion "pure." Many of these groups practice in secret to avoid the introduction of foreign elements, and part of the secrecy that officers may encounter is a direct result of the desire of the practitioners to keep the religion safe from intruders and those who would choose to exploit it.

SANTERIA—OFTEN MISUNDERSTOOD

Officers have reported finding such items as beads, coins, feathers, and candles at crime scenes. Many of these items are indicative of the religion of Santeria. The following is an excerpt from a 1997 police report taken in Raleigh, North Carolina:

Subject was reported walking through the woods and discovered some sort of shrine. A white sheet was found covered in blood. A black goat was found lying next to a large box. A wooden statue was found, surrounded by hair, ashes, and fruit. A decapitated sheep bound with yellow rope was also found.

Although the follow-up report on this incident used terms like "Satanic" and "devil worship," this site was purely Afro-Caribbean in nature and had nothing to do with European-based Satanism. The religion of Santeria is heavily practiced in such areas as Chicago, New York, and Florida. Officers in these areas have become accustomed to seeing the somewhat strange-looking artifacts encountered while on patrol. Some officials in the Miami area have even sent their officers to training that includes a tour of Santeria houses of worship and an animal sacrifice.

The public's perception of alternative religions can be shaped by the media. The show *NYPD Blue* featured an episode about a homicide suspect who practiced Santeria. While interviewing the subject, a white detective reaches into an iron cauldron and peers strangely at it. When the Hispanic detective tells him that the pot is used for spellwork, the white detective is disturbed and has an almost repulsed reaction to his partner's knowledge of the subject.

News stories involving Santeria easily capture the public's attention. One particularly disturbing example comes from an infamous 1989 incident in Matamoros, Mexico. A drug dealer named Adolfo de Jesus Constanzo used trappings of Santeria, Palo Mayombe (a Congo-based religion), and brujería (Mexican witchcraft) to hide and help his trade in the Mexican border area. He and his followers were responsible for killing at least 14 people and using many of their body parts in rituals to gain power. Constanzo's operation was ultimately foiled when one of his henchman was arrested by police.

When Constanzo's hideout was discovered, authorities found tons of ritual paraphernalia related to Santeria; however, the rituals performed by Constanzo were inconsistent with Santeria. This fact didn't stop the American media from spreading headlines about a "Santeria human sacrifice" and even a "Satanist human sacrifice." The incident was neither. However, this incident became a standard by which the American public viewed Santeria—animal sacrifices, human sacrifices, and drug running.

Sometimes the connection to the occult is not as publicized. In early 2000, America was held rapt by the struggle over the Cuban child Elian Gonzalez—the only survivor of a group of Cubans trying to escape to the United States by raft. While American television focused on the custody battle between the boy's Miami relatives and his father in Cuba, as well as the power struggle between the United States and Cuba, followers of Santeria were focusing on something different.

Elian was rescued by two fishermen who were fishing for mahimahi, also known as dolphin fish. The boy reportedly said he'd seen dolphins (porpoises), and soon the story became one of dolphins saving the helpless child. This story captured the imagination of Miami's Santerian community. To Santeria believers, the boy's "rescue" by the dolphins was a sign that Yemaya, the goddess over the ocean waters, had intervened. This belief was evident in the large mural of Yemaya that was painted outside of his home. A legend surfaced about the child, describing his arrival as the incarnation of the Santeria deity Eleggua, who is portrayed as a child in Santeria lore. Elian's arrival from Cuba was viewed as a sign that the favor of the gods was leaving Castro. It was also rumored that Castro was planning to sacrifice Elian once he was returned to Cuba.

ORIGINS

Santeria began in the area now known as Nigeria, where an ethnic group known as the Yoruba lived and built elaborate kingdoms. Under a king known as an *oba*, the Yoruba developed a strong culture of art, science, and religion. The Yoruba's fundamental beliefs surrounded a creator, known as Olodumare or Olorun. Under the creator, there are several "lesser gods" known as *orishas*. These gods govern all aspects of nature and human emotion. Beneath the orishas are the *eggun*, the spirits of the dead.

The Yoruba tribe flourished until the 1700s, when the Spanish took several thousands of Africans as slaves. The majority of the Yoruba were taken to Cuba, where they were forced to give up their religion and embrace the Catholic faith.

A Mixture of Christianity and African Religions

It was not uncommon to see a Yoruba slave bowing to a statue of St. Barbara of the Catholic pantheon, and later hear the same slave singing songs to Chango (also seen as Shango), the Yoruba god of thunder. In order for their religion to survive, the Yoruba syncretized, or linked, their gods with the saints of the Catholic Church. At night the Yoruba would secretly gather in houses called *cabildos* to sing and drum to their orishas. The

The artifacts found in Santeria are charged with ache, meaning that they have been given magickal power.

Details of initiations may be kept in a diary called a liberta. It is received after initiation and may contain instructions for worship.

Yoruba who practiced their native religion in secret used the term *lucumi*, which means "my friend."

This marriage of saints and gods continued into the 1950s, when the Cubans started to migrate to the United States. Cuban barrios developed in Chicago, New York, and Florida. The Santeria religion was introduced into the United States where it was eventually combined with European-based spiritism, which encourages a belief in spirits, ghosts, and seances. It also mixed with Haitian Voodoo in certain areas of the United States.

Today Santeria is a growing religion with millions of adherents in the United States. With the advent of the Internet, many in the religion are able to find other followers worldwide. Pictures and writings once kept secret are being displayed for the uninitiated to see. One particular article that was posted discussed the growing disgust that many in the religion feel about its exposure on the Internet. The Internet also advertises specialty shops, called *botanicas*, for Santeria spiritual supplies.

Beliefs

The power sources in Santeria are the orishas, who govern every aspect of life and nature. The creator orisha is Olodumare, who is father of the orishas. His son is Olofi, who is syncretized with the Christ Child. The orishas have distinct personalities, just like human beings, and possess special talents, have favorite foods, and even birthdays. It is believed that every human being has a personal guardian orisha.

It is the believer's first goal to find out whom they are born to serve. Believers can attain magick called *ache* (pronounced ah-chay) from the orishas. The concept of ache is seen as the manifestation of spiritual power in this physical world. It is power that spiritual beings carry that is higher than man.

To find out who his guardian orisha is, the believer must go to a priest or priestess (a *santero* or *santera*). Once initiated, the believer becomes the "godchild" of the priest or priestess, who then becomes known as *padrina* (godfather) or *madrina* (godmother). Once a santero has initiated someone into the religion, he becomes *babalocha* (father of a saint) or *iyalocha* (mother of a saint).

The high priest in Santeria is known as the *babalawo* (father of the secrets). This office is strictly reserved for males. The babalawo uses a necklace called the *opele*, which features round medallions made from coconut shells. The chain is "thrown" and the pattern in which the medallions land will tell the babalawo what is going to happen in the future.

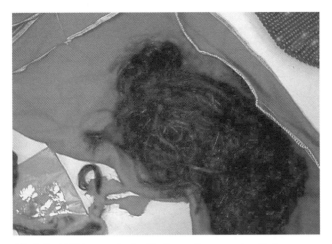

The hair of initiates may be kept by the santero or santera that performed the initiation ceremonies.

Ceremonial artifacts found at a celebration for an initiate of Yemaya. The author observed this celebration that focused on the initiatory birthday of a female worshipper.

The believer becomes initiated into a house of worship (*casa de santo*) that is composed of believers who have been initiated by the same santero. Many houses can trace their lineage back to original Cuban houses.

INITIATIONS

To begin on the path of Santeria, the believer must first become baptized into the Catholic Church. The initiate must then undergo a rite called *plante*.

Plante—Selecting the Guardian Orisha

The new initiate attends a ritual called *diloggun*, in which seashells are thrown to determine the initiate's guardian orisha. Sixteen shells are consecrated in animal blood, and a bone is taken from the sacrificial animal whose blood is on the shells. The shells are then tossed onto a flat surface where a priest interprets their pattern. This type of divination is used to find out what the orishas have to tell initiates all through their spiritual life. Many santeros perform divination services, called *registros,* in botanicas and are held in the same regard as doctors in the Santeria community. They can determine what kind of troubles a person is going to experience or the source of any current problems. Someone who is an expert in reading the shells is called an *italero*.

Obi

There is a tool for divination called an *obi*, which consists of four pieces of coconut being thrown and the patterns read to divine the will of the orishas. The process is also known as *darle coco al santo* (give coconut to the saint). The pattern in which the shells land, whether it be skin or meat up, will determine a pattern for the initiate to interpret. The obi is used in many ceremonies of Santeria. There are five possible combinations:

- **Alafia** (four white sides up): This means a positive yes.
- **Oyekun** (four brown sides up): This means no, and possibly death.
- **Itagua** (three white sides, one brown side up): This is an uncertain answer.
- **Ellife** (two white sides up, two brown sides up): This means a definite yes.
- **Okana sode** (three brown sides up, one white side up): This means no, but may also mean death.

Table of Ifa

Another form of divination used in these initiations is called the "table of ifa," used by the babalawo. This ceremony uses a wooden tray in which the babalawo sprinkles powder and is able to divine spiritual wisdom from the lines that appear from this powder.

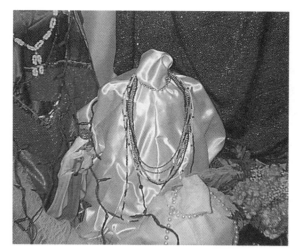 

Left: The elekes may be kept on the tureen or statue of the saint to give it ache.

Right: The warriors sit behind the doorway in a Santeria practitioner's home.

Eleke Necklaces

One of the first things a believer receives is a necklace called an *eleke*, also called a *collare*. These beaded necklaces come in different colors and combinations of beads, which correspond to the favorite colors and numbers of the orishas. The believer receives the necklaces as a means of spiritual protection, and the wearing of these beads publicly identifies the initiate as being dedicated to the particular orisha. The believer will initially receive the necklaces of Obatala, Chango, Oshun, Yemaya, and Eleggua. The cotton string that is used to make them is soaked in a special liquid called *omiero*, which is made from several different sacred herbs. These necklaces are then "fed" the blood of a sacrificed animal and are put through a series of rituals to attain ache. The initiate is then known as *aleyos*.

A law enforcement officer may encounter initiates wearing the beads of the orishas. They may also find the ceremonial necklaces draped over the necks of saint statues to give them ache. The color and bead patterns are common to most houses of worship.

This necklace is considered sacred, and if an officer is dealing with a suspect who is wearing an eleke, he should be cautioned that touching the necklace could initiate a violent response. By interpreting the eleke, an officer can determine the initiate's personal orisha and perhaps gain insight into the suspect's practices.

The necklaces are usually made from 2mm plastic beads. (It should be noted that many street gangs use similar necklaces.)

The following are some orishas and their corresponding elekes:

- **Eleggua:** black and red beads, usually in combinations of three
- **Yemaya:** white and blue beads, usually in combinations of seven
- **Oggun:** green and black beads. Many times a translucent green bead is used to indicate that the initiate has "received the knife" of Oggun. The pattern is usually in sevens or threes.
- **Chango:** red and white beads, usually found in combinations of six.
- **Orunla:** green and yellow; Orunla's number is one.
- **Oshun:** yellow and white beads found in combinations of five.
- **Babalu-Aye:** purple and white beads.

The Warriors

The new initiate may also receive the protection of three orishas called the warriors (*los guerreros*). They are Eleggua, Ochosi, and Oggun. In Yoruba lore, these three gods walked together. Osun accompanies the warriors. When an initiate receives the warriors, Osun is given as a "guardian angel."

The orisha Eleggua has many different manifestations. They are known as esu and may represent different locations such as graveyards and rivers.

The warriors. The orishas Eleggua, Oggun, and Ochosi are received in an initiation in which they are given to the initiate as personal guardians. These orishas protect the initiate against evil.

Offerings to the childlike orisha known as Eleggua may be in the form of candy and toys.

- **Eleggua** is presented in the form of a concrete head with cowrie shells for eyes, nose, and mouth, and is hollowed out and filled with dirt and herbs by the priest.
- **Oggun** is the orisha governing iron. He is depicted as an iron cauldron and as a chain of miniature iron implements.
- **Ochosi** is found inside Oggun in the form of a metal crossbow.
- **Osun** is given to the new initiate in the form of a metal cup with a rooster on its lid. If the tool of Osun falls over, this means danger is near.

Receiving the warriors gives the initiate the spiritual protection of these orishas. The warriors are kept around the initiate's house and are to be "fed" on a regular basis. Eleggua is the first to be fed because he is the orisha that opens the doorway to the spiritual realm. An initiate who neglects his warriors will suffer bad luck and possible harm.

Making the Saint

The ritual that gives the initiate personal protection from his or her guardian orisha is called *kariocha*, which is Lucumi for "seating on the head." This ceremony is also called "making the saint." This is a very expensive process that usually costs thousands of dollars in the United States; many Americans travel to Cuba to receive the orishas at a much cheaper rate. The ritual is a very complex ceremony that ends in a rite called the *asiento*. The believer undergoes several ritualistic actions, including the symbolic cutting of the head. The cut has several herbs applied to it to place the essence of the orisha into the head.

Iyawo

The believer then becomes known as *iyawo*, which means "bride of the orisha."

A witness records the details of the rites in a book called the *liberta*. This is a diary of spiritual occurrences in the life of the initiate. This book is given to the initiate after the initiation is complete.

Presentation of the Iyawo to the Santeria Community

The initiation process is very tedious. The climax of the ceremony is the presentation of the iyawo to the Santeria community. The iyawo spends seven days in a ritual room on a throne. The iyawo is then visited by members of the Santeria community on one of these days. At this ceremony the iyawo is dressed in a beaded, sequined outfit in the colors of the orisha; it is worn only three times in the life of the initiate—during the initiation, when the initiate is presented to the sacred drums of Santeria (*batas*), and at his or her funeral. The iyawo is given several restrictions regarding where he can go and what he can do for up to one full year. Restrictions can vary from house to house and typically include a prohibition against sex, shaking hands, or having his head uncovered in the rain.

PRACTICES

Sacred Stones

Santeria believers may later receive the protection of additional saints. They may acquire the tools and objects that represent the orishas. The orisha is represented by a stone called the *otane*, which is fed water and animal blood and housed in a tureen called a *sopera*. Believers will usually have these objects around their homes, placing them on shelves and under small tables. These are sacred objects and are treated as if the gods themselves were sitting in the soperas.

Patakis

Believers are taught about the orishas and how to serve them through stories called *patakis*. These are legends about the personalities and adventures of the orishas. These stories advise believers about the specific powers that orishas can also exert.

ORISHAS

Eleggua

Eleggua is syncretized with St. Anthony. Some houses may have Eleggua represented by the Spanish statue of Niño Atocha, the Christ Child. Some groups have a picture of a lady in fire, known as the "Lonely Soul of Purgatory," to represent Eleggua. Eleggua has 21 different manifestations or paths, so an officer may find large seashells, fruits, and other objects with shells for facial features to represent *esu*, his other paths. Eleggua is the guardian of doorways, as that is where he may be found. He represents destiny and is known as a trickster.

Oggun

Oggun is syncretized with St. Peter and is represented by an iron cauldron and iron implements. He is the orisha governing iron and vio-

lent death. Officers may find guns or knives inside the cauldron of Oggun.

Ochosi

Hunting and justice are governed by Ochosi, who is syncretized with St. Norbert. Officers may find a metal crossbow, deer antlers, and handcuffs to represent Ochosi. Some criminal groups hang the tools of Ochosi around their drug labs and hangouts to protect them from being "hunted" by the law. A traditional santera told me that this is very ignorant because Ochosi serves justice on those that do wrong; therefore this would hurt criminals in their endeavors.

Oshun

Oshun is syncretized with Our Lady of Charity and is the goddess of love, who governs matters of money and rules over rivers. Her shrines may contain peacock feathers.

Obatala

This orisha is syncretized with Mary, mother of Jesus, and is known as "father of the white cloth" and represents purity. Obatala owns everyone's head and is represented by anything white, such as cotton, doves, and eggs.

Chango

This fiery orisha is syncretized with St. Barbara and represents fire and thunder. Chango was a king in Africa who became a deity after his death. Officers may find wooden bowls filled with Chango's thunderstones, which are stones created by lightning striking the ground. Chango's shrine may contain his double-bladed ax and images of St. Barbara, who may have her sword pointed up in a defensive position. This indicates that the orisha is standing guard because of possible danger.

Yemaya

Yemaya is considered to be the mother of the orishas; her name means "Our mother whose children are the fish." Yemaya is represented by Our Lady of Regla (a province in Cuba). Yemaya rules over seas and will be found in the form of seashells, mermaids, boats, and

This tureen holds the secrets of Obatala, the father of purity.

This statue of St. Barbara is used to represent Chango. The horse that the saint rides is also found in the mythology of Chango.

other items associated with water. One manifestation of Yemaya is Olokun. Olokun is Yemaya of the deep seas and is depicted as somewhat of a mixed gender, holding a mask and a sea snake. Olokun represents the waters that slaves came across to the New World. Olokun cannot be "placed in the head" because he is so vast.

Babalu-Aye

This orisha presides over sickness and is syncretized with St. Lazarus. Officers will find Babalu-Aye in the form of crutches and sackcloth. In Africa, Babalu-Aye is the deity over smallpox.

Orunla

Presiding over divination, Orunla is syncretized with St. Francis. The babalawo will use the table of ifa, which is owned by Orunla.

Osain

Governing the forest and herbs, Osain is syncretized with St. Raphael and is found in the form of clay or stones with one eye. Osain has a gourd that brings money and good fortune to its holder. This is usually found in the form of a hanging gourd with feathers sticking out of it.

Other Orishas

The Ibeyiis are twin orishas. They are syncretized with St. Cosme and St. Damian and are the sons of Chango. They will be found as twin dolls or statues and can bring financial success.

Oya is the orisha over the cemeteries and the wind. She is represented by Our Lady of Candelaria. She rules over death and divorce. Officers will find her represented by a mask and sometimes sapphires.

Aggayu is the lord of volcanoes. He is usually found with Chango. Many houses view him as the father of Chango. He is represented by St. Christopher and is symbolic of transportation and rage of nature.

There are hundreds of orishas. There are also many other significant characters who are of great importance to those who follow the orishas.

One of those is El Negro José, who is used in orisha groups that use spiritism. José is a statue of an old black man sitting in a chair. Sometimes he may be found leaning on a crooked staff. It is believed that spirits speak through his assistance. He may be used for spiritual protection.

EGGUN: THE DEAD

The *eggun* are spirits of the dead that are honored so that they will not cause problems for the living. The eggun may be honored in a small indoor shrine called a *boveda*, which is usually a table on which glasses of water are placed.

Top: A shrine built for the orishas.

Bottom: A santera shows off her dress for Yemaya.

There may be seven glasses to represent spirits, with a central glass containing a crucifix to represent Christ. There are also pictures of the dead that are being honored. Usually the altar is covered with flowers, fruits, and food for the dead. Near the altar there may also be a doll that wears a dress the color of the orisha that rules its owner. Some houses that use customs from European spiritism may hold seances and may even channel the eggun.

Spiritism (Espiritismo)

The emphasis on spirits of the dead borrows much of its ideology from European spiritism, which is a belief system that focuses on communication with the dead. Ceremonies called spiritual masses are held to call upon and seek guidance from the spiritual realm. The writings of French spiritualist Allen Kardec (1804–1869) have influenced this culture greatly. Kardec authored many important texts on the subject, with his 1856 book *Le Livre des Esprits* (*The Spirits Book*) being one of his most popular. Kardec's books are still used as invocations to the spirits of the dead. The aspects of spiritism evident in Santeria today are such activities as channeling, which is the practice of a spirit speaking through a living human being.

ALTARS AND TOOLS

Because of a history of persecution, followers of Santeria may be very secretive about their practices. Many followers will publicly claim they are strictly Catholic, with no ties to the ancient African gods. Officers may first draw the same conclusion when they see statues and images of the traditional Catholic saints in the homes of practitioners. However, the presence of

additional items such as shells, coins, and African images may offer a different conclusion. It is important that officers recognize that all implements and objects that are used in orisha worship are viewed by its practitioners as sacred. If an outsider to the religion handles these items, it is viewed as spiritually damaging as well as disrespectful. The essence of ache may have been placed on the ritual implements in a costly and very sacred ceremony.

Officers arriving at homes of believers will usually find several shrines and altars. A small table may house the warriors, or they may rest behind a door. There may also be shrines for the orishas along with their tureens that house the sacred stones. The tureens are usually colored according to the orisha they represent. Tureens will be covered in beads called *collar de mazzos*. These large beads are very expensive and are also worn during initiation ceremonies.

The following is a list of orishas and items that officers might find alongside them:

- **Eleggua.** His image may be found along with a red and black beaded stick with a crook in it, and he may be wearing a small straw hat. His shrine may also have toys and candy in it for his childlike nature. He may have other manifestations in the forms of coconuts, seashells, and large rocks. A mousetrap found beside him may contain the name of someone that the initiate wants to trap with Eleggua. Officers entering homes may find him behind the doorway.
- **Obatala.** Officers may find a white cloth symbolizing his purity. His shrine may also contain a beaded horsetail, called iruke. He may also have cotton, eggs, and other white items in his shrine. He may also have a bell called an *agogo*.
- **Chango.** Officers may find his castle and mortar and pestle. He may also have his red and white beaded axe. Some altars have wooden tools of an ax, rocket, dagger, and other tools. His crown may also be found in his shrine. The rocket, also called a dart, is symbolic of both a metal

weapon and a penis (at one time, Chango was revered as a divinity of virility). His shrine may also include a figure of a white horse, which relates back to a story of St. Barbara in battle on a horse.
- **Oggun.** Found in his cauldron of iron, Oggun may have railroad spikes in his altar. Green and black items will be in his shrine along with ceramic or stuffed dogs. Officers may find guns or knives in the Oggun of criminal practitioners.
- **Ochosi.** Ochosi may be found with deer antlers, handcuffs, and keys. Officers may also find a deer head, deer hide, or other items related to the hunt. Violet is his color.
- **Babalu-Aye.** Officers may find sackcloth and crutches to represent this orisha.
- **Yemaya.** Seashells, boats, starfish, and other water items or any items that are blue may be found in the shrine to Yemaya.
- **Oshun.** Officers may find fans, mirrors, ducks, and boats or other river-related items. Yellow and white items will be found. Honey may be placed on the altar, as well as apple cider.
- **Oya.** Officers may find cemetery-related items as well as masks on her altar. Maroon and white items may be found.
- **Aggayu.** The shrine to Aggayu may have a large plastic volcano.
- **Osain.** Osain is found in the form of a gourd filled with rocks, herbs, plants, and implements. He is usually hung up in the home.

RITUALS AND CEREMONIES

There are several different types of ceremonies performed in the Santeria community. One of the most popular ceremonies is called the *bembe* or *tambor*.

Bembe

The bembe is held in honor of orishas. The days of celebration coincide with the Catholic

Left: The plaza for the orisha. The plaza is created on those days that celebrate initiations or feast days for the orishas.

Right: Animals such as goats or chickens may be found with their throats slit. Most animals that are sacrificed to the orishas are cooked and eaten. Animals that were used in workings to remove illness or to remove negative influences are not eaten by adherents; some may be disposed of in such locations as graveyards and railroad tracks.

days of recognition of the saints. The following is a list of orishas and their celebration days:

Orisha	Feast Day
Oya	February 2
Ochosi	June 6
Eleggua	June 13
Oggun	June 29
Yemaya	September 7
Oshun	September 8
Obatala	September 24
Orunla	October 4
Chango	December 4
Babalu-Aye	December 17

Sometimes the bembe may be held for other reasons, such as an anniversary of an initiation, or it could be for a special feeding by a priest/priestess. The bembe is usually open only to the initiated and invited friends. Certain ceremonies will only be open to immediate members of the casa de santo.

The bembe is traditionally marked by a spectacular drumming ceremony. Drums are considered sacred in Santeria and are used to call down the orishas with beats and rhythms that send messages into the spirit world. These sacred drums are known as *bata* drums. Drummers must learn special rhythms to play to call upon the orishas. The drums are considered

alive and have distinct sounds. One drum will call out and another will answer. Bata drums are constructed in a very elaborate ceremony involving prayers and animal sacrifices. Groups that specialize in ceremonial drumming are very popular in Latin culture and make a considerable amount of money performing at bembes.

One room of the bembe usually holds the throne of the orisha. This room is usually decorated in colorful banners and cloths spread across the walls and ceilings. There is also a tureen with the orisha inside of it in the throne. If the celebration is an asiento for the initiate, the iyawo will be found sitting in the throne. There is a large offering of cakes and other items, usually in the color of the orisha. This is known as the *plaza*. There are also fruits and vegetables for the orisha found on the floor. A basket called the *derecho* is usually amid the offering filled with money to help pay for all the food, tools, and time put into the celebration. At the base of the basket is a straw mat on which visitors must kneel and show respect to the orisha. A maraca or a bell will also be found to rattle or ring to call the orisha.

SPIRIT POSSESSION

Spirit possession by an orisha is a common occurrence at celebrations. The act of being pos-

The botanica serves as the supply store for spiritual goods relating to Santeria. The staff at the store typically serve as both pharmacists and counselors for patrons' spiritual needs. They supply candles, oils, statues, and powders for Santeria practitioners. Some even raise animals that can be purchased for sacrifices.

sessed is called "being ridden," likened to a person riding a horse.

During the bembe, songs are sung to call upon the orishas in hopes that they will manifest themselves within a person. As a person starts to show signs of possession, the songs become louder and more concentrated on that person. When an initiate comes under possession, he or she actually "becomes" that orisha. The possessed is given clothing and tools that the particular orisha uses. Miracles, healings, and amazing feats of strength may be exhibited by the possessed. While in this trance state, the possessed may speak in a different voice or, in some cases, may exhibit characteristics known to that orisha. One informant told me that every time someone becomes possessed by Yemaya, they start to manifest her characteristic high-pitched laugh.

During possession the orisha may give instruction to his or her followers. It may be in the form of blessings, or sometimes warnings. A story was related to me of a man who was in attendance at a bembe. The orisha Oggun manifested itself and possessed a man, who walked up to another participant and told him to "give Oggun a goat." For one reason or another the man did not heed the orisha's advice. During a later celebration, the man became possessed by the orisha Oggun. He immediately dropped to the floor like a dog and started to walk on all fours. He crawled into the room where an animal sacrifice was being performed and began to lap the blood falling from the sacrificial knife. The participants at the celebration looked on in disgust at the possessed man. A santero later told onlookers he was being punished by Oggun for not obeying him.

The act of spirit possession can be a very bizarre experience for those who have never seen it before. Officers coming into a ceremony where someone has been possessed may find themselves amid mass confusion. They should be aware that touching an individual being possessed may cause a violent or unpredictable response from the individual, as well as the onlooking crowd. Officers should seek out the leadership in the room to assist them before touching individuals who appear to be possessed. If it is necessary to lay hands on the possessed, officers should try to contain that person away from the crowd. Understand that touching the possessed is viewed as "touching the god." Also, officers should be aware of any tools or weapons that the possessed may be handling. Initiates may be wielding swords, axes, or knives. Additionally, implements that could be used as weapons may be available to the onlookers, so officers should always watch their surroundings, not getting fixated on the possessed individual.

THE SACRIFICE

A number of years ago a prominent physician in Miami was discovered on his knees among blood-spattered ritual objects and animal carcasses outside an intensive care unit. His wife was slowly dying, and the physician was earnestly pleading to the gods for her life. This is an example of a case in which traditional medicine has been tried, yet the believer feels there is more to be done in the spiritual realm. The animal sacrifice was in hopes the orishas would step in and intervene in his wife's recovery. Sacrifice of an animal is viewed as a small price compared with the enormous work that the orishas can return.

Although its practice is ancient and found in religions around the world, the use of animal sacrifices has become a focal point of controversy in Voudon religions. Followers of these religions claim that their gods cannot be properly appeased unless they receive blood. Animal blood is the powerful agent that the orishas ask for in exchange for ache.

Animal sacrifices are used for a number of purposes in Santeria. The most common is the gift of an *ebbo*, or an offering to an orisha. Sacrifices are also used in cleansing rituals and initiations. The animals used as sacrifices are usually ducks, chickens, goats, turtles, and doves. Dogs are sometimes given to Oggun. Many botanicas will raise and sell animals for sacrifices. While most of the animals used in rituals are animals that are considered livestock, there are some houses that will use more exotic animals. One Florida botanica was found to be selling Dalmatian puppies for sacrificial purposes.

Each orisha desires a particular ebbo.

- **Eleggua** is fed rum, cigars, turtles, goats, roosters, and opossum. A jungle rat known as *jutia* is sometimes given to Eleggua. These are very expensive animals, costing around $500. Powdered jutia is used in some rituals.
- **Chango** is offered fruit, coconuts, goats, turtles, quail, roosters, and rams.
- **Babalu-Aye** is fed toasted corn, tobacco, rum, goats, roosters, and pigeons.
- **Oshun** prefers pumpkins, honey, rum, yellow hens, and female goats.
- **Oggun** is fed rum, cigars, opossum, roosters, goats, pigeons, and sometimes dogs.
- **Yemaya** is given pork rinds, watermelons, ducks, turtles, coconut balls, syrup, rams, and roosters.
- **Oya** is fed female goats, pigeons, hens, and any black animal.
- **Aggayu** is fed a castrated goat, guinea hens, and pigeons.

The santero that performs the sacrifice must first receive the knife used in the sacrifice in a ceremony called the *pinaldo*. The knife is said to belong to the orisha Oggun. In fact, the ceremonial sacrifice is blamed on Oggun. The animal's blood is usually dripped onto the stones or tools that represent the orisha. During the sacrifice, chants called *oru* are sung by the group. These begin and end with a song to Eleggua. In most cases the animals that are sacrificed are eaten as well; however, those initiates who are children of a particular orisha may not eat of their orisha's sacrifice.

Sacrifice and the Law

In areas like New York and Miami, where there is a large Cuban community, sacrificed animals are commonly found in public places. The Society for the Prevention of Cruelty to Animals has led many campaigns against what they consider inhumane treatment of animals by the Santeria community.

In 1993 a Santeria church in Florida petitioned the U.S. Supreme Court for the right to sacrifice animals for its religion. In the decision of *Church of Lukumi Babalau-Aye v. City of Hialeah*, the subject of animal sacrifice in the church was given acceptance because of its comparison with the traditional Jewish practice of killing animals for kosher purposes. The decision had a few provisions that must be met in order for the sacrifice to be legal: the animal must not be an endangered species; the sacrifice must be accomplished with a swift severance of the carotid artery that causes the animal to go into shock before its death; and the sacrifice must not be left in a public place.

Addimu

Addimu are small offerings, which are not necessarily animals. Most of these are dishes of food that the orisha asks for during readings. They are usually found on plates and in bowls in front of the objects that represent the orisha.

- **Eleggua** is given cornmeal with palm oil, okra, coconuts, smoked fish and opossum, toasted corn, and candy.
- **Oggun** is given green plantains and the gifts that Eleggua requests.
- **Obatala** is given egg whites beaten with sugar. He is given rice and vanilla puddings, milk, and other white foods.
- **Chango** is given a dish of okra and cornmeal cooked together. Red apples and green bananas in groups of six are also given to Chango.
- **Yemaya** is given sweet plantains and pork rinds. Shrimp, dried coconut, white pears, and okra are found in her addimu.
- **Oshun** is given pumpkin, shrimp, eggs, spices, and raw fish. Honey is usually poured over the addimu.
- **Oya** is given eggplants and okra with cornmeal.

BRUJERIA

This is not to be confused with the Hispanic-based folk religion. Here the term "brujeria" refers to the use of traditional tools and aspects of Santeria in a malevolent form, where the saints may be used in a hex-type magick. This may also be called a *bilongo*. Sometimes dead animals and symbols of the saints are placed in public areas to frighten and curse the intended victim. During a trip to research Santeria, I found a statue of St. Barbara with her head split open with a nail. This was an intended "working" against someone who was a child of Chango. Sometimes amulets may be sent to the intended victim. A common amulet is a picture of the intended victim with thread tied around it to bind and cause the victim to be paralyzed. Victims of this type of magick may typically consult a santero at the local botanica to find out how to guard against this working.

RITUAL CLEANSING

Despojo

The ritual cleansing performed by a santero is known as the *despojo*. This is a ceremonial act of spiritual purification. These may be performed on the patient by brushing sacred herbs and plants on his or her body. Animals may also be rubbed on the patient. These animals take on the negative spiritual aspects that have developed as a result of the brujeria.

Rogacion de Cabeza

Because it is believed that the orisha reside in the head, there exists a special cleansing ritual of the head. Sometimes it is believed that evil spirits can attack and oppress an initiate. This cleansing ritual is performed by a priest/priestess by applying vegetables, herbs, oils, and fruits to the head.

ITUTU

When a santero dies, an elaborate ceremony called the *itutu* is performed. This ceremony, performed by the community santeros, takes one year to complete. The deceased is dressed in the clothing that belongs to his guardian orisha. The tools of the santero are broken apart and placed where the orishas dictate. I have found several of the warriors lying near riverbanks where they instructed to be placed.

MISUSE OF POWER

The majority of Santeria followers are law abiding and typically adhere to ethical standards in the Santeria community. However, a number of people have misused the power of Santeria for personal gain instead of spiritual satisfaction. Besides charging ridiculous amounts of money to rip off new adherents to the religion, some have become involved in perverse actions

Top: Investigators who must remove ritual items during investigations should use gloves to avoid possible biohazards.

Center: The tureen contains sacred items that represent the orisha. Officers should refrain from opening the tureens, as they are considered sacred. If the tureen must be opened by investigators, it is suggested that the contents be placed back inside the way they were found.

Bottom: The "Congo Woman" is a spirit that is recognized by some houses in Santeria. She represents the spirits of the dead.

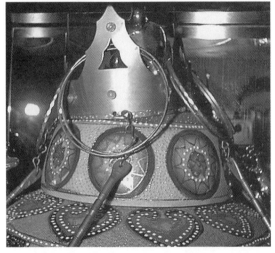

intertwined with traditional rituals. Consider the following report from the *Miami Herald*:

TEEN ACCUSES SANTERIA PRIEST OF RAPE

A Santeria priest was arrested and charged with sexual assault of a 17-year-old girl who said he raped her during a "ritualistic cleansing." Miami Dade Police said that during the course of the ritual, the subject had the victim disrobe, blindfolded her, and then sexually assaulted her. The victim fled from the botanica and contacted the police.

LAW ENFORCEMENT AND SANTERIA

Officers should not underestimate the role that Santeria plays in the Cuban-American community. Any disrespect toward altars, ritual implements, or shrines can cause a breakdown in communication and might cause a violent reaction. Unless an item presents a threat to the officer or plays a role in a criminal case, officers should not touch it. If an outsider touches ritual implements, they are considered desecrated. If an investigating officer must touch tools or altars, it is suggested that he or she remove any subjects from the immediate area and set up a perimeter to keep bystanders away. Implements should never be touched with bare hands due to contamination with animal blood.

Undercover officers should be cautious when trying to infiltrate the community. Many believers will ask what house, or casa de santo, the officer belongs to. The community is very tightly knit, and most priests and officials are very aware of other priests and officials. On the same note, because of the close relation-

Top: San Simón is a spirit that is found in some Mexican Santeria houses. He is believed to grant success to those that honor him.

Center: The Native Americans are honored for their deep spiritual roots and mythologies, and their images may be found in shrines and on altars.

Bottom: The family of orishas that live in this santera's apartment are considered to be living beings that guard her home.

ships that these groups have, it is very difficult for officers to gain information from them about their fellow believers.

Officers should exercise caution when interviewing subjects in the immediate proximity of altars. Knives and guns may be hidden inside the cauldron of Oggun. If detectives are investigating suspects who are involved in Santeria, it may be beneficial to perform surveillance on rituals, ceremonies, and funerals that are being performed by the suspect's house of worship.

Healing herbs and plants are a very important part of Santeria. Officers may find a number of powdered herbs and crushed plants at the home of practitioners. Many of these may appear as contraband; test powders when necessary.

When investigating a known criminal group that practices Santeria, some contraband may be hidden among the statues of saints. When probing a criminal group practicing Santeria, officers should look for the *liberta santo*, which is the book that shows consultations and the names of customers to the house. In order to use such a book in court, it should be secured through a search warrant.

I have had a number of officers tell me about ritual materials found while on patrol. The animal sacrifice will usually be found among other items that will indicate whom the sacrifice was made to. An animal found with its throat cut, and with a red and black ribbon tied around its neck, indicates its relation to Eleggua. A bag of coconuts with a red ribbon may be found on December 4 as a gift to Chango.

The sacrifice is analyzed by looking at where it is located, what is left, what god requires the sacrifice, how many items there are, and what the color of the items are.

Training Scenarios

Let's look at some sample situations and try to assess what is being done at each scene.

- **Scenario 1:** While on patrol, Officer John Doe makes a strange discovery along the local railroad train tracks. A large paper sack is found tied with rope. Inside there are 21 pennies and the body of a small goat with its mouth tied shut with a red and black string. What is going on here?
- **Scenario 2:** A concerned citizen calls in to report a bizarre display he has discovered in a local park in a wooded area. The responding officer finds six red candles in the grass arranged in a circle. In the center, the officer finds a dead rooster, six apples, and a picture of a girl in a beauty contest. What is going on here?
- **Scenario 3:** A concerned citizen calls in to report seeing a woman down by a local river placing several items into the water. She has thrown pumpkins and hens into the water. She has also been seen pouring a jar of honey onto the items before throwing them in. What is going on here?

Answers

- **Scenario 1:** The location of the train tracks is significant because they are considered crossroads. This is the home of Eleggua. The 21 pennies represent Eleggua because he is known to have 21 paths. The black goat is a normative ebbo for Eleggua. The tying of the goat's mouth represents the "binding" of someone. Obviously the victim of the binding needs to keep his mouth closed.
- **Scenario 2:** The location of this particular site does not really have bearing on the ritual. The number of candles suggest the orisha Chango because his favorite number is six. The apples are an ebbo to Chango. The picture of the girl represents an intended focus of the orisha's power. The girl in the picture may be the subject of a blessing or a curse in this particular site.
- **Scenario 3:** The location of the river is significant since it is the homeplace of Oshun. The gift of pumpkins and hens are an ebbo for Oshun. Honey is an aspect of Oshun because of her sweetness.

PALO MAYOMBE

The phone rings in the control center of the local emergency department. "911, how can I help you?" the dispatcher answers. A woman responds, "I think somebody has died next door. I can smell somebody or something rotting. I can't get anyone to come to the door!"

The dispatcher takes down the woman's address and sends a car out. The complainant lives in an apartment complex where local law enforcement receives many calls for various crimes, from domestic assault to drug sales. A unit arrives on the scene, and the officer can smell the stench the minute he steps out of his car. The complainant comes out to meet him at his car and says, "I think something bad has happened here—my neighbor won't come to the door. That nasty smell is coming from his apartment!"

The nganga *is the dark vessel that contains an entire universe. Trees, rocks, rivers, and spirits inhabit the cauldron. The palero is the master over this universe and commands it to do his bidding. Investigators should seek the assistance of a medical examiner in determining the origins of human bones found in the* nganga.

Left: The human skull used in the nganga is called kiyumba. *It contains the intelligence of the dead.*

Right: The crucifix in the center of this nganga may represent a path of Palo known as Palo Cristiano, *which is said to be benevolent. The cross may also be used to keep a spirit at bay.*

The officer walks up the flight of stairs in front of the apartment, and the stench grows stronger as he approaches. The officer taps his pen against the wooden door and shouts, "Hello? Is there anyone in there? Police officer." After no response, he contacts the manager of the complex, who opens the front door with his master key.

The smell nearly knocks the officer down as the door swings open. The apartment is dark. The officer reaches in and finds a switch. As he clicks the switch on, his eyes adjust to the light. He puts his hand on his gun as he sees a blackened shrine sitting inside an open closet. A large black pot is filled with machetes and sticks and is covered in some sort of black fluid. A grinning skull sits in the middle of the pot. Candles surround the scene; glasses of water sit close by. The officer calls for assistance. He's drawn to the kitchen, where a cloud of black smoke billows from the owner's stove. He opens the stove to find a dead skunk lying across the metal bars of the stove.

This incident recalls an actual event that took place in East Tennessee in 1988, where the responding officer discovered a shrine to ancient African gods. The man who owned the apartment turned out to be not only a priest in this African religion but also a well-known local drug trafficker.

ORIGINS

The implements that were found that day are still being found by officers in areas where the religion of Palo Mayombe is practiced. The implements of Palo are frequently seen in Florida medical examiners' offices because of the use of bones and skulls in its rituals. Palo is a very mysterious and secretive religion that originated in the Congo region of Africa. The word "palo" itself means "stick," referring to the magickal branches that are used in the religion; "Mayombe" is a sect that practiced the religion of Palo. The religion came into Cuba during the slave trade. The religion arrived on our shores with Cuban immigrants. Once it arrived, it remained a very secret practice that bonded Cuban families. While it is practiced covertly in America, the religion is practiced openly in Cuba.

There are several branches, or *ramas*, of Palo. Each has its own specific rites and ceremonies. Some of the branches practiced in the United States are Brillumba, Kimbisa, Mayombe, and Monte.

The practice of Palo is composed of two primary elements: herbs and the dead.

NGANGA: THE CAULDRON

The central focus of Palo is the *nganga*, a pot in which the spirits live. It is the universe

Top: Officers may discover drawings that represent the nkisi. *These drawings are called* firma.

Center: The bull represents the spirit of Siete Rayos. Bull horns may be found in his shrine.

Bottom: An offering to the spirit of Siete Rayos.

that the practitioner rules over. It is sometimes called *prenda*, which means "jewel." The cauldron contains spirits that are slaves to the owner of the pot. The pot is usually a large iron cauldron, but it may also be terra cotta; this will differ according to the spirits that reside in the cauldron. The nganga may also be found in a hanging burlap sack called a *boumba* or *muerto de saco* which means "dead who live in a bag." This type of nganga was very popular before Palo arrived in the United States.

Filling the cauldron begins with a stone and 21 palos. Herbs, dirt, water, shells, and animal blood are added to the pot to give life to the spirits inside. The bones of a dead human are placed in the cauldron to produce what is known as the *nfumbe,* which contains the spirit of the dead in its essence. There are stories of Cuban families coming to America on a raft carrying only the bare bones of family members to keep in their nganga.

The nganga may also have a skull in it to represent the intelligence of the spirits of the dead. The skull is called *kiyumba*. There are some ngangas, called *calderos espirituales*, or spiritual ngangas, that do not have human bones in them.

Other ingredients may include bamboo sticks. These are used as the "thermometer" of the nganga and are filled with river water, seawater, and mercury. The bamboo stick is sealed with wax and cement at both ends. They are used to stir the cauldron and move the spirit and also to keep coolness and stability.

The nganga can be dedicated to a specific purpose. The nganga that is ritually baptized with holy water is usually adorned with a crucifix in a practice known as *Palo Cristiano.* An intentionally unbaptized nganga is viewed as being capable of being used for good or evil purposes. This is called *Palo Judío.* The unbaptized nganga may contain a spirit entity known as *Kadiempembe.* This spirit has been likened to the Judeo-Christian concept of Satan.

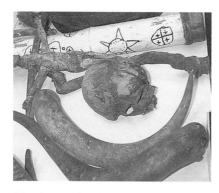

The elements found inside the nganga represent the nature of the spirit within.

Lucero is a spirit that is likened to Eleggua in Santeria.

A figure representing the spirit Siete Rayos.

The workhorse of the nganga is called the *nkisi*. The nkisi works for the owner of the nganga and is commanded to obey him or her. I have personally seen an initiate yell at her nkisi because it would not obey her. Some ngangas will have a bullwhip beside them to discipline the spirit to obey its master.

The nganga is usually kept hidden in a closet or may be kept in a small shed. This shed is called *nsu nganga*. This is usually found in the backyard of the *palero* (priest). Above the nganga may be a *gando*, which is a flag with a drawing on it. This drawing, the *firma*, is the mark that represents the spirit—a sort of signature.

Mpungo

There are also elemental spirits that inhabit the pot, called *mpungo*. Each mpungo rules over an aspect of nature and is syncretized with an orisha of Santeria. In the table on the following page are the mpungo along with their characteristics and powers, the orisha they are associated with, and the Catholic icon they are associated with.

The firma of the mpungo may be drawn onto the nganga or painted in the ritual area. The nganga will usually contain implements that represent the mpungo. For example, a nganga built to house a spirit over iron will contain iron implements, such as railroad spikes and machetes.

- **Lucero** is much like Eleggua of Santeria. He is usually formed of stone or shell, with cowrie shells for facial features. He is made from cement and ingredients such as bone and graveyard dirt. He is usually found next to the nganga. He is fed first before animals are given to the nganga, and he eats goats, black roosters, dogs, and guinea hens.
- **Siete Rayos** is a spirit associated with war. Siete Rayos rules over rain, wind, and lightning. In this aspect he is very much like his associating orisha, Chango. Some houses believe that you must build the nganga of Siete Rayos from the heads and bodies of 21 birds of prey. Lightning stones (made where lightning strikes the earth) should also go inside his nganga. Human bones, coins, and precious stones are also used in his cauldron. The nganga is buried for 21 days. It is fed red candles, red roosters, and water turtles.
- **Zarabanda** is equated with the orisha Oggun. Zarabanda rules over implements made of iron and is always made in an iron cauldron. His nganga is made with black dogs, black dog bones, black roosters, railroad spikes, machetes, and knives. He is fed black animals.
- **Mama Sholan** is equated to the orisha Oshun. She rules over the rivers and also over money and love. Mama Sholan is

Spirit name	Characteristics/powers	Orisha	Catholic icon
Nsambi	Rules over wind	Olodumare	Creator God
Tiembla Tierra/Mama Kengue	Rules over earth	Obatala	Jesus Christ
Mama Sholan/Choya Wengue	Rules over rivers	Oshun	Virgin of Charity
Siete Rayos/Mama Nsasi	Rules over storms	Chango	St. Barbara/St. Jerome
Centelle Ndoki/Centella	Rules over cemeteries	Oya	St. Teresa
Zarabanda	Rules over iron	Oggun	St. Peter/St. George
Lucero	Rules over crossroads	Eleggua	St. Niño Atocha
Calunga/Madre De Água	Rules over ocean/sea	Yemaya	Virgin of Regla

received in a ceramic-type pot. This pot is water-based and is characteristic of her aspects. Houses building her nganga use vultures, human bones, coins, stones, and feathers. She is fed goat, hens, and honey.

- **Centelle Ndoki** is associated with Oya. She can be built in an iron cauldron or a terra-cotta pot. Human bones, black cats, cemetery dirt, and many other ingredients are used for her nganga. She is buried in a cemetery and brought up in 27 days. I have an informant who is a practicing occultist who uses aspects of Wicca, Satanism, Santeria, and Palo. Beside his altar to the Horned God and Great Goddess he has a cauldron to Ndoki that contains the remains of a black cat.

- **Tiembla Tierra** is associated with Obatala. He is found in a large white bowl. The nganga is made with dirt, white stones, snakes, and birds. He is fed white goats, white chickens, and white pigeons.

- **Madre de Água** is associated with the orisha Yemaya. She rules the ocean waters, hurricanes, and water storms. Her nganga is kept in a large pottery jar. She is made from female human bones, stones, dirt, plants, and gems. She is summoned through songs and invocations. Her nganga is made with ram's blood, roosters, turtles, and guinea hens.

COMMANDING THE SPIRIT

The palero can command the nkisi to perform acts of magick and may call upon this spirit by going before his nganga. He may use a tibia bone called *kisengue* to wave like a wand at the cauldron.

The palero draws the sign of the spirit on the floor and begins to chant. After his incantation he will usually light small piles of gunpowder in front of the cauldron. The chants will eventually call the spirit to manifest itself. The palero will make his wishes known to the spirit, which may demand a sacrifice to carry out the request.

An informant of mine shared a story in which her nkisi would not perform correctly for her. She tried to bargain with the spirit over a bottle of rum. Her boyfriend finally persuaded the spirit to work by holding a live hen over the cauldron and threatening to let the hen go free if the spirit did not obey. This is an example of the personal interaction between the initiate and the spirit that lives in the cauldron.

Sacrifices

One of the most notorious criminal cases involving Palo Mayombe was the 1989 murders in Matamoros, Mexico. Adolfo de Jesus Constanzo led a ring of drug runners in a violent gang that utilized Santeria, Palo, and Mexican brujeria. Constanzo used Palo rituals to protect his drug trade, and the group sacri-

This nganga is dedicated to Madre de Água.

Ngurufinda is a spirit that uses the power of herbs to heal.

ficed several individuals to the nganga. The investigation into this group intensified when an American college student was kidnapped and tortured to death. The break in the case came when a member of the gang attempted to run a roadblock because he felt he was magickally protected and was invisible to his enemies. Constanzo and his gang died in a shoot-out with police.

Although this is a well-known case of paleros killing someone to use them in an nganga, this is not the norm. Some paleros explain that the use of human blood in the nganga will make the spirit a vampire and will only cause it to constantly thirst for human blood. This can cause the spirit to turn on its owner for blood.

The animals used to feed the nganga range from the small to the exotic. Ducks, chickens, turtles, goats, and other small animals are usually found. However, investigators have found zebra, peacocks, dogs, pigs, cats, scorpions, snakes, spiders, and even large cats such as tigers and panthers used in Palo sacrifices.

Sacred chants called *mambos* may be recited before offering a sacrifice to the nganga.

PRIESTHOOD

The priest in Palo is known as *palero*. (Priestesses are *paleras*.) He is also known as *tata nkisi*, which means "father of the spirit."

Palo is traditionally handed down through family lineage. The temple that is under a palero is known as a *munanso*.

The palero may perform divination rites with shells called *chamalongo*. These are used in much the same way as the cowrie shells are in Santeria.

Some traditions use the following initiatory structure:

- **Ngueyo:** Initiate has made a pact with the nkisi of his godfather.
- **Tata nkisi:** Initiate has acquired working knowledge of herbs and spells.
- **Yaya nkisi:** Female initiates.
- **Tata nganga:** Initiate who has received the nganga. May now initiate a munanso, a house of worship.
- **Tata ndibilinongo:** This is a tata nganga with godchildren.
- **Tata luwongo:** Godfather of the prenda (nganga). Highest grade.

INITIATION

The initiation into Palo differs according to houses and sources. Some sources tell of the initiate sleeping on a straw mat under a sacred ceiba tree during a full moon. The initiate wears clothes that have been buried in a graveyard. A ceremony is performed in which the initiate is given a

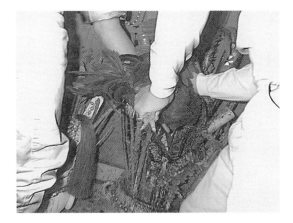

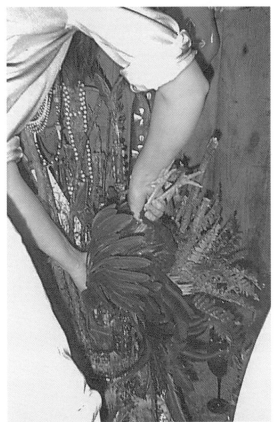

Top: Blood called menga *is given to the nganga. The nkisi is fed blood in exchange for work.*

Center: *Members of the munanso recite chants called mambos that ask the spirit to receive the blood.*

Bottom: *The sacrifice is given.*

human tibia bone. This is used to rule over the spirits of the dead. The initiate goes under *rayado*, in which the initiate is cut on several points of the body and has the spirit of the nganga implanted into his or her skin. Blood is dripped into the nganga to bind the initiate to the spirit. The initiate is blindfolded during this process. Gunpowder (*fula)* may be placed into the cuts, as well as rum poured into them. Drums and chants are used to invoke the spirits. The initiate also is given a secret name and a secret symbol that is carved into his or her flesh.

Some branches of Palo decide during this ceremony if the initiate will serve good or evil. This is by worshipping Nsambi, a good deity, or Ndoki, a devil.

The initiate will receive a large strand of beads called the *bandera*. These are worn during certain Palo ceremonies.

Eggun

As in Santeria, the eggun, or spirits of the dead, are part of the religious ideology of the palero. The palero may be given a staff known as the *palo muerto*, which means "stick of the dead." This wooden staff will usually have nine colored strings hanging from it with small bells attached to them. A boveda shrine to the dead like the one used in traditional Santeria will also usually accompany the staff.

Possession

During the "scratching in" of Palo, the initiate may be "mounted" by the spirit of the nfumbe. This is spirit possession that changes the abilities of the initiate.

Once the palero receives his nganga, he becomes the master over the spirit inside. The palero uses powdered eggshell (*cascarellia*) and draws the symbol (firma) of the spirit he is calling.

The palero then uses a stick or a bone and bangs it on the ground to start calling the spirit. Chants are spoken in Bantu, the language of the Congo, and call upon the spirit to manifest itself.

Officers may discover traces of gunpowder called *fula*. The powder is used in rituals to foretell the future.

The remains that officers find in the nganga may be very bizarre. Agencies have reported finding the remains of cats, dogs, snakes, spiders, monkeys, and horses, and even animal excrement inside these vessels.

The palero may use a liquid called *chamba* (usually alcohol and peppers) to make the spirit act. The palero drinks some of this liquid and spews it onto the nganga. One palera shared with me that she had burned her throat lining with the liquid. Cigar smoke may also be blown onto the nganga to wake it.

Once the spirit has manifested itself, the palero tells the spirit what it is going to do for him. The spirit is "fed" an animal in exchange for its power. Mercury may be added to the nganga to give it speed and easy movement in its power. Officers may also find a bull's horn, called *mpaka*. This may be used to call upon the spirit in the nganga. It may also be used to transfer the spirit of the nganga if the palero needs to move it into another pot. It is filled with dirt from various locations such as police stations, jails, or graveyards. It is sometimes filled with human bones, fingernails, toenails, and cigars. It is usually capped off with a mirror.

ITUTU

Just as in Santeria, when a palero dies, the *itutu* ceremony is performed. His tools are gathered and dispersed where the spirits dictate. The ritual has three parts:

1. The palero is prepared for his journey into the spirit realm. The chamalongo shells are read. The palero is buried with his mpaka, money, and his chamalongo shells. Sometimes the spirits will be willed to another person in the same house of worship.

2. In a ritual for the eggun, prayers are made to the ancestor spirits. The palo muerto is tapped on the ground during the prayers. Coconut shells are consulted to see if the eggun are pleased with the ritual. If they are, a white plate will be broken to symbolize the breaking of all ties with the living.

3. A spiritual mass is performed to make sure the spirit will be accessible as an eggun spirit. After this ritual, the spirit will be contacted during masses and consultations. This ritual takes place one year and nine days after the palero's death.

LAW ENFORCEMENT AND PALO MAYOMBE

While most exist to perform herbal healings and benevolent spellwork, paleros are very secretive about their practices. Officers

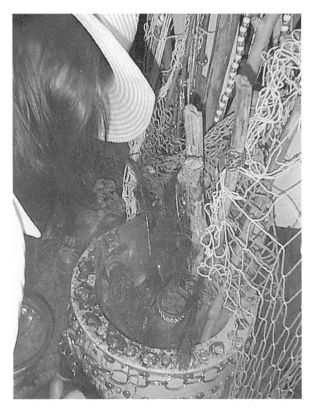

Top: The palero blows smoke into the nganga to invoke the spirit that lives inside.

Bottom: This is an nganga dedicated to Mama Chola, a water spirit whose nganga is presented in a water-based material such as terra-cotta. At the bottom of the image is the ceremonial liquid known as chamba. This particular chamba is made from cayenne peppers and pure grain alcohol.

will probably find it difficult to gain access to intelligence about rituals and inner workings of the Palo religion.

Very little has been written in the English language about the practices of Palo, but the advent of the Internet and the popularity of Voudon religions in America is changing this. Recently there have been a few mainstream publications about Palo.

If a nganga is discovered in the course of an investigation, officers should look for the presence of human remains. The origins of these remains should be analyzed by a local medical examiner. Remains may have been attained from illegal trafficking or grave robbing; although it is unlikely, the remains could be from a homicide. If the materials are found to be legal specimens, they should be returned to the proper owner.

When examining a nganga, use gloves to prevent possible contamination. Blood, feces, animal remains, and other contaminants have been found in the nganga.

When analyzing a nganga, officers should use caution. If possible, allow medical examiners to X-ray the cauldron. Blades, guns, and booby traps could be inside. Many paleros use gunpowder in rituals, so be careful about using anything that could ignite the powder.

Officers may find connections between those involved in the drug trade and the use of Palo, which is seen as a very powerful and dark religion. It can be used to create fear in enemies and faithfulness in followers.

Animal sacrifices to the nganga may be illegal in your state. Check with state statutes regarding the use of animal sacrifice as it pertains to religious rites.

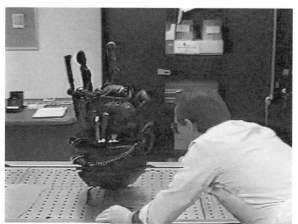

Left: This nganga was used by a drug dealer to protect his cocaine trade.

Right: Officers should use caution when moving a nganga as evidence. Besides carrying sharp implements and animal blood, the cauldron may contain mercury, which is used to give the spirit speed and flow.

Crime scenes

Police departments report discovering elements of Palo in some high-profile incidents. The November 2002 *The Wall Street Journal* reported that police in Kearny, New Jersey, charged a Palo priest and several followers with the theft of the remains of an infant who had been dead for 83 years.

Another case involved grave robbers looking for the corpse of a mobster in hopes of gaining extra power. They mistakenly robbed the grave of a tavern owner. Informants led police to a botanica where the officers discovered three skulls and the bones from five corpses.

There are a number of paleros who contend that these are the exceptions to the rule. One palero told me that he was concerned that authorities would begin to dismantle any ritual implements found among Afro-Caribbean practitioners because of these types of incidents.

Palo Mayombe Sources

Much of the information that has been made available about Palo has been tainted with false reports. An excellent classic source of information on the subject is the article "Brujeria: Manifestations of Palo Mayombe in South Florida" by Charles Wetli and Rafael Martinez, which appeared in the *Journal of the Florida Medical Association* (August 1983).

Early documentation about this obscure religion is found in Spanish in the writings of anthropologist Lydia Cabrera and writer Fernando Ortíz. Ortíz, in his classic *Los Negros Brujos*, shares early Cuban news reports on Afro-Caribbean religions.

Many of the incidents that Ortiz documents are identical to the ritualistic implements and evidence found here in the United States. Ortiz tells of stories of police finding "casseroles" of bones and sticks; one consisted of cat skulls, necklaces, and two human skulls.

VOODOO

Voodoo altars may contain images of saints that represent the loa.

The word "Voodoo" conjures up many dark images—dolls pierced with stickpins, curses, and human sacrifice. The real practices of Voodoo are far from what Hollywood has portrayed them to be. Practitioners of modern-day Voodoo usually practice in secret because of the negative images associated with the religion.

ORIGINS

The religion of Voodoo comes from West Africa. Different ethnic groups of Africans such as the Yoruba, the Fon, and the Ewe each held distinct religious practices and philosophies that are best described as "Afro-Paganism." Beliefs in gods and goddesses and the practice of magick were staples of these religions. When the Africans were captured by slave traders and sent to the Caribbean islands, they were forced to adopt French Catholicism, which led to a syncretism between the religions that can still be seen today in modern Voodoo.

This altar contains aspects of the loa Erzulie.

The slave trade also brought many practicing Voodooists to America. Slave owners saw how this religion acted as a bonding force and a power base for the slaves to draw from, and this led owners to prohibit any form of the religion. Slaves caught with any sort of paraphernalia were abused or killed immediately. But this abuse only seemed to light the fires of those who secretly practiced Voodoo. Families sought protection from the spirits, and some even magickally attacked their masters through the spirits.

Voodoo managed to survive the onslaught of American slavery and still exists in homes and temples across the United States.

The word voodoo means "spirit." Some scholars use the term "Vodou," which basically means "a look into the unknown."

Voudon rites come from a number of regions. The sects that developed from these geographical areas spread beliefs in different rites and deities. The sects do have some common patterns in ritual practices but are very distinct. Officers will find that "Voodoo" means something very different to different areas. Voudon sects from Florida will differ in practices from those in Chicago, and Voodoo as practiced by Haitian immigrants will be very different from that found among groups made up of American citizens.

Some common elements found in most sects will help in understanding the beliefs and practices of this religion.

PANTHEON OF SPIRITS

Voodooists believe in a creator spirit called Gran Met Bondye. In Haitian Krio, *Gran Met* means "Great Master," and *Bondye* means "Good God."

The following of spirits, called *loa*, is the key element to Voodoo ritual. The loa are broken into families with different aspects and different purposes. The loa are present in all aspects of nature—they are in trees, rocks, water, and fire. Most loa belong to three separate classes identified with ethnic groups in Africa. They have distinguishing characteristics in ritual, dance, and sacrifices.

Loa may cause problems such as pains and troubles for initiates if they ignore or forget to appropriate them at scheduled times.

Loa may be called *zanj,* meaning "angel." They may also be called *djab,* meaning "devil." During the course of interviewing practitioners, you may encounter the loa called "mysteries." This is a common term used to describe initiation into the loa. There are also loa that are spirits from ancestors, called *loa racine.*

Rada

The loa that come from the holy city, Arada, of the Dahomey (now Benin) region of Africa are called *rada*. Rada loa are considered "cool" and benevolent spirits. The following spirits are considered rada:

- **Legba:** Father of the Crossroads. Legba is called upon first to open the doorway to the spiritual world. He is syncretized with St. Peter and St. Anthony. His favorite color is red. He is symbolized by an old man in rags.

- **Azaka:** Loa of agriculture. Azaka is syncretized with St. Isidore. Azaka's favorite colors are blue, red, and green. Azaka's shrine may contain a straw bag called a *djakout*. This bag symbolizes Azaka and is used to hold and carry items by initiates. The bag is usually decorated in colored ribbons. He may be represented by a small reptile called a *mabouya*.
- **Damballah:** Loa of goodness. Damballah is syncretized with St. Patrick and symbolized by a serpent. He is often paired with Ayida Wedo. His favorite color is white.
- **Ayida Wedo:** Loa of wealth and happiness, Ayida Wedo is represented by a rainbow. Ayida Wedo is syncretized with Our Lady of Immaculate Conception and favors blue and white.
- **Erzulie:** Loa of love. Erzulie is represented by a heart and is syncretized with the Virgin Mary. Erzulie's favorite colors are blue and pink, and she is symbolized by a heart and a mirror.
- **Ogou Feray:** Loa of the fight against miserable conditions, blacksmiths, and war. Ogou is represented by a sword stuck in the earth and is syncretized with St. James. Ogou's favorite color is red. Ogou's shrine may also hold a machete with a red cloth tied around the handle.
- **Agwe:** Loa of the sea. Agwe, represented by a boat, is syncretized with St. Ulrich. Agwe's favorite colors are white, green, and pink.

Kongo

The loa that come from the Bantu region of Africa are known as *kongo loa*. Many of the kongo loa demand dogs as sacrifices. Some of the loa are Grande Alouba, Canga, Zinga, and Man Inan.

Petro

The loa that come from the colony of Saint Domingue are known as *petro loa*. Petro loa take their name from a man named Don Pedro. These spirits are "fiery" and sometimes malevolent and are used in destructive magick. Some of the petro loa are:

- **Simbi:** Loa of clairvoyance. Simbi is represented by a pond of water and is syncretized with the Magi that visited Christ. Simbi's favorite colors are black and gray and a pond represents him.
- **Gede:** The gede family are a group of loa that rule over the cemeteries. The gede are represented by a cross (representing the crossroads) and are led by a figure known as Baron Samdi. Samdi is pictured as a man with a black hat and coat, smoking a pipe, and with a face that is white like death. The gedes' favorite colors are black and purple.
- **Marassa:** These loa are twin spirits that appear in rada and petro rituals. The twins may be invoked after Legba in rituals. They may have other spirit offspring known as *marassa dosu*, which means "boy." The sacrifices are in the form of foods served in a terra-cotta bowl called the *mange-marassa*. The bowl looks like three small bowls connected together.

SPIRITUAL WORK

The soul is seen as an "angel." The conscience is called the *ti bon ange*, which means "little good angel." The psyche is known as *gros bon ange*, which means "big good angel."

The soul is placed in the initiate during a ceremony called *mette n' anme*. This brings a balance between the two souls.

At the death of the initiate, a ritual called *dessounen* is performed to separate the protective spirit from the body.

HIERARCHY

The priestess in Voodoo is known as the *mambo* or *manbo*, and the priest is known as the *houngan* or *oungan*. The leader of the

Voodoo temple carries a tool called the *asson*. This is a maraca covered in beads or snake vertebrae, and it is a symbol of power in the temple and can only be carried by the leadership.

In traditional Voodoo there are several offices in the temple. Offices are designated for a variety of duties including singing, preparing the food, performing as musicians, and keeping order.

The following is a list of some of the traditional officers in a Voodoo temple:

- **Voudouisant:** An uninitiated attendee.
- **Housni:** A person who affiliates with a house of worship.
- **Housi Kanzo:** A member who is initiated into a fire ceremony.
- **Sur Point:** An initiate who becomes a mambo or houngan and receives the asson is called "on the point" of a single loa. This means the initiate is serving one particular loa.
- **Asogwe:** An assistant to the priests in the temple.
- **Ongenikon:** The choir director of the temple, also called the "queen singer."
- **Bête-charge:** The animal keeper.
- **Lafla:** The master of ceremonies.
- **Bokor:** The sorcerer who works with the dead. He is said to be working with the "left hand," which is a term to describe black magick.

THE TEMPLE

The Voodoo temple is called the *oumphor*. The area in which the majority of ceremonies occur is called the *peristyle*, which is usually decorated with drawings of the saints, hanging calabashes, and a large wooden boat that represents the loa Erzulie. It may contain pictures of the president of the country that the group originated from, such as a picture of the leaders of Haiti. There is usually an area that contains a fire pit wherein resides an iron bar that represents the spirit of iron.

In the center of the peristyle is a pole called the *poteau-mitan*. This is creole French for "pole in the middle," and it is used by the loa to climb down from the heavens. The top of the pole represents heaven, while the bottom represents hell. It is usually decorated with paintings of Damballah and Aida Wedo, the serpent and the rainbow.

There is also an altar called the *pe*. The *pe* is usually square shaped and holds several personal ritual objects that are considered sacred to the members of the temple. This may even include a snake representing Damballah.

The temple also contains chambers known as *kay-miste*, or "huts of the mysteries," which are reserved for worship of a single loa. These chambers may contain images and tools used by the particular loa.

- **Asson:** This is a rattle similar to a maraca and is usually carried by those who have been initiated into a priest or priestess position of leadership. This rattle is usually made from a large calabash. It is sometimes filled and covered with snake vertebrae to symbolize Damballah. When the rattle is shaken it causes the spirits to appear.
- **Baka:** This is usually found in the form of a statue of a devilish-looking creature. The *baka* is a malevolent spirit that can be used to spiritually harass and attack enemies. Although the baka may be found, it is not a common item in temples.
- **Govi:** A spirit can be called through a vessel of water using a white sheet or cloth. It is then placed inside a jar called a *govi*, which is used to call down the loas. These jars are found in the temple and may be decorated with symbols of the loa.
- **Pakets:** The *paket* comes from the Congo region and is a bag that contains bones, herbs, stones, and other ingredients. The bag, usually decorated with satin cloth and sequins, may have one stem sticking out of it. This is a male paket. Female pakets will have two arms, rounded, pointing down. The paket is found in the temple and is used to "heat up" the loa for ceremonies.

The ve-ve is a symbol that represents the spirits of the Haitian pantheon. The image is drawn in cornmeal.

- **Flags:** Multicolored flags may be found during a search or observation of a residence in which Voodoo is practiced. Flags announce the spirits that will attend a ceremony and are usually made on fine cloth with sequined images of the spirits sewn into them. Flags may be kept on the poteau-mitan to give them power.
- **Swords:** Swords are used in Voudon rituals as symbols of the iron spirit, Ogou. There is a ritual procession of the sword known as the "Sword of La Place." The La Place is the swordbearer who helps begin the rituals of Voodoo.
- **Ogan:** The *ogan* is a cowbell-type instrument without a clapper. It is struck during ceremonies to summon the spirits.
- **Triangle:** An iron triangle that is a musical instrument is used in rituals as well. When it is struck, it opens spiritual doorways.
- **Conch shell:** The shell is blown like a trumpet to call the loa of the ocean, Agwe.
- **Zins:** These are three-legged cauldrons that can be used to burn incense and offer sacrifices in.
- **Drums:** Drums are central to the Voudon ceremony. The rhythms call the spirits into the ceremony. The drums are considered alive, and their creation and preparation is a very involved process.

Drums are treated as living beings and are given power and even fed sacrificed animals. They are broken into different categories according to the type of spirit being called. The three types of drums are rada, petro, and kongo. Each drum has its own particular style of play, and each has its own physical characteristics. Rada drums are three in a set. They will typically have small pegs that stick out the sides of the top of the drum; petro drums come in sets of two with one drum larger than the other; the petro do not contain pegs. Kongo drums usually come in sets of three.

Personal Altars

The devotee may keep a personal altar in his or her home. This is called a *rogatoire* and usually contains a picture of the saint that corresponds with his or her personal loa. Candles, crosses, and other Voudon icons may be on this altar. Food may also be left on the altar for the loa.

CEREMONIES

Voodoo ceremonies are referred to as services. Most traditional services fall on the celebrated dates of the Catholic Church's liturgical calendar.

The traditional Voodoo ceremony has several components that must occur before the loa appear to the temple. The two main parts of the service are the procession of the flags, drums, and sacred ritual tools to the temple, and the invocations of loa.

One of the most common items found in the Voodoo ceremony is the *ve-ve*—an image that is universally recognized as the symbol of a particular loa. The symbol is drawn on the ground with cornmeal, coffee, powdered brick, or chalk. It is usually placed where a spirit is to manifest, with food sometimes being left on the drawings for the spirit. This image originally came from the Congo region, where they utilize drawings and symbols in many of their ceremonies and rites.

Entrance
The ceremony begins with the parade of the oumphor's flags. These flags are decorated with the symbols of the loa. The oumphor's drums are then greeted. The center of the temple is entered and the four points—north, south, east, and west—are recognized. The loa are called upon, as well as the Catholic saints. Drumming and dancing begins to call the loa. Ve-ve are drawn in cornmeal and powders on the ground to represent the loa that are manifesting.

Manje Loa: The Sacrifice
The loa are believed to eat as human beings do. The second part of the service is known as *manje loa*, the ritual feeding of the animals.

Plates of food and the animals to be sacrificed are left at the poteau-mitan. The animals may be dressed in colors of the loa. The person in charge of the sacrifice (*commanditaire*) usually wears a red cloth on his head. He eats some of the food on the plates and feeds the animals some of the food. If the animals eat the food, this means that they have accepted the sacrifice. They are then rubbed with sacred herbs and killed.

The person who kills it drinks some of the animal's blood and then carries it to the four points of the ritual area. Devotees may rub the animal's blood on their foreheads in the shape of crosses. The animals' bodies are then taken outside to be cooked.

Rites of Passage
There is a ceremony known as the *leve nom*, in which the initiate will receive the name of an ancestor for protection.

The ritual of *garde* is performed after the leve nom. This is a sacrifice to the spirit that protects the initiate.

Lave-tête is a ritualistic washing of the head. This "baptism" places the loa inside the initiate's head.

To become an initiated priest or priestess, a ceremony called *haussement*, or the "lifting" of the initiate, is performed. The devotee is lifted in a chair three times, then swears allegiance to the loa.

Spirit Possession
Possession is a normative practice that temples observe. The initiate is "mounted" by the loa, similar to the possession in Santeria. The initiate actually becomes possessed by the loa, speaks as the loa, and takes on its characteristics. For example, those possessed by the loa Damballah may act like a snake; possession by Ogou will usually make the initiate wield a sword; devotees who are possessed by the gede loa will wear sunglasses, a hat, and will be given strong drinks like rum. They will usually curse and begin acting in a sexually promiscuous fashion.

Initiation
The initiate is called the *ounsi*. The ritual to becoming ounsi takes one to two weeks. The initiate is dressed in white and is taught about the loa and how to function in the temple. The initiate is then presented to the temple. If the initiate becomes possessed, it is a sign that the initiate is connected to the loa.

Marriage
To gain additional power from the loa, initiates can be married to the loa in a ceremony. The ceremony is conducted like a traditional wedding ceremony, and the initiate signs a marriage certificate to the loa.

INTERNATIONAL POWER

The use of Voodoo for political power is clearly seen in the history of Haiti. The dictator François "Papa Doc" Duvalier used Voodoo to bring the people of Haiti under his control. Duvalier dressed in black and carried the tools of the loa Baron Samdi. This made many citizens believe Duvalier was the spirit of death. His private police—the Tontons Macoutes—were violent enforcers who often were well-known practitioners of black magick.

These tactics were successful in inflicting fear of the supernatural on the citizens of Haiti.

ZOMBIES

The idea of "zombies" sounds ludicrous to Western thought. However, in the world of traditional Voodoo, the zombie is a very real concept. Through the use of various toxins and powders, such as the venom of the puffer fish and various tree frogs, Voodoo initiates may create an altered state of consciousness. Though the use of these items is actually not different from the use of an anesthetic in surgery, it is considered "magickal" to those in Voodoo. An oungan who uses these powders is said to make zombie slaves.

The powders actually slow the heart rate and produce a trancelike state that can mimic death. The subject is buried and is later exhumed to show the "miracle" of zombification.

These exotic powders can produce harmful results if used recklessly. A Miami police officer reported seeing the results of some toxic Voodoo powders that had been blown into a woman's face, which caused serious nerve damage.

SECRET SOCIETIES

The practice of Voodoo is very secret. This stems from the abuse that slaves incurred when they practiced the religion. This is also because of contemporary views and distortions of Voodoo. However, even though the majority of Voodoo practitioners are not involved in criminal activities, there exists a number of secret societies that operate in the Voudon community.

These groups have adopted the name *secte rouge*, or red sect, so named because of their shedding of human blood.

Most of these groups operate using fraternal structures that include secret passwords and ceremonies. These societies generate a climate of fear in the Voudon community.

Most of these groups utilize the powers of the petro loa. Some of the sects are known as *cochons sans poils*, meaning "hairless pigs," with one sect known as *vin bain-ding*, which eloquently means "blood, pain, and excrement."

These sects dress in red clothing and wear ceremonial jewelry. Red sect ideology teaches that Legba was crucified on the center of the cross so that he may become an edible human sacrifice.

Members of one sect, known as the *bizango*, are said to have the ability to transform themselves into animals, just like werewolves.

LAW ENFORCEMENT AND VOODOO

The growth of traditional Voodoo is becoming popular among outsiders. However, Voodoo in its purest form is found primarily among those who have come from Haiti and the areas of Africa in which it is a common family religion. Officers with a background in working with the Haitian population will most likely see the subtle outward signs of traditional Voodoo. Officers should be reminded that Voodoo has a very rich tradition among Haitian families and is considered sacred. Intelligence on criminal activities from this community might be difficult to obtain.

Officers are advised to use caution when handling sacred objects; handling them in front of practitioners could produce violent behavior. If officers must investigate items, it is suggested that they keep practitioners away from the area.

Again, respect tempered with caution is the rule. Be sure that you have sufficient probable cause or a real emergency before disturbing *any* religious ceremony.

Officers encountering rituals may find such tools as swords and blades that are used in the ceremony. Always use caution when entering ceremony areas.

Law enforcement personnel may arrive during a spirit possession. If possible, allow the leader of the group to stop the possession. Remove other followers from the ritual area when laying hands on the possessed subject.

Officers should use caution when examining altars and ritual jars and bottles. Toxic powders may be present that could harm the investigating officer.

Officers should also be aware of state statutes regarding the use of animals in religious sacrifices.

Chapter 5

OTHER VOUDON RELIGIONS

In addition to the Voudon-based religions that we have already examined, there are several other derivatives of the Voudon tradition that are not so well known. These are particularly secretive, with some sects having been involved in criminal activities.

ABAQUA

The sect of Abaqua came to Cuba with an ethnic group known as the Calabar. The Calabar were seen as the "second wave" of slaves into the New World. Because of this, the group that formed Santeria, the Lucumi, looked down on them as second-class citizens. So the Calabar formed the Abaqua—a secret brotherhood dedicated to serving a deity known as Ekue, who is known as the "power of the leopard."

Researchers have debated whether Abaqua is a religious movement or only a secret society, similar to freemasonry. The Abaqua have sometimes been referred to as the "leopard people" because the leopard plays an important role in the religion, symbolizing masculine power. The deity Ekue is served, as well as a deity known as Sikan, who is represented by a fish. For this reason, many Abaqua lodges are built near water.

Men who join the Abaqua are required to be "honest, honorable, and strong" and must go through a series of trials and initiations to be accepted. The priest is known as *iyamba*; the second in command is known as *mocongo*.

When Cuban dictator Fidel Castro came into power, he sought to overthrow the Abaqua because belonging to this brotherhood gave strength to the dockworkers and helped them stand up to Castro and his security forces. Because of their incredible powers, Castro allowed the Abaqua to govern themselves.

Abaqua rituals are very secretive. They use sacrifices of large animals, ranging from goats to cattle. The Abaqua also take part in the ritualistic blood-drinking ceremony called *macuba*, which bonds the brotherhood of the group.

Part of Abaqua ritual is the "masquerade." This is a drama of sorts in which key figures in the group play spiritual characters. Elaborate masks and costumes decorated with leopard spots are part of this rite.

A Santeria initiate who visited Cuba shared some of his experience with contacts in the Abaqua. He told me that Abaqua rituals are kept on cryptic texts that demand a secret code to interpret. He went on to tell me that any attempt by law enforcement to crack the code to such texts would be nearly impossible because of its intricacies.

Abaqua ritual areas are usually marked by yellow chalk drawings called *nsibidi*, which are symbols of the Calabari people. They are usually found in an area where a tree has had the earth around its base cleared away.

Members of the Abaqua secret society were said to be responsible for a number of homicides in the Miami area in the early 1980s. These deaths were attributed to "unfinished business" that started in Cuba.

Abaqua is a very closed tradition. Informants advise that most Abaqua lodges will not put up with destructive behavior by members, and that not just anyone can join them. There is a code of honor that regulates Abaqua, and justice is handled by the group, not by outside agencies.

BRUJERIA

Police officers in Texas were called to a residence in response to an anonymous report from a woman who claimed to have seen a human skull on an altar while at a party. The responding officers talked to the resident about the skull and asked to look around the house. The resident was a Hispanic hairdresser who frequently traveled into Mexico. He took the officers into a closet area where he showed them an altar. Officers found the skull alongside jars, bottles, oils, candles, and photographs. The subject gave officers a receipt from an individual who was purported to sell magickal implements. It was during this time that several incidents of illegal trafficking in human remains were rumored to be occurring on the Texas-Mexico border.

The officers found bits of hair and blood on the altar and confiscated the altar and its tools for investigation. The evidence inventory list includes these items found on the altar:

- 1 dried frog inside a glass jar
- 1 bottle of King Solomon's Oil
- 1 dried frog wrapped in black cloth
- 1 picture of a white female with stickpins stuck in it
- 1 book, *El Libros Secrets*
- 1 picture of a Catholic saint
- Several bags of herbs
- 1 pack of Mexican tarot cards
- Several white candles

The items found in this case were used by a practitioner of Brujeria, which has traditionally been used as a generic term meant to denote witchcraft of any kind. However, there is a recognized religion called Brujeria. This is a belief system that focuses on the powers of a Catholic saint, Mother of Guadalupe, and an Aztec goddess, Tonantzin. The religion combines aspects of Catholicism, Aztec religions, and European witchcraft.

Beliefs
Some basic knowledge of Our Lady of Guadalupe is needed to understand the deities

of this religion. On December 9, 1531, an Indian named Juan Diego, who had been converted to Catholicism, saw a manifestation of the Virgin on a mountainside. She informed Diego that he was to build a church to her. Her appearance was marked by the sudden growth of roses in winter weather and the appearance of the Virgin's image on the Indian's clothing. Her appearance is celebrated every year by a huge procession of believers in a grand church in Mexico.

Tonantzin was known as "Our Mother." She was also known as "Eater of Filth." One of her many manifestations was as "Mother of the Gods."

The Aztec religion is perhaps best remembered as a savage culture that practiced human sacrifice. The pantheon of Aztec gods is large; however, it was the goddess Tonantzin who was revered when Spanish missionaries decided to baptize the followers of the Aztec religions. The Aztec pagans took the Virgin Mary and the saints as simply "children of the Mother." The Virgin of Guadalupe and the Aztec goddess became syncretized like the saints and orishas of Santeria. This syncretism became the standard source of power for what we see as modern-day Brujeria.

Followers of this religion are known as *brujas*, meaning "witches." (Males may be called *brujos*.) The religion began to change more when it combined traditions from the Yaqui Indians. Herbal healing became an art with the bruja. Like the Cuban santeros who found European spiritism in America, the brujas added aspects of spiritism to their beliefs. What has evolved is a belief system that remains popular among many in the Hispanic community.

Witches who work in herbal healing and bone setting may be called *curandaros*. Some brujas may also even be called santeras.

Practices

One of the most important practices of the bruja is divination, the ability to forecast the future. The most popular form is through the reading of tarot cards. Tarot cards are broken into suits of wands, cups, swords, and penta-cles. Each suit has 10 numbered cards from the ace through 10, as well as court cards of knight, queen, page, and king. There is a section of cards known as "major arcana." These are 22 "trump" cards that contain pictures and words on them. Cards like the fool, the princess, the magician, and others make up the arcana.

The cards are shuffled and a card is laid out to represent the person who is getting his future told. Other cards are laid out by the bruja that explain the past, present, and future. Cards are typically laid out in a form called the Celtic cross. Brujas may lay cards in a manner known as the santa cruz, or "holy cross," or in the shape of a heart known as *el santisimo corazon de la Guadalupana*, "the most holy heart of Our Lady of Guadalupe." The end result of the card pattern tells what is to come in the future for the subject. It may also reveal aspects of the subject's character during the reading.

There are hundreds of types of tarot cards; most brujas use Mexican or Spanish tarot cards.

Brujas also use astrology in performing spells and important workings. The location of the planets is important in providing extra energies for the bruja's powers.

Spell Casting

The practice of performing spells is accomplished in a number of ways by the bruja. The use of sympathetic magick is very popular in Brujeria. Brujas' altars contain photographs, hair, nail clippings, and clothes of intended recipients of healing or harm.

Love magick is very popular among the brujas. Brujas will perform spells that will bring lovers together or tear them apart. Some will charge enormous fees for spellwork, while some offer to help for meager payments.

Candle magick is very popular in Brujeria rituals. Officers may find candles in a glass, such as the votive candles most often found in supermarkets. Taper candles may be also be found in brujas' homes, along with candles with photographs under them for magickal operations. Candles may also represent victims of magick operations.

Left: The priest in a Candomble ceremony.

Right: Officers that have the opportunity to interview any members of the Candomble religion will find a rich religious heritage. There have been very few deviant activities connected to any Candomble houses. The tradition is very guarded by its practitioners.

Altars

The altar of the bruja may differ according to which avatar, or manifestation, of the goddess she is calling on. A typical altar will be a small table or counter space. The altar is usually covered in a white cloth along with votive candles. An incense burner is there to call spirits and create a ritual atmosphere. Holy water and a statue of Our Lady of Guadalupe are important elements used on altars as well.

Some altars may contain a knife, or *cuchillo*, to cut herbs and plants for use in spells and magick.

Brujas keep a diary of spells and thoughts, like the Wiccan *Book of Shadows*. It is called a liberta. It is kept in secret and is not to be seen by the uninitiated. When a bruja dies, it is to be destroyed.

Ceremonies

Ceremonies may be performed on the dates of the classic European witches' calendar (e.g., equinoxes, solstices) Ceremonies may also be observed by the Catholic calendar; however, the meaning of the holidays will usually differ. The most important dates of December 8 and 9 are the Vigil and Feast of Our Lady of Guadalupe.

Diablera

The bruja uses her powers for healing and for the good of others. But there are malevolent witches known as the *diablera*. They do not serve the Virgin, but instead serve *el diablo*, or Satan. These followers are considered outcasts in the Brujeria community.

CANDOMBLE

The 1999 U.S. Department of State annual report on international religious freedom concluded that in the country of Brazil, 5 percent of the population followed tenets of spiritism-based religions, particularly the religion of Candomble.

The word *candomble* is possibly derived from *candombe*, which means "dance" or "invitation to celebrate." The Yoruba tradition that became Santeria in Cuba, mixed with traditions from the Ewe and Fon people, became Candomble in Brazil. Those groups were brought over as slaves and were divided into sects known as "nations." These different cultural groups are distinguished by the ethnic origins of their rites. (Note: In Brazilian Portuguese, the letter x is pronounced "sh.")

Deities

The spirits of Candomble are known as *orixas*. They are identified with the Catholic saints that were taught by the slave owners. Each represents an aspect of nature and a human emotion.

- **Exu** is the messenger to the spirit world, the orixa over crossroads. He receives an offering so he will not interfere with ceremonies. Exu is identified with the Judeo-Christian image of the Devil; however, Exu is an example of a deity that must be looked at in context of a religious ritual before immediately identifying it as such. Exu is sometimes represented by a pitchfork, and his colors are red and black. He acts as a mediator between the physical and spiritual worlds.

- **Ogun** is the orixa over war and iron and is identified with the images of St. Anthony and St. George. He is known as the orixa who can clear all paths and is represented by an iron sword. His favorite color is dark blue.

- **Omolu** is the orixa over diseases and cures and is identified with St. Lazarus. He is covered with straw to hide his smallpox and disease scars and is represented by a bundle of palm leaves covered with cowrie shells. His colors are red, black, and white.

- **Xango** is the orixa over fire and thunder and is identified with St. Jerome. He is represented by an axe, and his favorite colors are red and white. He is actually a deceased king of the province of Oyo. His presence as an orixa is a reminder of the Yoruba origins of the religion.

- **Oxossi** is the orixa over the hunt in the forest and is identified with St. George and St. Sebastian. He is represented by a bow and arrow, and his favorite color is light blue.

- **Iemanja** is the orixa over the sea and is identified with Our Lady of the Immaculate Conception. She is represented by metallic fish, and her favorite color is crystal clear.

- **Oba** is the orixa over female hunting and is identified with St. Catherine. She cut off her ear to put in Xango's stew to make him love her more and is seen clutching her ear. She is represented by a sword, and her favorite colors are red and yellow.

- **Nana Buruku** is the orixa over swamps and stagnant water and is identified with Our Lady of Mount Carmel. She is represented by palm leaves covered in cowrie shells.

- **Oxala** is the orixa over creation and is identified with Our Lord of Bonfim. He is represented by a sword and a metal shepherd's rod, and his favorite colors are white and blue.

Inside a terreiro, the Candomble temple. There are a few Candomble houses in the United States, including some in California, Florida, and New York.

The spirits of the dead Brazilian Indians are also part of the Candomble pantheon. The *caboclos* may also speak through states of possession.

As in Santeria, the ancestor spirits of the eggun are given recognition in the Candomble religion. Shrines and altars will be set up specifically for these ancestral spirits.

Temple
The temple is known as the *terreiro*. This was traditionally the building where slaves could dance and celebrate their normal folkways and traditions. Upon entering a terreiro, there is usually a pot full of water to be splattered on the front step to cool whatever the visitor is bringing in off the streets.

The main room where the feasts and rituals are held is known as the *barracão* (barracks). There are several small rooms where the orixas are kept. The sacred pots that house the saints are known as *igbas*. These are not to be viewed by the uninitiated.

The warrior orixas (Exu, Ogun, Ossayin, Oxossi) are visible to the public eye in the main ritual entrance. In South America the orixas and ritual implements are very rarely found in the devotee's homes. However, due to the lack of terreiros in the United States, implements may be found in the homes of practitioners.

Ceremonies
The initial ceremonies of Candomble are very similar to those of Santeria. As in Santeria, the priestess must perform a consultation of the shells (*jogo de buzios*) to reveal who owns the initiate's head. The initiate receives colored beads similar to the elekes in Santeria and then begins the spiritual journey by having a series of ritualistic animal sacrifices made to his head. These will strengthen the power in the head and make the initiate more open to the eventual "possession" of the orixa.

Candles and powders used in southern folk magick.

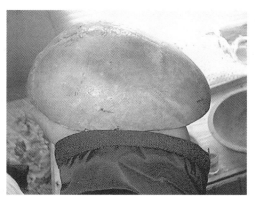

These bones were discovered by a southern Hoodoo practitioner who inherited the tools of a famous mojo maker.

Stores in the southern United States carry candles, oils, and powders for the practice of magick.

During the initiation, the initiate is placed in a solitary environment inside the group's temple for several weeks. During the last days of the initiation, the initiate will have his head shaved and his body painted in colors of the orixa that rules him. The initiate is then presented to the Candomble community. The orixa will give the initiate a name to speak when the spirit possesses him.

Drums and chants are frequently used in Candomble ceremonies. There are also several different feasts throughout the year that celebrate the orixas and fellowship among believers.

Animal sacrifices (the ebbo) are used in Candomble. Animals such as hens, goats, and doves are sacrificed.

Hierarchy

The high priestess is known as *mãe de santo*, which means "mother of the saint" (Iyalorxha). The high priest is known as *pai de santo*, which is "father of the saint" (Babalorixa). The mãe de santo leads the congregation of followers in rituals and ceremonies for the orixas.

Houses of worship do allow attendees who have not been initiated. These people are typically known as *abians*.

Initiates who become possessed by the orixa are known as *filhos/filhas de santo*, which literally means "sons/daughters of the saint." During possession by a female orixa, the initiate may wear a headpiece of stringed beads called an *ade*.

Those female initiates who do not become possessed are called *ekedis*. Males who do not receive possession are known as *ogans*.

The Candomble celebration to *iemanja*, the orixa of the sea, takes place on January 1. This event is televised across the world by Brazilian television. Followers of the goddess place small boats containing gifts and candles into the sea. If they sink, it is viewed as an offering accepted by the goddess.

HOODOO

I was contacted by a local deputy about a woman who he had seen "performing Voodoo." The deputy reported that a little old lady had entered a local store and had walked around the inside of the store shaking a ring of keys. She told the owner, "This is to get rid of the Voodoo." Store patrons reported to the deputy that the women held strange powers and had even healed a local judge of some knee problems.

I decided to contact the woman. When I visited her, she told me of several cases in which she healed others. She claimed her powers came from God and from her deceased grandfather, who was a Cherokee Indian. Her house was decorated with pictures of Jesus and photographs of dead relatives. She told me about how she used a pendulum to find money and tell the future. A pendulum is a weight or stone attached to a string that sways back and forth freely. When the user asks the spirits a question, the string swings in a pattern that is interpreted as a "yes" or "no." She also talked about how she mixed herbs and roots together to heal others of sickness. Her specialty was using the healing powers of a root known as John the Conqueror, or "polk root," in the South. It is believed to contain magickal properties and is used universally by those involved in southern folk magick.

Southern folk magick is sometimes called "Hoodoo." Hoodoo combines elements of European spiritism, Voodoo, Native American practices, and Protestant icons and beliefs. It may also be called JuJu or Rootwork. Hoodoo is not an organized religious group, nor are there Hoodoo churches. There are groups that gather to the practice Hoodoo, but there is not a leadership or hierarchy in Hoodoo. Practitioners of Hoodoo typically belong to Protestant churches, and most don't even consider their practices as religious or magick-based workings.

Stores throughout the South sell such items as oils, candles, powders, and herbs. Many of these stores sell exotic items such as black cat bone, frog eyes, and even the entrails of certain animals. Most of these stores do not necessarily advertise these goods, but in fact hide them in the back of pharmacies and convenience stores.

One of the largest selections of Hoodoo supplies in the state of Tennessee is available from a beauty supply house. The items are kept in the back of the store.

Some of the practices of the Hoodoo use candle-burning rituals for love, money, and protection. Some use very primitive practices like rubbing urine on the steps of their houses to keep evil away. Many followers use small bags known as mojo bags, which are filled with herbs and roots. The bags give powers to their holders. Luck in gambling, luck in love, and even protection from the police can be attained from the bags. In the South these bags may be called "nation sacks."

One Hoodoo faction that has distinct characteristics is that of the South Carolina Gullah. This is a collection of beliefs and practices that came to the coast of the Carolinas from slavery. Use of roots and herbs known as *gris-gris* or the "mojo" is universal in Gullah. One of the most famous root doctors was a Dr. Buzzard, who was said to be able to raise the spirits of the dead and heal the sick.

Most Hoodoo practitioners are not largely involved in criminal activities although some grave theft may occur because some believers use items like coffin nails or human bones.

MACUMBA

The Congo slaves in Brazil were broken into groups known as nations. After slavery the nations tried to regroup and organize. The Congo religions that survived slavery transformed into what is known as Macumba, which is divided into two factions—Umbanda, the sect that practices white magick with powers of the orixas, and Quimbanda, a sect that practices black magick and uses the powers of the orixas for malevolent purposes.

Umbanda

Umbanda is said to mean "divine principle" and "the art of healing." The Umbanda religion follows principles of understanding spiritual beings and their places in everyday life. Sources say the creation of Umbanda is a result of the combination of African religion, local Indian religion, European spiritism, and Catholicism. The spiritual deities of these groups are recognized, as well as the ancestral spirits of these cultures. It is the ancestral spirits that serve as liaisons between humans and the spirits.

In Rio de Janeiro, it is believed that the spirit realm is divided into seven different lines under the creator spirit. Each line has a four-star general who commands seven divisions. There is also a three-star general who commands seven battalions. There is a two-star general who rules over two subdivisions. Each four-star general has a favorite food, color, day, number, chant, and symbol.

- Line 1 is Oxala. He is represented by Jesus.
- Line 2 is Iemanja. She is represented by Mary.
- Line 3 is Ogun. He is represented by St. George.
- Line 4 is Oxossi. He is represented by St. Sebastian.
- Line 5 is Zang. He is represented by St. James.
- Line 6 is Oxun. She is represented by St. Catherine.
- Line 7 is Omulu. He is represented by Lazarus.

The ancestral spirits manifest themselves in three forms. The first are spirits known as cablocos, the spirits of dead Brazilian Indians. These spirit beings work in the forest with herbs and plants. *Preto-velhos* are spirits of "old black slaves." These spirits bring ancient wisdom to ceremonies. The third spirit is a child spirit called the *ere*. This is a child who died at a young age.

There are trickster spirits known as Exu and Pomba Gira. Exu is represented by the Judeo-Christian Devil and has many manifestations, such as Exu Worldspinner and Exu the Piercer. Pomba Gira is an interesting spirit who is considered the wife of Exu. She is known as the seductive harlot and is represented by a statue of a nude or scantily dressed woman. Initiates call her the "Devil Woman." Exu and Pomba Gira are to be given a sacrifice before rituals to keep them from interfering with the rituals.

Hierarchy

Priests of the religions are known as *pais de santo*, the "fathers of the saint." Under the priest is the *pai pequeno*, who is the "little father." The assistants to rituals are the *cambonos*. The cambonos also act as mediums for spirit possession, being persons who let their consciousness be taken over by a spirit. Once in this state, the initiate will give wisdom to the other initiates. The medium may pick up the tools and clothes of a spirit. The medium who is possessed by a preto-velho picks up a tobacco pipe and a crooked staff while displaying the characteristics of an old black man. There are also offices, such as secretary and president, for the temple.

Symbols

Those viewing an Umbanda ritual will see symbols from other occult religions such as European witchcraft and even signs from European Satanism. These symbols have distinct meaning in these religions that differ from their more popular associations. The pentagram, moon, triangles, circles, and even pictures of the inverted pentagram are found at rituals. Each temple has its own personal symbols called "risked points."

Quimbanda

The religion of Quimbanda is said to be the Afro-Caribbean version of Satanism. While the orixa Exu is viewed by most as just a trickster identified with the Christian version of the Devil, the Quimbanda Exu is "King Exu" or "King Lucifer," the dark angel.

Satan has three manifestations, Lucifer, Beelzebub (Exu Mor), and Ashtaroth (Exu of the Crossroads).

The Pomba Gira is the female manifestation of Exu in Quimbanda. The European spellbook *Goetia: Key of Solomon* has many of its rites and symbols taken from it that are used in conjunction with the religion's deities.

ZULU

In 2001 the British newspaper *The Guardian* reported:

A boy whose dismembered torso was found floating in the river Thames last month may have been the victim of a ritual killing by witchdoctors, Scotland Yard said today. Officers are exploring the possibility that the boy was killed in order that African witchdoctors could use his body parts for magic potions.

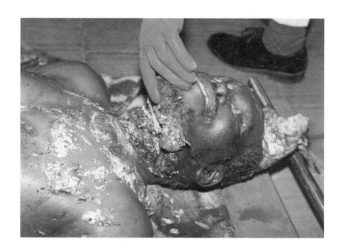

The discovery of the child's body led detectives into a bizarre world of clandestine rituals and dark magickal workings. A Southern African tribe, the Zulu, were key suspects in the case. The Zulu are a people that inhabit the areas of South Africa, Zululand, and Swaziland.

The Zulu have a very complex religious system that uses tribal healers known as *sangoma*. These healers follow a concept known as *muti*, which is the power of magick in the Zulu culture. It can be produced by sacrifices and offerings to the deities; the sacrifice of a human being is also included in these offerings.

One South African researcher has determined that at least five homicides in Swaziland have been attributed to Zulu human sacrifices (H.J. Schotz, "Muti or Ritual Murder," *Forensic Sciences International*, Vol. 87, June 6, 1997).

In one case the decapitated body of a 5-year-old boy was found in a village dump. The child's body had been used in a Zulu ritual in which his brain matter was extracted and placed in a muti charm bag. The sangoma who murdered the child was deemed unfit for trial by a local court, but was found "guilty" by local followers, who killed him by "necklacing." (Necklacing is the act of placing a gasoline-filled tire around the neck of a man and setting it on fire.)

LAW ENFORCEMENT AND VOUDON RELIGIONS

Most of these Voudon groups are very scarce in the United States. Among communities with a strong ethnic base will be found some of the purer forms of these religions.

Most true practitioners of these religions are very secretive about their involvement in these groups. Officers may receive misleading information about the groups to intentionally throw them off true group practices.

Remember that the degree of superstition and belief in magick that follows practitioners of some of these religions may override any threat of physical threat by officers. This could result in dangerous situations when dealing with a call involving such people.

SATANISM

"I hope your God likes you ...you're gonna need Him!"
—Warning from a local Pagan priestess to
the author about investigating
a local black-magick group

The inverted cross is used to blaspheme the cross of Christianity.

The following incident happened in 1997 in western Tennessee. A white female, 27, walked into the local police department to report a crime. Her clothes were torn, and she was crying hysterically. She kept mumbling something about the "dark angel." An officer asked her to sit and calmed her down. She told a story about how she was leaving a local bar and was approached by two males she had attended school with. They asked her up for a drink, and she followed. After a few shots of whiskey, she blacked out. She woke to find herself tied up on a wooden cross, with several robed figures in the room chanting and pointing at her. She managed to break free and run for help.

The men involved in this incident were under investigation on drug-related charges. They were discovered to be employing animal tranquilizers to sedate victims to be used in various black-magick rituals. This is just one of many incidents involving criminal black-magick groups in the United States.

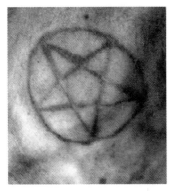
Some deviant Satanists may carve symbols into their flesh. Self-mutilation may be an indicator of deeper emotional issues than simple occult involvement.

Some Satanists get tattoos that show their affiliation with the religion.

This mural was discovered inside a clubhouse for group of dopers. The group embraced a mixture of Satanism, ceremonial magick, and Egyptian mythologies.

The practice of Satanism is made up of a very diverse set of beliefs that has a few common philosophies. Its followers' traditional focus has been on a total inversion of Judeo-Christianity. Rituals, symbols, and doctrines are reversed by the Satanist faith.

SATANIST THEOLOGIES

Satanism is the most complicated religion to explain because there is no central dogma. However, there are several common ideologies used by Satanist religions. Understanding a group's theology can tell officers a lot about the group's motives and behavior patterns.

- **Satan as a symbol:** The deity of Satan is viewed as a symbol of the ego and indulgence. This belief is popular with many of the Church of Satan groups.
- **Satan as a sibling:** Satan and Jesus Christ of the Judeo-Christian faith are viewed as brothers. God found favor in Christ; therefore Satan is the underdog. His followers will one day take back his throne, which is in heaven.
- **Lucifer:** Satan is followed in his beginning phase of evolution. He was viewed as an enlightened angel. Followers are seen as moving forward toward being

spiritually enlightened and becoming gods themselves.

- **Many Satans:** Some groups use a pantheon of deities that show "Satanic characteristics." Usually this is a god that is considered evil or the rebel of a religion. Some examples of this are Legba of Voodoo, Set of the Egyptians, or Loki of Norse mythology.
- **God of this world:** Many follow the belief that while a benevolent God may rule over the heavens, Satan rules over this physical world. The path to riches is obtained by serving the "god of this world."
- **Satan as a literal evil being:** Some followers of this concept believe that Satan is evil incarnate and can grant power to those that choose to turn their backs on Judeo-Christianity.
- **Satanic Neo-Paganism:** This category of believer takes the basic tenets of Goddess-oriented religions and gives them dark aspects. May be called Satanic witchery.
- **Public Satanists:** Followers of this category are very public about their belief in the "dark side." In fact, most public Satanist groups have filed with the U.S. government as tax-exempt religious organiza-

Left: The Baphomet. The goat-headed deity invented by occultist Eliphas Levi (1810–1875) is the most used and perhaps the most misunderstood symbol used by Satanist groups.

Right: Many Satanists believe that inverting or defiling Judeo-Christian symbols will bring about power from a force known as Satan.

tions. Most members of these groups consider themselves the "alien elite," a term that refers to the group mentality that they are above the rest of society in regard to intelligence and spiritual knowledge. These groups, in spite of their blatant hatred for organized religion, claim to be nonviolent and noncriminal in their actions and practices. Groups such as the Church of Satan, Temple of Set, and their splinter churches are part of this category.

History of Classical Satanism

No one knows the origins of what is considered classical Satanism. The practice most surely has its origins in what we think of as classical Judeo-Christian tenets. However, any religious group that ever went against the theology/ideology of the established Christian churches was sure to be accused of Devil worship, among other things.

For instance, the Bogomils (People of God's Grace) of the medieval Balkans and the Cathars (cf. cathartic, which has to do with cleansing, purification) of early medieval southern France became targets of the established Orthodox and Catholic churches. Naturally, these religious movements were accused of heresy, first and foremost (the Eastern Orthodox and Western Catholic churches were also accusing each other of the same thing at that time). Both the Bogomils and the Cathars followed Manichaean-influenced tenets: that the material life (i.e., existence on this Earth) was corrupting and corrupt—a thing of the Devil—and was to be transcended by pure, ascetic living. (These Manichaean precepts had been floating around the Middle East and the Mediterranean since the third century A.D.) Both groups were accused of worshipping Satan by the established churches, and that propaganda exists to this day.

The matter of the Knights Templar is entirely different: a case of a French king's need for funds. It's a long story, mostly honorable for the Templars, who were an idealistic band of monk-warriors who escorted and protected pilgrims in the Holy Land during the period of the Crusades. While still acting as noble knights, however, they'd also managed to become the operators of a mighty loan and banking firm as early as 1148, even though usury was not permitted by the Church. Later, when a Templar renegade ran around Europe accusing the Templars of such abominations as blasphemy, sodomy, homosexuality, bestiality, idolatry—and Devil worship—he was not believed, even by the pope. Philip IV (the Handsome) of France, however, was interested. In 1307 Philip got hold of the order's chiefs, had them tortured horribly, making them confess to everything and anything, and got what was left of the order's fabled riches. The Templars who survived were burned on charges of heresy and blasphemy, and the order was suppressed in France in 1312.

Another public sect that performed "devil worship" is the Arab Yezidi. This group splintered from Islamic culture and has followers in Iran. The Yezidi were followers of Yezid bin Unasia, who believed that God would reveal to him a book that has been written in heaven. Unasia left Islam to follow the religion of the Sabians mentioned in the Koran.

Yezidi mythology tells that Adam and Eve placed their seeds in jars—from Adam the Yezidi sect was born; from Eve were born rotten worms. Adam was given a mother's nipples and fed his child, the Yezidi.

Adam and Eve had two children, the Jews and the Christians. These groups were viewed as inferior religions. Yezidi texts tell that Paganism existed before Christianity. The Yezidi also followed an incarnation of evil symbolized as a peacock.

In the 1800s, a French occultist named Eliphas Levi came on the scene. His concepts of magick were penned in such books as *Transcendental Magic*. His drawing of the Baphomet is still regarded as one of the most influential occult sketchings of all time. Levi's writings became the catalyst for several occult study groups. Out of these groups came some very influential occult writers and leaders. One of the groups that was formed under much of the Levi influence was the Order of the Golden Dawn. The order followed concepts of ceremonial magick, the tarot, and the Jewish mystical system, the kaballah. The order's members included William Butler Yeats, Algernon Blackwood, and a young man named Aleister Crowley.

Aleister Crowley

Crowley was born into a Puritan family. His father became a traveling salesman, while his mother remained a stern parent who encouraged the reading of the Scriptures. Crowley's interest lay far beyond the Bible. He started at a young age reading tomes about magic, witchcraft, and the occult. His interest in "things of the devil" repulsed his mother, who nicknamed young Crowley "The Beast." Crowley proudly took this nickname with him as he became known as "the wickedest man in the world." His marriage to a young British girl began with a honeymoon inside an Egyptian pyramid in Cairo. During the evening, Crowley's wife was overtaken by a demon named Aiwass. This demon dictated to Crowley the contents of a classic occult book called *The Book of the Law*.

This book dictates that mankind is passing through three aeons of existence.

- **The Aeon of Isis**: This was the time period when man was to be ruled by a female deity.
- **The Aeon of Osiris**: Begun in 500 B.C., this is the time of male gods being worshipped.
- **The Aeon of Horus**: This is the aeon that should begin. This is the time that man will worship "self" as a god.

Crowley's other writings, such as *Magick in Theory and Practice*, are still the backbone of many modern occult groups. His concept of Thelema, or will, dictated in his classic statement "Do what thou wilt, shall be the whole of the law" is the creed of many modern-day Satanists. Crowley's notoriety grew, with rumors of sexual perversions and animal sacrifices. He was told to leave Italy by Mussolini because of his perversions. One group that Crowley was associated with was a group known as the Order Templi Orientis, or O.T.O., a sect that followed Germanic teachings and sex rituals. Crowley also created another group that is also in existence today known as the AA, or Silver Star. Crowley died of a heroin overdose in 1947. His influence on the occult world and on modern culture was phenomenal. He has been immortalized on the cover of the Beatles album *Sgt. Pepper's Lonely Hearts Club Band*, in a song by Ozzy Osbourne, and lectures by drug guru Timothy Leary. His home is now occupied by the rock legend Jimmy Page, who is a current member of one of Crowley's orders.

Left: The Church of Satan, based in San Francisco, is very public about its activities. Members of the church are open about their affiliation and have historically turned away criminal elements. This is a public ceremony held at a Church of Satan grotto.

Right: The most popular primers on religious Satanism available to the public include the works of Church of Satan founder Anton LaVey. While officers may find deviants clutching to the teachings found in these books, the true teachings of these texts endorse a philosophy of self-preservation and pop psychology.

THE CHURCH OF SATAN

Crowley's influence was spread to North America by the Golden Dawn and other sects. His beliefs were to be later picked up by a man known as Howard Levey. His interest in the occult sparked him to initiate counterculture gatherings at his home in San Francisco. These gatherings would start the core group that would become the Church of Satan (COS). Levey later changed his name to Anton LaVey, and on April 10, 1966, he opened the doors to the Church of Satan on California Street. LaVey declared himself the high priest. The church became fully functional, offering weddings and funerals for the Satanist citizen.

LaVey's church chooses to view Satan as a symbol of man's ego and selfishness. LaVey's tenets were described in the infamous *Satanic Bible*, with its own Ten Commandments.

Nine basic philosophical statements, the Nine Satanic Statements, appear in the book as "statements of faith."

I. Satan represents indulgence, instead of abstinence!
II. Satan represents vital existence, instead of spiritual pipe dreams!
III. Satan represents undefiled wisdom, instead of hypocritical self-deceit!
IV. Satan represents kindness to those who deserve it, instead of love wasted on ingrates!
V. Satan represents vengeance, instead of turning the other cheek!
VI. Satan represents responsibility to the responsible, instead of concern for psychic vampires!
VII. Satan represents man as just another animal, sometimes better, more often worse than those who walk on all fours, who, because of his "divine spiritual and intellectual development," has become the most vicious animal of all!
VIII. Satan represents all of the so-called sins, as they all lead to physical, mental, or emotional gratification!
IX. Satan has been the best friend the church has ever had, as he has kept it in business all these years!

Although not as popular as *The Satanic Bible*, LaVey's other books, *The Satanic Witch* and *The Satanic Rituals,* are still considered basic primers of modern-day Satanism. Members of the Church of Satan say their group is not involved in criminal activity, and as of this writing there have been no crimes connected to the church. What is common is for a pseudo-Satanist youth to be discovered falsely claiming

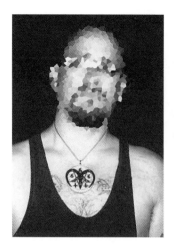

affiliation with this group. Ex-Satanist Linda Blood, in her book *The New Satanists*, criticizes notions that "there exists a benign version of the Satanist religion represented by organizations such as The Church of Satan."

In 1997 LaVey died of a heart attack. His church now rests in the hands of his daughters, Zeena and Karla. Both of the leaders are very youth-oriented in their recruitment. The church is also currently publicizing mass propaganda on the Internet. One of the famous offshoots of The Church of Satan is a sect known as The Temple Of Set, focusing on the Egyptian god. The temple is the brainchild of former Church of Satan member Michael Aquino. One of the most controversial things about Aquino was his position as a lieutenant colonel in the U.S. Army. The temple is still very active and has groups in California, Missouri, and Texas.

THE WORLD OF CONTEMPORARY SATANISM

The Internet has introduced the mainstream population to several different public Satanist groups. The membership of these groups can be up to several hundred, or the group may consist of two individuals with a post office box. Criminal activity among these groups is unknown; aliases are frequently used on Web pages and in magazines. Several are offshoots, or "grottos," of the COS. There are grottos in

almost every state in the nation. Following are some of the more popular groups that are not affiliated with criminal activities as groups, but officers might find some of their materials during investigations:

- **The Grotto of Shaitan.** Located in Baltimore, Maryland, this group's affiliated members include Ron Mephisto and Magister Luminosus. However, these may be the same individual. The group is an official Church of Satan grotto. The group's newsletter is *The Watcher*.
- **The Luciferian Light Group.** Located in Tampa, Florida, this group's membership materials warn the curious that,

> "armed with the truths of Satan, through his emissary Lucifer, you can be your own master; your own god. But keep in mind the secrets to which you will be exposed require great responsibility. Those who toy with such powers foolishly will only hasten their demise. Only you will be brought to bear for your own failure. Once you embark on the path less traveled, there is no turning back."

The group newsletter is known as *Onslaught*. The advertisements for this group feature a nude woman with the motto "You can't win if you don't play!" The group sells rituals tools such as candles, robes, and athames.

- **Order of the Evil Eye.** This now-defunct group known as the OOEE was in Tampa, Florida. However, the group's literature and propaganda frequently continue to show up on the Internet and in magazines. OOEE was created by heavy metal musician Vincent Crowley, who was leader of the death metal group Acheron. The OOEE wins the prize for some of the most creative anti-Christian propaganda. One of the most inventive pieces is a flyer that members are encouraged to nail on the doors of traditional churches that tells members of the existence of Satanic groups in their area and promises the destruction of Christianity. Group literature tells members that "Worshippers of the Nazarene are the OOEE's mortal foes, and this movement plans to fight them until the war between good and evil is over." OOEE is defunct, but Crowley is still very active in the Satanic community.

- **Infernal Garrison.** The Infernal Garrison has locations in Ottawa, Toronto, and Hamilton, Canada, and in New Baden, Illinois. Led by Doug Richards, the group has newsletters called *The Devil's Tavern* and *The Black Pun-kin*. This group is an official Church of Satan grotto. Group literature tells of the nine infernal laws that the group is built upon. The laws are rehashes of *The Satanic Bible*'s philosophies. The group encourages group participation but asks members to "display idealism and individuality instead of sheepish attitudes."

- **Ancient Brotherhood of Satan.** The ABOS was located in Marston Mills, Massachusetts, and was led by Damien Egan. He is now leading a group in Salem known as The First Church of Satan. It is unknown at this time if the ABOS is completely defunct. The group's newsletter is *Brimstone*. ABOS was very

bold in the early 1990s and produced several public-access shows. One of the sleazier productions from this group was an audiotape that contained classical music, satanic sermons, and in the background a man and a young boy discussing sex and masturbation. The tape concluded with two men talking about oral sex with each other. Egan's Web site now contains weekly satanic sermons.

- **Illuminati of Satan.** Located in Allen Park, Michigan, this group publishes the newsletter *Diabolica*. Membership kits are signed by a person known as Azazel. The group's newsletter claims that "Satanism is alive and well in Detroit" and is very Church of Satan oriented This group does not advertise as heavily as it did in the early 1990s.

- **Temple of the Vampire.** Located in Lacy, Washington, this group is led by Lucas Martel. The group's newsletter is *Lifeforce*. This group is an affiliate of the Temple of Set with a focus on "evolving into a vampire." The group theology teaches "psychic vampirism." There is another level of initiation mentioned in the group's literature called the Inner Temple.

- **Order of the Trapezoid.** The Order of the Trapezoid is a subgroup of the Temple of Set and claims to be a "Knightly Order of the Temple of Set." It has small groups broken into lodges. Except for one in Texas, no lodge locations are specified, but they are said to be "centrally located." The group was founded by Michael Aquino of the Temple of Set but was later handed over to Stephen Flowers. Flowers' research centers on Germanic-based sex magick. The order's Web site talks about the main areas of concentration within the order. The Black Flame is the area of inspiration by the spirit of the Prince of Darkness. The Grail Quest is the path to truth that the initiate must find. The Trapezoid is the central figure, concerned with magickal practices. The last area is the area of Walhalla, the evolving of initiates in magick.

- **Legion of Loki.** Located in St. Louis, Missouri, this group proclaims itself to be the "Stormtroopers of the Infernal Empire, the Special Forces of the Age of Fire." An official grotto of the Church of Satan, the group uses the god Loki from Norse mythology to symbolize Satan. The group's site offers a clean image as it proclaims:

> We believe in fully supporting principles set forth in *The Satanic Bible* by Anton LaVey. We believe in fully supporting the Constitution of the United States. We believe in fully supporting law enforcement authorities in legitimate exercise of authority. We believe in promoting personal responsibility.

- **First Church of Satan.** Formed in 1999 by Karla LaVey, daughter of Anton LaVey, the church is located in San Francisco, California. The church uses the tenets from *The Satanic Bible* and discusses a "Black Xmas" celebration in which there were "blasphemy and Christ-raping" performances.

These groups represent a growing number of public organizations that tend to steer away from criminal activities. The Church of Satan has released a set of instructions for those interested in Satanism to keep them from falling into the hands of criminal and unstable groups. This set of criteria is known as the Satanic Bunco Sheet, which says, in part:

1. When someone claims to have a direct line of communication with Satan, watch out. Selling that kind of mysticism is exactly how Christianity has kept people enslaved in ignorance for centuries. It's one of the things we're fighting against.
2. Look out for jargon and secrets to which only the "initiated" can be privy. Once you're processed through the lengthy and strictly enforced "degree" system, you'll discover there are really no answers, just more gobbledygook. If they have something worthwhile to say, they'll say it. If they don't, they'll pretend they do anyway.
3. Check the copyright date. Much of the esoterica you may receive from supposed Masters as "wisdom" or "revelation" comes directly from Anton LaVey, the Church of Satan, or our affiliates. Don't accept the inducements you may receive as emanating from some great brain, when they most likely were cribbed from material released by us weeks, months, or years ago.
4. The most parasitic "Satanic" newsletters invariably contain a liberal dose of LaVey-baiting. … When responding to such transparent tactics, it's our policy to preface rebuttals with two acknowledgments: A) "I know you're a masochist and delight in hostile banter," and B) "Anything I write or say to you will keep you going for another six months." *The Satanic Bible* advises us to "question all things"—but it helps to be able to think, first.
5. Most pseudo-Satanic groups are short-lived, running out of money, enthusiasm, or suckers before too long. An easier game comes along and they're off in a new direction.
6. How do they deal with Anton LaVey and The Church of Satan? This is tricky—some current groups play the Christian game of handing out laurels with one hand while stabbing their progenitors in the back with the other. Others aren't so subtle, boldly claiming to be the "true" or "evolved" Church of Satan. To make their rationale work, they must somehow convince you that the author of *The Satanic Bible* isn't practicing pure Satanism and their brand is the straight stuff. Still others just ignore Anton LaVey altogether and hope you won't notice.

6. Be wary of the approach of "You probably aren't smart enough to join us." True Satanism builds the ego, it doesn't tear it down.

7. Beware of cults offering sex orgies and drugs, or killing animals in the name of Satan. As you well know, these are not part of Satanic practices. The leaders are copying the lame-brain spook stories from Geraldo and Oprah and obviously know less than you do.

8. Some other groups to watch out for: A) Feminist, Wiccan-oriented, consciousness-raising groups who practice more male-bashing than magic; B) New Age groups that promote LaVeyan concepts, but shun the dreaded "S" word; C) Jargon-laden Christians masquerading as Satanists; D) Pen-pal or lonely hearts social groups pretending to be elitists performing powerful Satanic rituals.

One of the most notorious Satanist groups that started out as a very public organization, but had many splinters alleged to be involved in criminal activities, is the Process Church. The church is also known as the Process Church of Final Judgment, Process Church of the Millennium, and the Foundation Faith of God. The church was started in London in 1963 by Robert and Anne DeGrimston. The DeGrimstons were dissatisfied with the Church of Scientology and left to begin their own church. The church originally began with materials from the Golden Dawn. A "spiritual experience" in Mexico led leaders to change church theology. The new theology taught that Jehovah and Lucifer were joined together by Satan. The belief is that the deities work together to provide a universal justice. Christ would judge, while Satan carried out His judgment.

The group's church would become formal, even holding public moonlight Satanist rituals. It broke into three sects: the Jehovahs (this group is not related to Jehovah's Witnesses), who were uncompromising; the Luciferians, who focused on sex, peace, and drugs; and the Satanists, who focused on violence.

There is an animal sanctuary being run by the group called the Best Friends Animal Sanctuary. The church is also currently recruiting on the Internet on a Web site run out of San Francisco, with contacts listed in Vancouver, British Columbia.

MEDIEVAL SATANISTS

These followers usually are very well versed in philosophies, symbols, and rituals of the Satanist faith. These groups may be generational in nature with a high propensity for criminal acts. They are very secretive, and most rituals that are inversions of Judeo-Christian rituals are done literally. Whereas a public group may use wine to symbolize the blood of Christ, these groups will use actual blood. Membership in these groups is for serious followers only. Most members are members for life. Narcotics trafficking, murders, and ritualistic abuse of children may be evident in this belief system.

Medieval Beliefs

Satanism is a very self-centered practice. Adherents are usually involved for what they can get from rituals, as opposed to a deep spirituality. Most rituals are ego driven, performed for the gaining of power or for the destruction of others, and are performed usually in a barter-type fashion. The concept of the initiate giving blood, sacrifices, or his soul for a spiritual gift is standard for the traditional Medieval Satanist.

Medieval Satanism appears to have three common types of rituals:

- Demonic assistance
- Necromantic assistance
- Satanic assistance through distortion of traditional religions

Demonology

Demonology is a medieval practice concerned with the cataloging and researching of demons.

The traditional concept of demons is that they are assistants to Satan. Classic literature talks of demons being scapegoats for man's shortcomings. Demons were blamed for such emotional aspects as lust, sloth, and pride. Demonology concerns itself with those fallen angels taken from Judeo-Christian beliefs. Demons are believed to hold a special talent and power.

Here is an example of a group of demons and their talents taken from the book *The Magus* by occultist Francis Barrett.

- **Mammon**—Prince of tempters
- **Asmodeus**—Prince of vengeance
- **Satan**—Prince of deluders
- **Belzebuth**—Chief of false gods
- **Pytho**—Prince of the spirits of deceit
- **Belial**—Prince of iniquity
- **Merihim**—Prince of the spirits of pestilence
- **Abbadon**—Prince of war
- **Astaroth**—Prince of accusers and inquisitors

In rituals demons are called upon, or "summoned." Once a demon is summoned, it must be bound. The Satanist then appeases the demon by giving it an object or a living creature. Requests are made to the demon. Then the demon is banished.

The Satanist must first decide which demon to call. Many practitioners rely on printed books called grimoires to give them instruction. Many utilize grimoires that have been handed down through groups and are not available to the public. There are several still available through mainstream and occult bookstores. Some of the more commonly used grimoires are these:

- *The Keys of Solomon (Lesser and Greater)*
- *The Arbatel*
- *The Grimoire of Honorius*
- *The Black Pullet*
- *The Book of Sacred Magic of Ambra-Melin*
- *The Red Dragon* or *Le Dragon Rouge*
- *The Sacred Magick of the Angels*
- *The Grimorium Verum* or *True Grimoire*

These books contain the names of demons, the types of magick they perform, the symbol that represents them, and the types of sacrifices needed to call them.

Over the years I have been told of a number of spell books that exist in the "occult underground." I have no hard proof these documents exist. Officers may find similar reports of "mysterious tomes." The unavailability of these books can be explained in a few ways: They do exist and are extremely difficult to obtain, they existed at one time and are no longer available, or they were created by a group and used only by the group.

Or the books may be known by different names. In one case I worked on, a group of juveniles were "mesmerized" by a mysterious "black book." This book supposedly had the power to raise demons, manipulate spirits, and kill enemies. It turned out that the book that "no mortal could obtain" turned out to be the mass-published *Necronomicon*.

Some of the books mentioned by ex-members are as follows:

- *The Book of Generations*: Lists who's who in Satanism.
- *The Goat's Book of Life*: A mockery of the Christian Book of the Lamb with blood from a child and sewage used as ink. Those who become traitors to Satan will disappear from the book.
- *The Scroll of Destruction*: No information available.
- *The Book of Ages*: Lists demons by powers.
- *The Great Mother*: Tells how to use the powers of the female aspect of Satan.
- *The Book of Death*: Rumored to have survived the Salem witch trials. The accused were said to have signed their names in this book.

One of the most famous sources that demonologists take their rituals and ideologies from is the *Keys of Solomon*. The name is taken from a Biblical reference to the "keys of heaven." The keys are broken into several sections:

- Goetia: The first section, known as the "lesser key." Goetia means "magical arts," and it tells how to conjure demons for specific powers. The "greater key" tells how to hold and bind spirits.

- Theurgia Goetia: The second section describes various spirits and powers.
- Pauline Art: The third section covers angels and signs of the zodiac.
- Almadel: The fourth section covers angels and their various powers.

These books are readily available from most bookstores and on the Internet. The formulas for the potions that many of these demons must be called with include some very obscure elements. Perfumes, oils, and some very elaborate ceremonial tools are needed to properly call upon the demons of the Goetia. If the occultist does not perform proper ritual instructions, it is believed that the demons can turn against the summoner.

The preparation to conjure a demon is very involved. The right area, the right colors, symbols, incense, and time are all imperative to the summoning. Many grimoires dictate that the occultist abstain from such things as sex, alcohol, drugs, or types of food before preparing to summon a demon. Common symbols that are used to summon demons are called seals. These seals may be drawn on paper or painted on the floor. A crime scene was found to contain a seal painted on a rolled-up mat that was found hidden under the victim's couch.

One of the principal symbols used in conjuring a demon is the Star of Solomon. It is said that King Solomon was given a ring by God that contained two interlocking triangles. This ring was used to control demons and to enslave them to assist Solomon in building the Temple of Solomon. It is also said that the demons rebelled against this slavery and hid a number of magickal occult books under Solomon's throne. This was to lead the public into believing Solomon was an occultist, and not a man of God. This symbol is many times drawn on the ground to conjure and control demons. Most ritual sites that contain areas where a demon may have been summoned will contain Hebrew names for God. It is believed that names like Adonai,

Tetragrammaton, Elohim, and others are used to control demons. The name of the demon, as well as its seal, will bring the demon into the physical world.

A triangle may also be used in conjuration of demons. The demon is invoked, or called to appear in the triangle, which represents the trinity of Christianity. A sacrifice may also be found in the triangle. The following is a sample conjuring dialogue:

"I conjure thee to come at once and fulfill my desires, by the powerful name of Him who is obeyed by All. By name of Tetragrammaton, Jehovah, come speak to me clearly, come in the name of Adonai, come, linger not, I command thee." Demons may appear in a glass or stone mirror. They may also spiritually appear to the summoner. If the demon does not appear, it is said to be because the demon is busy somewhere else, or the ritual was not done correctly.

Rituals may happen in places where it is believed that energy resides. Ceremonies may happen at a physical crossroads. They may also take place in churches, graveyards, and locations where spiritual activity is high, such as a burial mound.

There is an understood hierarchy in the demonic world. The following is a chart of that hierarchy followed by many contemporary Satanists.

SATAN
MASTER DEMONS
LESSER DEMONS
EVIL SPIRITS
MAN

Occultists who engage in demonology may keep a book of spirits that contains invocations and formulas to call spirits. Early versions of the books include an area for the spirits to autograph once the occultist has properly summoned them.

KABBALAH

The *kabbalah* is an occult system of magick based on Jewish mysticism. It is a form of magick that teaches, through various stages of initiation and process, that man can climb the tree of life and become one with God again. The kabbalah emphasizes a spiritual evolution, or building up of power.

Some Satanist materials describe using the dark side of the kabbalah. The traditional kabbalah has branches that are identified with angels of the Judeo-Christian traditions. The dark kabbalah identifies branches with demonic entities. The process of the dark kabbalah creates the ultimate separation from the Christian deity.

NECROMANTIC RITUALS

The art of using the spirits of the dead is known as necromancy, from the Greek words for "dead" and "divination." This practice can be performed through rituals that harness "death energy." In New Orleans there is a museum known as the Westgate Gallery that is totally dedicated to necromancy and the dead. This practice may be followed by those devotees who have a death fetish.

SELF-MADE SATANISTS

Many consider people in this category, composed mostly of juveniles, to be following a fad. These are those individuals commonly termed devil worshippers.

While these groups may not be as organized as others, it does not reduce the propensity for violence among these groups. In fact, the lack of responsibility to a governing church or body makes these groups more susceptible to criminal activities.

Self-made Beliefs
Most homemade groups do not have a concrete ideology. Most followers of these groups are fringe personalities who are hell-bent on self-destruction or deviant behavior.

Most of these members are not familiar with any ideology except the concept of Satan as a deity. This member is usually not patient or disciplined enough to seriously study the tenets of

black magick. While the music, movies, and literature that people in this category use to "create" a religion are cultural fads, their actions may be anything but harmless. These followers are usually 15- to 21-year-old white males. Many inform themselves of rituals through books like *The Satanic Bible*, the *Necronomicon*, and other store-bought materials. (Note: This group will be covered in more detail in the chapter on juvenile occultism.)

Common Elements
In researching Satanist groups, there appears to be a distinction among the types of magick involved in rituals. There is a type known as lesser magick, which is concerned with everyday needs such as immediate power. Greater magick is used in destruction, sex, and compassion rituals and utilizes greater powers like demons and deities.

One of the most common symbols used in Satanism is the inverted pentagram. This figure may also include the goat's head, sometimes called the Baphomet, inside of the star. The points of the pentagram are said to be provinces of spiritual entities: air is ruled by Lucifer; fire is ruled by Satan; water is ruled by Leviathan; earth is ruled by Belial; and spirit is ruled by the deity of Man.

Altar tools may represent these elements and spirits on the altar. Incense may be burned to represent air. A candle may be burned for the element of fire with a chalice of water to represent water. The element of earth may be represented by a depiction of the inverted pentagram. The element of spirit may be represented by a sword.

Black Mass
One popular ritual practiced by Satanist groups is that of the black mass—an inversion of the Catholic mass, which is a celebration of taking communion. The ritual is said to have three objectives. One is the inversion of Christian elements to bring about power. The second is to liberate the participants from those elements that the church has bound in dogma. The third is a building of raw energy that can be used and directed.

A Satanist altar.

A ritual site.

The priest who performs the rite is known as the celebrant, and he may wear a priest's garb. A priestess may also be present, and she may be acting as the "altar." She is usually nude and becomes the central part of the ritual. She usually holds two black candles in her hands. Her legs are spread, and the area between them is usually where the mass takes place. There is usually a ritual assistant known as the Mistress of Earth.

After the followers come in, the ceremonial kiss of shame (pax) is given. This is a kiss to the buttocks of someone representing Satan, or a statue of Satan, to show allegiance to Satan in a humiliating fashion. If the group is involved in criminal rituals, animals may be sacrificed to Satan. The blood of the animal, or from the participants, is placed in a chalice to form an unholy communion of sorts. A black piece of bread or a black turnip will be blessed and taken as bread. Demons are called forth to join the ritual. A female member is asked to urinate into a cup or vessel. This is used in an aspergeant, a tool used by priests to sprinkle holy water. The directions of north, south, east, and west are acknowledged. A communion wafer is blessed. This wafer represents the "body of Christ" and is placed in the vaginal area of the altar. The wafer is then dropped on the ground to be trampled by the group. The blasphemous aspects of the rite are based on the concept that during a regular Catholic mass, a degree of spiritual energy is raised. The black mass raises that energy and then twists that energy for dark purposes.

Most public Satanist groups will use the elements of ritual nudity, the unholy kiss, and the communion wafer in the vagina, but will not use the blood or urine elements. In 1983 a video was taken by the Texas Department of Public Safety of a grotto observing the Black Mass. The ritual does appear to be very blasphemous, very dark, but does not contain any criminal acts.

Another ritual that is performed by many magickal groups is that of the grand rite. This is a fertility rite that combines the male and female element. It is used by many neo-Pagan noncriminal occult groups, and it's usually presented using the athame (ritual knife) and the chalice (cup) as the male and female elements.

One criminal Satanist group was reported having a man and woman actually act out the rite. Sexual acts were performed within a circle, and during intercourse the couple was lifted up and placed on an altar and sprinkled with the blood of animals.

Chants

The use of the voice to build energy and call spirits is universal in magickal religions. The

---

Satanism

Satanist use of chants may include using languages like Enochian, which sounds a little like Chinese. It is a magickal language that is said to change spiritual realms when spoken. Those who observe a Satanic ceremony may hear the word *shemhamforash* spoken. This expression was made popular by the Church of Satan and is fabled to have been used to create this universe. When used in a ritual context, it is said to mean "bring into being."

Chants may be words or the names of spiritual entities. To call for the entity Beelzebub, one might drone, "Bee-el-ze-bub." The vibration of the name produces energy to build the ritual. The pace of chanting may be used to produce energy or induce frenzy.

Here are some examples of ritualistic chants used by Satanist groups:

- *Ad Satanas qui laetificat juventutem meam.* ("To Satan, who gladdens me with youth.")
- *Veni, omnipotens aeterne diabolus!* ("Come, almighty eternal devil!")
- *Pone, diabolus, custodiam!* ("Devil, set a guard.")

A close friend of mine who is a police officer in the Midwest had been working a case involving a Satanist group. He had started receiving strange phone calls at his office from members of the group. One message left on his machine was a recorded chant from the late Aleister Crowley—an invocation in the Enochian language intended to induce fear in the officer.

Destruction Rituals
Unlike Wiccan groups, there is no concept of karma or any creed that keeps the initiate from harming others. In fact, the majority of Satanist groups are so self-centered in their practices that revenge and destruction of enemies are encouraged. Destruction rituals may be performed using homeopathic magick to bring harm to enemies.

The following is an example of a ritual of destruction:

Gather cobwebs from your house. Place them all a-tangle upon a black cloth. Procure then a fly, recently dead, and set it down upon the mass of webs. These words should then be written down on paper:

> North, South, East, West
> Spider's web shall bind him best.
> East, West, North, South
> Hold his limbs and stop his mouth.
> Seal his eyes and choke his breath
> Wrap him round with ropes of death.

Fold the paper four times and wrap it, the fly, and webs in the black cloth, forming a small bag. This should then be bound up with the end of a long cord and suspended from a hook in a dark corner of the home. Do not disturb it, but let it hang until it is thickly covered in dust. Then take down and bury it in the earth to work its influence in perpetual secrecy.

The investigator may find pictures, dolls, puppets, or other images of a person at the scene. The image may be burned, cut, pinned, or drawn on. Animals may be found mutilated or tied to serve as representation of the victim.

A recent incident involved the high priest of a very public Satanist group and the suicide of an enemy of the priest. The priest's enemy was a member of an opposing Satanist group, and he ended his life by shooting himself. The priest now takes credit for throwing a curse on the suicide victim. This magickal threat could possibly be investigated as a motive if the death was not proven to be a self-inflicted gunshot.

Group Structure
Depending on the type of Satanists, groups' structures may differ. Organized public Satanists call their groups grottos. Some groups use the term circle or coven. Some groups are led by a high priest and high priestess; others are led by a charismatic individual. Those individuals are perceived to possess spiritual knowledge and are seen as powerful. This can be simply attained by someone who reads a lot of the historical books on Satanism.

Ritual Tools

- **Altar cloth:** Usually store-bought, sometimes handmade, this cloth usually contains the symbol of the inverted pentagram or of Satan. This covers the altar during rituals.
- **Athame:** Unlike the Wiccan use of this ceremonial dagger, the Satanist athame is used in casting a circle, as well as in cutting animal and human flesh.
- **Bell:** The bell is rung for the purpose of clearing the ritual area of demons as well as to begin a ritual.
- **Bones:** Used in divination rites to tell the future, they are also used as elements in spells. Bones can also be used to decorate an altar. Many sources have reported that wearing a bone on a necklace shows authority in a group.
- **Candles:** Traditionally black candles have been used in Satanic magick.
- **Chalice:** The chalice is used by Satanists as a mockery of the communion cup of Christianity.
- **Gong:** This is used to begin a ritual.
- **Incense:** Incense is burned to call on spirits and to create a ritual feel.
- **Mirror:** The mirror is used to peer into the future. This is also to see demons that may manifest themselves.
- **Oils:** These are used to anoint candles.
- **Parchment:** Paper may be needed to write sigils and names to invoke curses.
- **Phallic symbols:** Various items are used to represent the male sexual organ and are used to represent the male in ritual.
- **Salt:** This is used to create areas where demons cannot go. Salt is considered pure and is hated by demons.
- **Staff:** The staff is used to cast a circle and to direct energy.
- **Sword:** Used like the athame, the sword can also be used to stab flesh.
- **Wand:** Used to send energy forth, the wand can also be used to represent the male organ.

Satanic Sexuality

Deviant sexual behavior tends to lean toward the dark and macabre. There is now an entire market of publications and videos that cater to the black magick mind-set. This subculture brings together those on the fringe of society and actually provides a structure for loners who would otherwise remain solitary. The Internet has bred an underground that can now add a degree of dark spirituality to their sexual preferences.

One Internet discussion group, HomoHellions, spreads information about gay Satanist groups. The group's site contains pictures of Satan and Jesus Christ having sex, as well as numerous cartoon pictures of demons raping muscular young men. The group has a very violent slant on sex and Satan. Consider one of the following messages sent by a member:

"White male, 34, bear seeking mate. I love to jack off and think of fucking Christ in the mouth. I swallow cum and love pain. Any takers? I have fucked Satan on a number of occasions, his presence is extraordinary."

Several artists have found the combination of sex and Satanism to be a popular topic. One of the most famous is visual artist Nigel Wingrove, who has produced a series of videos called the "Redemption." This series shows numerous images of nuns, sado-masochistic sex, inverted pentagrams, and blood fetishes. As a result of his activities, Wingrove was brought up on charges of blasphemy in the United Kingdom. His "Visions of Ecstasy" film was about Saint Teresa having sex with a crucified Christ. His film was eventually banned in the United Kingdom.

Another Internet site that combines sexuality and Satanism is the GothErotica site. Photos show nude women laid across Satanic altars and under inverted crosses. The nudity is rather softcore in contrast to the hard-core imagery that is known to be for sale.

Generational Ties

Families that practice the religion of Satanism usually do so very clandestinely. These

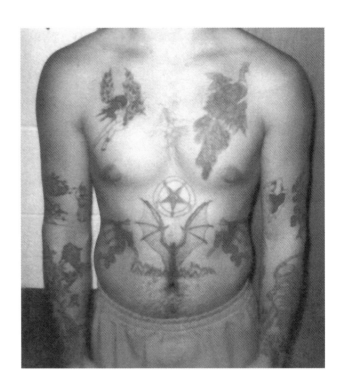

This subject raped and murdered an elderly woman. The religion of Satanism seems to attract a number of sexual deviants, psychopaths, and homicidal maniacs. The archetype of Satan as the enemy of mankind seems to be an attractive source of comfort to those who live on the fringes of society.

families include those that have practiced the Left-Hand Path for generations, and those that have just picked up the religion.

Recently a number of periodicals have begun to print materials exclusively for those families. Consider the following bedtime story for Satanist parents to tell their children:

Billions and billions of years past, our world never existed. However, in another place in the vast recesses of our universe, or perhaps even on another plane of existence, lived the demons. The demons, being wise and powerful beings, and able to harness the elements and powers of the universe, kept mostly to themselves from what we are told. That is until they heard something distant and disturbing. From the blackness in our corner in the universe something wondrous occurred. There was a storm in the blackness, of fire and debris, an implosion, a rumble, and from it was birthed our solar system. The demons heard the commotion, and by bending time and space, ascended to the new system. As they touched each mass the elements blended together and dissipated. But then the demonic elements (Lucifer, Leviathan, Belial, Flereous, and Satan) touched the earth and, because of its existing condition, the combined elements created an atmosphere that would harbor life. It was Satan who told his hierarchies they should protect all life that began here. For he was fully aware

that the demonic elements, all parts of the whole, were responsible for its creation and all life upon it. Since then, any human who chooses to recognize the demons for who and what they truly are will understand. The demons are more than willing to teach and guide us if we only ask. After all, they are largely responsible for our existence.

Incidents involving sexual deviancy and criminal acts have been found in those generational Satanist families. The veil of secrecy surrounding the families' religion also covers the criminal acts. Officers may only discover these groups after investigation for peripheral crimes that have nothing to do with the religion. However, officers may find that those involved in this generational group could also be connected to criminal acts.

A case that started in Kentucky involved a man who was brought up on charges of child molestation involving his daughter. Members of his family were questioned about his actions and behaviors, and his sister told investigators

A Cop's Guide to Occult Investigations

Initially the perpetrator in this case claimed to be a Wiccan. Investigators began to look through the cultural artifacts that were used in the crime. The seemingly benign tools that were connected to traditional Wicca were found to be customized with an element of malevolent occultism. These gemstones were used to charge an inverted pentagram.

that when they were children, the suspect was forced to perform sexual acts on his own mother. His grandfather had also forced sex upon the suspect's father at a young age. The entire generation had been affected by abuse that included strange visits to Christian churches after hours. The investigator started to question the motivations behind the church visits, and family members told several bizarre stories of bloody rituals and ceremonies involving demons. The investigators checked with clergy at these churches and found that there had been several break-ins without any items reported stolen. The father of the group confessed to the sexual abuse along with the murder of a hitchhiker the group had kidnapped. Documented police reports show that there was a severed head found in a wooded area that was designated as a ritual site.

The allegations about these groups are often sensational. The subject of Satanic ritual abuse is considered taboo by many in the law enforcement field because there have been so many false allegations and cases based on "repressed memories" that it has ruined the credibility of verifiable incidents. It is my experience that the actual abuse that takes place is not of the front-page story variety featuring global Satanic conspiracy theories by multiple perpetrators, but rather happens

in the local trailer park among the lower social classes.

Consider an incident that took place in Arkansas. A suspect was found guilty of torturing and raping his 5-year-old niece. The crime was transmitted to a group of watchers on the Internet. The perpetrator used a video camera connected to his home computer to broadcast his torture of the young girl. Interviews with other residents of the trailer park where the act took place revealed that many residents knew there was something going on, but no one dared say anything. One female resident told a news reporter, "We saw him and that young girl acting out like they were a couple or something, but that ain't none of my damn business!"

LAW ENFORCEMENT AND SATANISM

Officers should exercise discretion when dealing with possible Satanic groups. As readers may find throughout this text, there are several strange-looking practices in America; however, many of them have nothing to do with Satanism. Officers should thoroughly investigate situations before immediately labeling them Satanic.

Anyone investigating incidents involving criminal Satanist groups should be very cautious because many of these people are dangerous and may be a threat to anyone who seeks to expose them.

Because the religion is so subversive and diverse in its practice, it is nearly impossible to put all the beliefs and movements into a box;

therefore, officers should avoid claiming to be experts on Satanism. But there is nothing wrong with an officer claiming to be proficient in understanding occult groups and basic magickal concepts as long as he or she is prepared to show credentials of study, research, and training if called into court. A well-written report outlining the case in detail will speak for itself without the officer having to show any particular expertise.

The evidence found in ritual sites and on altars that show a connection with a crime should be handled with caution. Ritual tools may be contaminated with human or animal blood.

JUVENILE
OCCULT GROUPS

*"I don't care what you need to do to me—you'd better be
scared of what I can do to you!"*
—Fifteen-year-old occultist to an Oklahoma police officer

A young woman attends a convention for vampire aficionados. The prospect of being accepted by a group has lured many people—juveniles and adults alike—into occult pursuits.

The number of juveniles involved in occult activity is growing. As a result, several non-criminal occult groups and spokespersons are prospering by providing books and Web sites for youths wishing to practice magick, with numerous materials geared toward "teen witches." Recent occult-theme television shows and movies have also contributed to popularizing occult practices.

But because becoming a sincere follower of a neo-Pagan religion takes time, study, and discipline, many juveniles take the shortcut and simply embrace the dark side of the occult, hoping the symbols will imbue them with an aura of mystery and power. They reduce the ancient pentagram to a trendy logo, like the Nike swoosh.

REASONS FOR INVOLVEMENT

There are a number of reasons that juveniles become involved in these groups. Most of these reasons are very

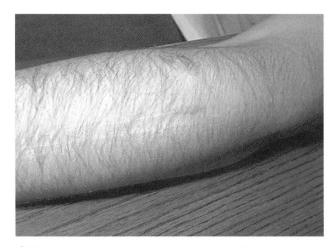
Self-mutilation may appear among juveniles involved in the occult.

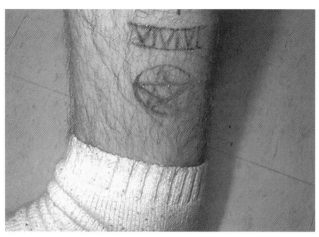
Crude tattoos of occult symbols may be found on juveniles dabbling in the occult.

similar to those that influence youths to become involved in street gangs.

Identity

Juvenile occultists tend to be on the outside of the social circles in their age group. Those young people who are considered "nerds" or "stoners" find identity in belief systems that accept anyone. Sometimes knowing that a juvenile has developed an interest in the more negative aspects of the occult can be a sign of trouble. After the school shootings at Columbine High School in Littleton, Colorado, investigators learned that one of the shooters had visited the Church of Satan Web site. There is nothing, however, to indicate that the murders were linked to occult involvement.

Structure

Street gangs and juvenile occult groups maintain a family type of atmosphere. The group member feels wanted and protected by his family. There are rules and regulations in these groups that give a young person a feeling of boundaries.

Power

Many juveniles who become involved in the occult are seeking power. Many occult religions promise power over circumstances. This is very appealing to those youths who have been victims of abuse. The rage and pain of the abuse can be released in rituals and spells. The power of magick can give them the feeling of protection.

Rebellion

Juvenile occult involvement can provide an outlet for rebellion against authority, parents, and traditional religion. Many juvenile occultists have been hurt by traditional religion and have a need to act out against that hurt. Occult belief systems such as Satanism endorse reversal of Judeo-Christian ideals and rituals, which is quite appealing to juveniles who are trying to rebel.

Recognition

I recently assisted in a case involving a juvenile who cut himself during class and started calling out the names of demons to come to his side. This youth is a prime example of a juvenile occultist trying to shock mommy and daddy. Officers dealing with juvenile occultists will discover many who want to shock and offend. Most youths indulging in this behavior are seeking attention.

Protection

A young man was seen in his high school carrying a copy of *The Satanic Bible*. He was known to be an excellent student, and the school guidance counselor found it very disturbing to see him involved in such a destructive practice. The counselor contacted the boy's family and arranged a counseling session. When the boy was questioned about his involvement with Satanism, he smiled and shook his head, saying, "If you're talking about that book I carry around, I don't even know what it is about. I just know that it scares people. I used to get beat up by these guys in my class, but ever since I started carrying that book around, nobody messes with me!"

Using the occult as a security blanket is very popular. I have had teachers, parents, and even police officers tell me that they were scared to deal with juvenile occultists.

Acceptance

Young people who feel that they are not accepted by any other social groups find acceptance in the occult. Magick plays no favorites and can be practiced by anyone.

Justification for Violence

Those with violent tendencies and aggressive behavior find a niche in such occult belief systems as Satanism. With its philosophy of dog eat dog, Satanism can provide troubled youths with a justification to act on their tendencies.

Curiosity

The world of the occult is very intriguing. Kids have always played with Ouija boards and held seances at slumber parties. But there are some don't treat these activities as simple games. Some young people become so curious about using magick that they seek out literature on the occult. Some may even contact established groups.

DEALING WITH JUVENILE GROUPS

Juvenile occult groups may come to an officer's attention through school personnel, juvenile probation officers, or other agencies. Youth groups involved in the occult tend to be loosely structured; when there is some sort of leadership, it is usually a very charismatic leader who commonly has some basic knowledge of the occult and appears quite impressive to the rest of the group. The saying "A little bit of knowledge is a dangerous thing" applies to these leaders. Many times, a leader may have a few store-bought occult books and know enough to combine occult philosophy with his or her own views. The group will usually form around the leader and the practices he or she espouses.

In one example, a group formed around a 14-year-old girl who claimed to be "the greatest, strongest Wicca in school." She promised to give followers power and protection. She managed to take traditional Wiccan philosophy and mix it with her own "homemade theology" regarding magick and demons.

On Their Own

Juveniles involved in finding their own religious paths should be respected; however, the majority of youths that create their own occult groups tend to create a negative atmosphere. The possibility of having some sort of power can create dangerous situations. In one case I recently worked on, a young girl had made contact with a group of teenagers claiming to be Wiccans. She had appealed to the group for assistance in harming her mother, telling them that her mother had tried to keep her from her friends and needed to be stopped. The group gave her a recipe for a poison that she could slip into her mother's drink to make her go crazy. The components for the spell were actual poisons and could have caused death.

Another danger that can develop from a youth occult group is the use of blood in rituals. There is a very real chance for any number of infections, including hepatitis and HIV. Common incidents involving self-mutilation and animal cruelty have also occurred in juvenile occult groups. The ultimate danger is that a group could participate in murder.

Adults

Young people may become involved in adult groups in a number of ways. Many families practice an occult religion and teach their children to follow their faith. This is common in the

Voudon religions and in many neo-Pagan religions. However, many magickal religions that practice noncriminal activities are very careful about allowing minors into the group.

In situations where adults are involved with minors in an occult group, officers should be cautioned to look for sexual offenses.

Consider the following news item: A self-avowed witch was convicted of molesting two girls and raping another at his home. The victims were 15 years old. Religion is what the suspect used to entice young girls to his home, an investigator said. The suspect claims to be a Wiccan priest.

The use of the occult by sexual predators can present a danger to young occultists. Some of the noncriminal occult groups publish guidelines for youth and adults looking for membership into a magickal group.

Suicides

I received a call from a local police department regarding a suicide being investigated. The suicide victim was a 16-year-old white male who was found alongside railroad tracks about a mile from his house. He had shot himself in the head with a small handgun. Investigators questioned the boy's father, who couldn't recall any obvious signs of depression, but mentioned some strange changes his son was going through. The boy was wearing black a lot, his taste in movies and music was leaning toward violent, aggressive themes, and he had begun to hang out with some very questionable groups.

The father gave officers boxes containing hundreds of books, tapes, and CDs found in the boy's room. The officer who called me over to the department showed me a diary he had found, which was filled with occult symbols and dark writings. The boy wrote about dreams he was having, which started out as standard boyhood dreams of sexuality and teenage love. However, a progression into dark, violent themes later came upon him. Dreams about Satan and demons started to fill his mind.

A photo album found in the inventory revealed pictures of the boy and his friends dressed in black, hanging out in graveyards, and drinking blood. A large collection of occult manuals and occult jewelry was found as well.

The issue of occult involvement can play a major factor in contributing to youth suicide. Youth surrounding themselves with dark music, movies, and books will find themselves becoming more cynical and depressed.

Warning Signs

The American Psychological Association has detailed some warning signs that a juvenile may exhibit before he/she becomes violent:

- Daily loss of temper
- Frequent physical fighting
- Significant vandalism or property damage
- Increase in use of drugs or alcohol
- Increase in risk-taking behavior
- Detailed plans to commit acts of violence
- Announcing threats or plans for hurting others
- Enjoying hurting animals
- Carrying a weapon

Long-term symptoms that violence may be brewing in a juvenile may also be present. Some of these symptoms may be the following:

- A history of violent or aggressive behavior
- Serious drug or alcohol use
- Gang membership or strong desire to be in a gang
- Access to or fascination with weapons, especially guns
- Threatening others regularly
- Trouble controlling feelings like anger
- Withdrawal from friends and usual activities
- Feeling rejected or alone
- Having been a victim of bullying
- Poor school performance
- History of discipline problems or frequent run-ins with authority
- Feeling constantly disrespected
- Failing to acknowledge the feelings or rights of others

Juvenile ritual sites may lack sophistication. This site of alleged hard-core Satanists turned out to be a copycat scene from the movie The Blair Witch Project.

Music

The issue of music has long been controversial when discussing juvenile issues. Sex, drugs, and rock and roll have long been the scapegoat for negative behavior and even criminal activities by destructive youth. Allegations of backward messages and Satanic evangelism may or may not be the downfall of today's youth. However, just as the popularity of gangster rap music has been observed as being a contributor to youth gang involvement, music groups that adopt a "Satanic" persona have been found to have a profound influence on juvenile occultists.

The genre of heavy metal passed with the 1980s. Where musicians like Ozzy Osbourne and Mötley Crüe were cited as playing satanic music, new icons such as Marilyn Manson and the Electric Hellfire Club have taken over. While subtle hints of occultism were evident in heavy metal music, the advent of industrial and thrash music has opened the doors for a less kind, less gentle generation.

The industrial genre consists of music that is usually characterized by heavy electronic music, chaotic keyboard sounds, and electronic beats that pound aggressively. Industrial music is not occult in nature, but the genre has a large share of groups that have lyrics that espouse anti-Christianity and black-magick invocations. Groups like Electric Hellfire Club, Fields of Nephilim, and others are very vocal about their dark philosophies. Some groups have combined music and stage drama to form a performance art theater. One popular example of this is the group the Genitorturers, who use occult imagery and sadomasochism together in a musical stage show. One show includes a nun crucifying members of the group, as well as self-mutilation and genital mutilation.

Excuses, Excuses

Some researchers feel that the occult is simply a scapegoat for destructive activities. The antisocial stance that some facets of the occult portray may give juveniles a feeling of justification and endorsement to commit heinous acts.

Consider the following case that took place in a Job Corps camp: A 19-year-old woman was murdered—found with an inverted pentagram carved into her chest with a meat cleaver. When two people were arrested and charged in the crime, the motive turned out to be a love triangle, but investigators still needed to check into the occult aspect of the crime.

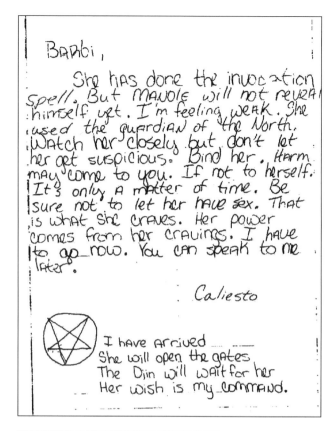

Accusations of occult activity can be used by those who are seeking attention and help. An officer shared with me a case in which officers were called to respond to an incident where a young woman said her father-in-law was assaulting her.

She showed officers evidence of marks on her body that resulted from a struggle with him. She told the officers that he was a high priest of a Satanist group and had forced her to cut her wrists and give blood for ceremonies. She showed officers marks on her wrists as evidence.

Investigators were given two Bibles that had "occultic writing" in them, which was alleged to be evidence of "sacred ceremonies" that had been performed by the group. The Bibles included words written backward, inverted pentagrams, and other symbols. Investigators noted that the writings appeared to be very elementary for "sophisticated ceremonial writings." An in-depth investigation into the physical evidence conflicted with the testimony. The result of investigations concluded that the plaintiff had written in the books. The scars on her arms were from an ink pen she had rubbed into her flesh. All allegations about Satanic involvement were determined to be false. However, the power of the occult worked to accuse and to condemn.

JUVENILE OCCULT GROUP ASSESSMENT

Knowing what to ask and what to look for can help officers in investigations of juvenile occult groups. Using the following questions the officer can get a basic assessment of what the group is doing.

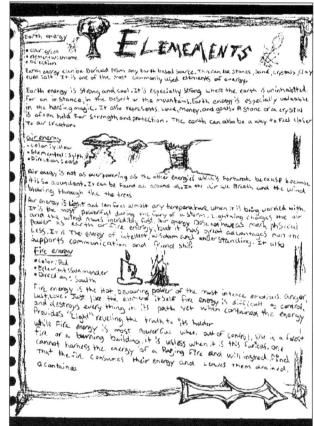

Officers may find juvenile occultists talking about the infamous Necronomicon. This legendary tome is nothing more than a well-written piece of fiction.

- What name does the group go by?
- How many members does the group claim?
- How many actual members are there?
- What belief system do they profess?
- Do they claim affiliation with an established group?
- Are they an official charter group?
- What is the group structure, leadership?
- What are the common symbols of the group?
- Does the group have any hand signs or signals they use to identify themselves?
- Does the group have any tattoos, brands, or cuttings that identify its members?
- Does it have a particular geographical turf or ritual area? Why did members choose that location?
- If any, what books are used in rituals?
- Do the members have ritual tools, homemade or manufactured?
- What is the group's goal?
- Does the group show animosity toward other religions or toward society or authority?
- Are drugs involved? What types? In what context are they used? In rituals?
- Where are the drugs coming from?
- Are adults involved?

- Have any criminal acts been tied to the group? What kind?
- Are there any adults involved in the group?

THE *NECRONOMICON*

One of the most commonly found books among juvenile occult groups is the *Necronomicon,* also known as the "Book of the Dead," the "Black Book," and several other nicknames. At first glance this seems a very demonic-looking tome. It is available in several different versions, the most popular of which is available in most major chain bookstores. Youth occult groups seem to be very fascinated by this book. It claims to include instructions on calling up spirits of the dead.

The Story

The book tells the story of the Mad Arab, Abdul Alhazred, who tells the reader how to call upon spirits known as the "Ancient Ones." The book tells the reader how to travel through the spiritual gates of the otherworld. Each time the reader performs one of the rituals required to walk through a gate, the reader will gain the power from that gate.

The book purports to be a legendary document that will actually call up spirits and give the book's owner power.

The Truth

The truth is that the *Necronomicon* is fiction created by several authors but based on a mythical book invented by horror writer H. P. Lovecraft (1890–1937). The controversy over the authenticity of the book has been going on for years between die-hard occultists and *Necronomicon* fans. An excellent book on debunking its history is *The Necronomicon Files* by Daniel Harms and John Wisdom Gonce III, published by Weiser Publications.

How It Affects Youth

The book has several rituals and practices that have been attempted by youth occultists. Some of the rituals call for the use for blood. The book can also add to the paranoia and delusions of people who are already unstable or on drugs. One youth group that used the book claims to have "conjured" up something that attacked them. The back of their copy of the book has writing in it that claims "we called up something and we couldn't make it go back."

INTERVENTION

Many juveniles who become involved in occult groups are told they are trapped in the group. The concept that they can never leave strengthens the power of the group's leadership. I have worked on cases involving juvenile occult groups where the leadership kept their members trapped by threatening to harm them magickally. Fear is a major factor in keeping some juveniles involved.

Teachers, law enforcement, and mental health professionals should network to communicate regarding juveniles found in this type of group. Juvenile groups should be monitored on school property for any propensity for violence. It should be noted that authorities should not infringe on those juveniles who are freely practicing their freedom of expression and religion.

Signs and Symptoms of Destructive Occult Involvement in Juveniles

There are a number of signs that school resource officers and juvenile officers can observe and document in assessing juveniles involved in destructive occultism. The following is a list of symptoms that may appear in these juveniles. The observance of a few of these symptoms does not make a teenage Satanist. All of these indicators should be taken into consideration.

- Depression and withdrawal
- Hatred toward traditional religion
- Secretiveness about new friends and activities
- Possession of occult books and ritual tools
- Alcohol/drug use
- Cruelty to animals
- Self-mutilation
- Drawings of demonic imagery
- Drop in grades
- Display of occult tattoos or jewelry
- Suicidal tendencies
- Obsession with death, demons, Satan
- Lack of emotion or uncontrollable anger
- Nightmares and sleep disorders

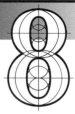
MISCELLANEOUS GROUPS

People are strange,
when you're a stranger...
—The Doors

This is a traditional Asatru ritual blot. The practice of Norse-based Paganism has become very popular in the United States.

ASATRU

Law enforcement agencies are discovering new groups involved in the white supremacist movement—a blending of Norse Pagan religions and racist-based philosophies. Texas corrections officials claim there are close to 200 practitioners of the Asatru belief system in their inmate population. (*Klanwatch Intelligence Report,* Spring 2000 Online Edition)

Asatru is an Icelandic word that means "true to the Aesir." The Aesir is the collective name for the pantheon of Norse deities. The myths and legends of Nordic deities like Odin, Thor, and Loki are followed in ritual and practice. Asatru is a revival of religions practiced in Europe when the Scandinavian Vikings were among the original followers of these

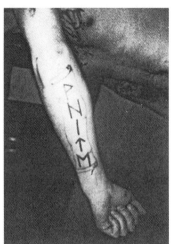

Left: The hammer of Thor is traditionally found on the altar in Asatru.

Right: A number of racist groups have begun to use Asatru as a religious structure to interject hate, racism, and antigovernment sentiment into a nonracist belief system. This federal prisoner is a practitioner of racist Asatru.

religions, prior to the Christian domination. The character of the "raiding barbarians" is easily identifiable with many in the white supremacist movement. The new hate-group version of Asatru identifies the Vikings as "defenders of racial purity." However, most adherents to Asatru are not racists. Asatru is sometimes known as "Odinism."

Asatru practice focuses on "ancestors" and traditional virtues. There are typically three general categories of Asatru:

- **Ethnics:** These practitioners feel that only people with a Germanic or Norse ancestry can be involved.
- **Open:** These practitioners follow Asatru with a belief that anyone may follow even if they do not have an ancestral tie to Germanic or Norse heritage.
- **Racists:** The racist-based Asatru are the minority in the community. Skinheads and neo-Nazi groups fall into these groups.

Members of Asatru may be known by the term "heathens," taken from the name given to those country dwellers who lived "on the heath" and used magick in everyday life and religion.

The Nazis used elements of Asatru to bond Hitler's followers and to obtain spiritual power. The infamous sigil of the SS is taken from the Norse runes.

Beliefs

There are three distinct races of spirit beings found in Asatru.

The first race is the Aesir. These are gods of the tribe or clans. Second are the beings called Vanir. Vanir represent the forces of nature and the elements. The third spirit race is Jotuns, which are giants who are battling with the Aesir spirits.

The gods that reign in Valhalla (heaven) are led by the god Odin, who is the founder of the runic alphabet. He gave up one of his eyes to drink from the fountain of wisdom. Odin hung upside down from Yggdrasil, the ash tree that holds the universe together, to learn the runes. The son of Odin is Thor, the god of thunder. He rides the skies and creates thunder with his hammer. There are many other gods used in today's Paganism and in conjunction with hate groups, such as Freya (Goddess of Love) and Loki (The Trickster).

It should be noted that the modern-day movement of Asatru is very different from most traditional Norse Pagan religions. Most Asatru groups are not hate groups, but there does exist a racial subculture.

Asatru teaches that the human race was created from the gods Odin, Vili, and Ve. Humans were created from two trees and called Ask and Embla.

After humans die, they are taken to Valhalla

by beings known as Valkyries. While in this hall, they will feast on sacrificed boar with the gods.

Stories about the deities are written in books called Eddas. There are two books, known as the poetic Eddas and the prose Eddas. Stories regarding the Norse deities have also been recorded in stories called sagas.

Principles

Followers of traditional Asatru religions adhere to a group of tenets known as the Nine Noble Virtues, which are courage, truth, honor, fidelity, discipline, hospitality, industriousness, self-reliance, and perseverance.

Group Structure

Asatru worship groups may be known as kindred or hearths. Groups usually meet in member's homes, although some groups may have public houses of worship. The area of worship is known as a *ve*.

Asatru rituals are led by a priest known as *gothi* and a priestess known as a *gothia*. These are central figures in rituals that provide guidance and instruction in Norse-based religions.

Rituals

One of the most common rituals in Asatru is called a *blot*, which is an animal sacrifice to the gods for the purpose of sharing the object of the hunt with the gods.

The blot usually begins by calling on the gods that are being honored by the sacrifice. A rune may be traced in the air by using a staff or wand. Ale or mead may be offered to the gods for blessings. The drink is passed around the group and shared by all. The sacrifice is then presented, blessed, and eaten by the assembly.

Many traditional Asatru groups celebrate blots on specific dates of the year.

Some of these dates include the sabbats observed by many other neo-Pagan religions. The following are some of the dates observed by Asatru:

- Disablot, January 31
- Ostara, March 21
- Valpurgis, April 30
- Midsumarsblot, June 21
- Freysblot, July 31
- Haustblot, September 23
- Vetrnaetr, October 31
- Jol, December 21

Another Asatru ritual is called the Sumbel, which is a drinking celebration. A horn is filled with beer or mead and passed around the fellowship, and songs and poems are shared with the group. This is a fellowship and bonding ceremony.

The act of profession is a dedication to the gods. The initiate may dedicate himself to his kindred. The initiate may swear himself to the gods, the kindred, and to the Nine Noble Virtues.

Altars

Outdoor altars are known as *harrows*. The traditional harrow is usually made from a pile of stones or a stone slab. Indoor Asatru altars are known as *stalli*. These may be placed on wooden boards or stone slabs.

The typical Asatru altar implements include a hammer representing Thor's hammer, which is used in consecrating a sacred area or sacred tools.

A drinking horn, usually fashioned from a cow's horn, may be found on the altar. The horn is used to pour and drink libations for the gods.

A tree branch may also be found on the altar to bless or asperge the altar.

Figures of the Norse gods or goddesses may be present, along with candles. A ring may be found on the altar, which is used to take oaths and agree upon decisions. The altar may also contain bags of sacred herbs and totems, which are used to empower the celebrants. Fur or antlers from animals that were hunted and killed may appear on the altar.

A ceremonial knife may be found that is used to perform sacrifices and carve runes into magickal items. A spear may be used to represent the Norse god Wotan (Odin).

A wooden bowl called the *blotbolli* is used to hold the sacrifice (blot). Ceramic or wooden runes may be found on the altar in a bowl or bag. Banners that represent the runic symbols of the gods may also adorn the temple area, or ritual site.

Hate Groups and Asatru

Law enforcement agencies discovered the role that Norse Paganism played in the criminal hate group called The Order that was led by white supremacist Robert Matthews. The Order was responsible for several bank robberies committed to build up a war chest for the white supremacist movement in America. The Order was also responsible for the murder of a Jewish radio talk show host in the 1980s.

Members of the Order gave blood oaths to the gods of Norse Paganism, mixing the concept of racial survival with the ideology of the Norse warriors. Matthews' faction of The Order ended in a shoot-out with federal agents in Washington State in 1984.

White Order of Thule

Today there are several racial identity organizations that are active in the United States that use Asatru ideologies and concepts. A group calling itself the White Order of Thule is active in Washington State. This group mixes Asatru, Nazism, and Satanism. The White Order claims to be carrying on The Order tradition that Robert Matthews started. The White Order claims to have several degrees of membership. Members must attain a working knowledge of the writings of Carl Jung and Adolf Hitler.

Fourteen Word Press

The racial symbolism of the name Fourteen Words is the following 14-word saying used by racists: "We must secure the existence of our people and a future for white children." This group stems from racist David Lane, who was a member of Robert Matthews' Order. According to the members of the Fourteen Word Press, the Norse god Wotan is an acronym for "Will of the Aryan Nation." This is a perfect example of how traditional Norse Paganism is being used as a propaganda tool by race groups.

Racist Rock

Many of today's racist rock bands are using the symbols and trappings of the Asatru movement. Resistance Records carries bands like Odin's Law, Thor's Hammer, Freya, and several others.

There are several nonracist Norse groups that are protesting these hate groups. Heathens against Hate and Pagans against Fascism are rallying to educate the public about what they feel is a perversion of their beliefs.

Asatru Terminology

Many corrections officials and those working investigations involving Asatru groups find correspondences and writings using cryptic words. The following names and terms are used by many in the Asatru religion.

Aesir: Active gods

Ager: A giant, the brewer of mead for the gods

Alf: The soul

Alvis: A dwarf who was with Thor's daughter

Asgard: Court of the gods, home of the Aesir

Asmegir: A potential god

Asynja: An active deity

Audhumla: Symbol of fertility, a cow

Balder: The sun god

Barre: The sacred grove of peace

Bele's Bane: The sword of Frey

Bifrost: The Rainbow Bridge between men and gods

Brage: Wisdom

Brimer: The ocean shore, an aspect of Ager

Brisingamen: Freya's gem, intelligence

Brock: A dwarf

Budlung: A king

Buri: King Buri, personifies winter

Byleist: The destructive side of Loki

Draupnir: Odin's magic ring, ongoing cycles

Dvalin: The solar disk

Dwarves: Souls less than human

Edda: Great grandmother, or the name of one of two collections of Norse writings

Eldrimner: One of the Great Boars

Elf: The soul in between dwarf and man

Eli-Vagor: Cold streams of matter

Fenja: One of the goddesses that turn the magic mill grotte

Fenris: Loki's son, a wolf that devoured the sun

Fimbultyr: The highest divinity, god of secret wisdom

Fjolsvinn: Odin as instructor, and initiator

Forsete: Karma

Freke: One of Odin's wolfhounds

Frey: Planetary spirit of Earth

Frigga: An active deity who is the consort of Odin

Frode: A legendary king

Frodefrid: The golden age of peace

Frost giant: Represents age of stillness between an active cosmos

Galder: An incantation

Garm: The hound that guards the gate of Hel, queen of death

Gerd: Spouse of Frey

Gere: One of Odin's wolfhounds

Giant/Giantess: Matter in form of divinity

Gladsheim: Location of Valhalla

Grimner: Odin as teacher of young Agnar

Grotte: Magic mill of change and creation

Gudasaga: A divine fable, a gospel

Gunnlod: Giantess who served Odin in the mountain

Gymer: Father of Gerd, a giant

Hamingja: A guardian spirit

Heidrun: The goat that nibbles on the Tree of Life

Heimdal: Guardian of Bifrost, winter

Hel: Guardian of the dead, daughter of Loki

Hel's Road: Road from life to death

Hermod: Son of Odin

Hoder: Brother of Balder

Honer: Part of creative trinity, water principle

Hostage: An avatar from the higher world in the lower world

Hugin: One of Odin's two ravens

Hvergalmer: Source of the river of life, one root of the tree of life

Idun: Goddess who feeds the gods apples of immortality, soul of the earth, wife of Brage

Ifing: River that separates man and gods

Iormungandr: Offspring of Loki, serpent of Midgard

Jarnsaxa: Mother of Thor's son Magne; Earth in the Iron Age stage; in space, one of Heimdal's nine mothers

Kvasir: Hostage given to the Aesir and whose blood is epic poetry

Lin: Odin's consort

Lodur: One of the trinity, the fire principal

Loki: Trickster, the Devil, the enlightener

Magne: One of Thor's sons

Menja: The other giantess who turns the mill grotte

Midgard: Our physical planet

Mjolnir: Thor's hammer of creation and destruction

Mode: One of Thor's sons

Mundilfore: Giant father of sun and moon

Munin: One of Odin's two ravens

Nagelfar: The ship of death, built of dead men's nails

Nanna: Soul of the moon, died when her husband Balder was killed

Nidhogg: Serpent undermining tree of life

Nikar: Odin as misfortune

Njord: Father of Frey and Freya, sea god

Odin: Divine principal embodied

Ofner: Odin at the beginning of a cycle

One-Harrier: Odin's warrior, one who has conquered himself

Orgalmer: The big bang

Ragnarok: End of a world, when gods withdraw to their grounds

Ratatosk: Squirrel in the tree of life

Rind: Earth in winter

Rodung: Father of the early races

Runes: Wisdom gained by living

Saga: Sacred wisdom in form of a story

Sarimner: One of the boars that feed the one-harriers

Sif: Thor's wife, her hair is the harvest

Sigyn: Loki's wife

Sinmara: Hag who guards the cauldron of matter

Skald: A bard

Skidbaldnir: Ship created by dwarfs for Frey, the planet Earth

Sleipnir: Odin's eight-legged steed

Officers investigating vampire groups may find items relating to the classic vampire such as coffins, capes, fangs, and even human blood.

Svadilfari: A stallion who is father of Odin's eight-legged Sleipnir

Svafner: Odin at the end of a cycle

Svipdag: A successful initiate

Svitor: Sweden

Tables: Stars and planets where the Aesir feast

Thor: God of power, Jupiter, god of lifeforce

Trudgalmer: Cosmic Thor

Tyr: A god who sacrificed his hand to bind the wolf Fenris

Valhalla: Odin's hall of warriors

Valkyries: Odin's agents

Vidofner: Cock in the Tree of Life

Vigridsslatten: Battlefield of life

Yggdrasil: The Tree of Life

VAMPIRISM

The character of the vampire has undergone many changes. It was a foul creature in folklore and legends, and its first appearance on film was as a ghoulish wraith in the German film *Nosferatu* (1922). The vampire's image was polished into Eastern European nobility with Bela Lugosi's portrayal in *Dracula* (1931), but he was still an evil presence.

Years later, after dozens of vampire movies, books, and television programs of various quality, a portion of our society has a different opinion of the "undead." Vampires are no longer feared by many but embraced as misunderstood characters who are seeking peace but only find violence.

Many feel empathy toward the vampire because they feel, like him, they must play the hand they are dealt. The vampire's violent acts are his only option to keep him alive.

Anne Rice's popular character Lestat has redefined the vampire. No longer is he seen as the devil incarnate but is now a charismatic hero of sorts. Portrayed by Tom Cruise, Lestat has become a sex symbol to many of his followers.

While many find the vampire to be chic or trendy, his character is also being discovered by a new breed of followers. These followers do not only want to admire the vampire character, but also want to become actual vampires themselves. This subculture embraces vampirism as a religion, a philosophy, and most important, a reality.

In 1996 a journalist named Susan Walsh began to research the vampire phenomenon in New York. Her studies took her from strip clubs that specialized in blood fetishes to underground Goth clubs that catered to vampire types. While immersing herself in the vampire subculture, Walsh mysteriously disappeared. Stories of abduction by vampire clans and Goth Satanists filled the papers. Author Katherine Ramsland writes a fascinating exposé on the vampire underground movement in her book *Piercing the Darkness: Undercover with Vampires in America Today*.

In her attempt to find Walsh, Ramsland went undercover into the vampire underground. Her book tells of secret societies that exist in America that have their own "feeding circles," where blood is shared in erotic sessions by men and women. While many in the movement are

Left and center: This store in New York City sells artificial fangs and other novelty items that are of interest to members of the vampire subculture.
Photos courtesy of Dawn Perlmutter.

Right: With its dark theme and Old-English lettering, this T-shirt appeals to modern "children of the night."

mere aficionados of the vampire genre, Ramsland tells readers about the secret occult circles that many of the vampires occupy.

One member shares with Ramsland some of the inner workings of the groups. "The taking of a life for the renewal of a coven—it's said that such things happen all across the country. It's so infrequent and well planned that vampires such as these are hard to catch or convict. It's called a 'Sacred Death.'" The informant also tells Ramsland of other types of murders. "Traitors. It's a lifetime contract once you're part of the coven, and outcasts are hunted down. Sometimes there's just thrill-killing."

Research into the vampire subculture reveals that participants are classified by their level of involvement. Some are mere "hobbyists" who observe the vampire culture in movies and books and are not associated with any criminal or destructive elements.

Because of the popularity of books like Rice's and movies and TV shows like *Buffy the Vampire Slayer*, vampires are being embraced by many as harmless fun. However, there are many who are serious about vampirism. The vampire subculture takes a dark turn as the subject matter in magazine articles changes from "vampire movie trivia" to "the caloric value of blood."

Blood Fetishists

There are those involved in the blood fetish community who find the act of drinking human blood a sexual turn-on. These members may or may not be involved in the vampire subculture. Many are strictly involved in S&M activities with clubs and swinger groups where "blood-sports" are common activities.

The act of cutting may be found among members of the S&M groups. This is the use of scalpels and surgical blades to cut thin layers of skin to produce erotic emotions. There are also groups that practice piercing the body with sharp objects and burning with candle wax to produce "painful pleasures."

Blood fetish groups have their own periodicals, clubs, and networks to fellowship with other blood drinkers.

Experimenters

Some juveniles interested in the vampire subculture may cut themselves as an experiment. The amount of bloodletting is usually limited, and the "bleeder" usually drinks his own blood.

Sanguinarians

Those who identify with the vampire in clothing, dress, and lifestyle, and who drink human blood, may be known as sanguinarians.

Some of these blood drinkers may actually have a medical condition known as porphyria, a disorder that makes the person's face, teeth, and eyes turn very red. Their skin is sensitive to light and can even crack when hit by the sunlight. A craving for blood may also follow these symptoms. The hunger for blood may become an

Officers may find members of the vampire subculture reading publications that contain information on obtaining blood and how to safely ingest blood.

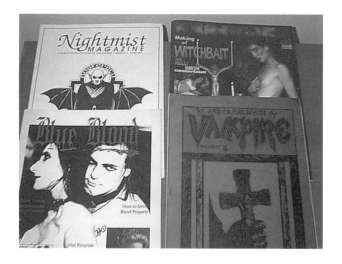

addiction to the "vampire." Some have tried to fight the urge to drink blood from animals or blood from rare steaks.

The following is a letter to a vampire forum from a young man who realized his addiction.

Hello my friends, it is good to back! I have been away for a couple of days but my cousin finally posted my bail so here I am. It seems that 3 nights ago my blood lust got the best of me and I was incarcerated. While shopping in the 24 hour Wal-Mart, I happened upon the pet section. It seems that a family was looking at a particular hamster and the store clerk let them handle it to make sure it was tame before they purchased it. While in the hands of the mother the hamster turned on her and bit her on the hand. It immediately drew blood and it was too much for me to take. The second I saw the blood on the woman's hand instinct took over. I jumped over 3 bags of dog food and sank my teeth into the woman's skull!!!! It was more than I could take! Her husband and children all screamed and the store clerk grabbed the phone and made a 911 call. By the time the law arrived, the woman and I were covered in blood and her skull was exposed. The children and husband were crying and I was taken immediately to jail. I was kept in a cell by myself and they would not even let me use the phone. So beware children of the night … this world does not welcome our kind and we are strangers in a strange land. Until next time dark ones. …

Donors

There is an element that finds satisfaction in being a "donor" for blood drinkers. Many advertise on Web pages and in periodicals to offer their blood for vampire groups. Some donors can make money by donating blood at "blood orgies" at blood fetish clubs.

Obtaining the Blood

One particular article in a vampire journal advises readers on how to safely obtain blood. Drinking blood is done in a number of ways. One vampire suggests using a butterfly needle to hook up to a tube in an arm and suck on the tube like a straw.

Blood may be drunk from a cup in a communion-like ceremony. Blood may also be "mixed" by cutting open two subjects and taking the blood from one of the cuts into a hypodermic needle and shooting it into another subject's cut.

Philosophies

There are many different philosophies that flow through the vampire underground about how vampires are created. Some believe they were born as vampires, and the lifestyle is as natural as breathing and eating. There are also those that believe that one must be "embraced" or "turned" to become part of the vampire race. This embracing or turning is attained by being bitten by some-

104 A Cop's Guide to Occult Investigations

The Temple of the Vampire is a religious organization that uses the vampire archetype as a model for mankind. The Temple has some loose affiliation with the Church of Satan.

one who is already a vampire. Some have vampire-like tendencies such as dislike for sunlight, loner tendencies, and desire to taste blood.

VAMPIRE CULTS

There are vampire sects that meet in a religious context. These groups may practice blood magick. There is a Bible verse that is used by many groups that says, "For the blood is the life," which some people believe means that a life force or energy resides in blood drinking.

Temple of the Vampire

One religious vampire sect is the Temple of the Vampire in Lacey, Washington. The temple began in 1989 and bases its beliefs on various books known as "bibles." There is a *Vampire Bible*, a *Vampire Predator Bible*, a *Vampire Adept Bible*, and a *Vampire Sorcery Bible*. The group teaches that the vampire is his own god. Vampires can draw life energy from others through psychic and astral vampirism.

Membership in the temple comes in two forms. The first is outer membership. This membership is easily attained by making donations to the temple. Inner membership must be obtained from those in leadership positions in the temple. Once inside the temple, initiates may become initiated in a step-by-step process.

The temple teaches that the Earth was created by vampires, and that one day, vampires will rise again and rule the Earth in a vampiric armageddon called the final harvest.

According to the temple, there are two types of vampires. The living vampires are members who have realized their "godhead" as vampires. The second are the vampiric gods, also called the undead gods. The living vampires give energy to the gods as sacrifices. This is called vampire communion.

The temple has five grades of initiation:

- Vampire initiate
- Vampire predator
- Vampire priest or priestess
- Vampire sorcerer or sorceress
- Vampire adept

Temple of the Vampire members claim no affiliation with criminal or destructive organizations. Members may be identified by their use of jewelry or altar cloths that feature the temple's stylized "winged skull of Ur." This is an image of a skull with wings coming out of its upper cranial region.

According to temple documents, the Temple of the Vampire claims to be the *only* authentic vampire-based religion. The temple advertises in Satanist journals and vampire fan magazines.

Another public vampire sect is a splinter from the Satanist group Temple of Set known as the Order of the Vampyre. This is a faction of the TOS that uses magickal practices to obtain its goals and desires. Public interviews with leaders of the order tell of the powers of invisibility and manipulation that members hope to

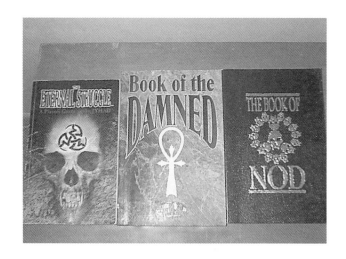

A number of juveniles have become involved in the role-playing game Vampire: The Masquerade. The game does not endorse or teach violence; however, some misguided youths have used the game to structure deviant activities.

attain. Members of the Temple of Set must have been members for two years and have attained certain initiatory status in the temple to be eligible for membership. The order has two grand masters as leaders. The group meets a few times a year at international conclaves.

Psychic or Astral Vampires

Psychic vampires may or may not drink human blood. The term psychic vampire was made famous by Satanist Anton LaVey in his *Satanic Bible*. LaVey referenced those individuals who stand in the way of those who choose the path of "only the strong survive." It refers to those that live off others and drain their life energy and resources. Psychic vampires in the vampire subculture may live to drain others of spiritual energy through rituals and psychological intimidation.

Vampire Culture

Cases such as the infamous Kentucky Vampire Murders that occurred in 1996 are bringing the vampire subculture to the attention of law enforcement. Sixteen-year-old Rod Ferrell led a "vampire clan" patterned after clans in a game called Vampire: The Masquerade. His clan broke into local animal shelters, dismembered animals, and drank their blood. The group practiced Satanist rituals taken from books and mixed them with vampire ideology. Ferrell and his group escalated to killing a couple in Florida and burning their clan's symbol into the victims with cigarettes after beating them to death.

VAMPIRE: THE MASQUERADE

The game Vampire: The Masquerade

(VTM) has been blamed by the media as a catalyst for several vampirical acts, including murder. While the game may have several questionable facets, its primary intent was to introduce a new level of game playing. The game can be played on a tabletop or acted out. This novelty was welcomed by a generation of Dungeons and Dragons players and other role players who were looking for something new and challenging. Soon, teenagers and young adults were spending their hard-earned dollars on purchasing Goth clothing, medieval weaponry, and other increments to enhance the game play. The company that distributes VTM also publishes guides to making scenery and props for play.

For many the game remains nothing more than a game, but for some it has become a nightmare. Consider the following news release from a public health clinic in the Southwest:

The health department is advising that parents and older preteens be alert to the fact that the game "vampirism" is being practiced in our area. The game starts innocently enough but then in some participants, it progresses to actual sucking or licking of blood from a willing partner. Normally, blood is brought to the surface through a prick or cut. The department is aware of one case in which the blood was obtained through a bite.

News reports from around the globe started to expose the world of the dark subculture of vampirism. In many cases, VTM was cited as a possible reason that the acts were committed. The game itself does not insist that violent or criminal acts be committed, but many followers of the game utilize its trappings, symbols, and beliefs in their practices. The game is sometimes used as a "framework" of sorts to enhance and even build juvenile occult groups. It is important for investigators to understand the game and how it can be used as a framework within juvenile criminal occult groups.

The Story

The following is an independent study of the game. It is intended to familiarize readers with the game's myths and legends. It is not intended as a criticism of the game or its creators.

The legends of the vampires are found in a tome called *The Book of Nod*. The birth of the vampire race begins with the Biblical character Cain, who was born a son of Adam and the brother of Abel. After killing Abel in jealousy, Cain is cursed to walk the earth in bloodlust. He is approached by Lilith, Adam's first wife, who had turned against God, who teaches him the ways of magick. Cain becomes immortal and is seen as a "god" by mortals. He takes over the city of Enoch and is believed to possess superhuman powers. Cain goes on to produce children. After the great flood swept the Earth, Cain believed it was a punishment for his actions.

Cain rules that no vampire may reproduce and continue the wicked race. The children refuse to listen and reproduce with humans to create Cain's grandchildren. There is a great rebellion, and the grandchildren murder their parents. The rebellious children build a city and separate into 13 tribes. As time moves on, the children start to notice the differences in the tribes. This begins a war called the Jyhad. Vampires, known as the Kindred, start to use humans to strike and attack each other. The

vampires carry on this war in secret from mortal society.

The Masquerade

The Kindred's existence was threatened by the Catholic Inquisition. Many vampires were unknowingly killed according to the record. After the Inquisition, many vampires decided to form a secret network called the Camarilla. Founders of this network created laws and rules that vampires must follow in order to survive. The first law is that of the masquerade. This is the vampire's pact to live in secret and to learn all the ways of humans in order to blend into contemporary society.

The second element is to purposely steer mortals away from the supernatural to avoid discovery. In order for a vampire to reproduce, he must be a Prince. He is elected into the office of Prince by his clan. His offspring give him status and strength in the clan. To become a vampire, a human must take part in the Embrace.

The Embrace

The Embrace is the act of becoming a vampire. This requires a human to be drained of blood and, at the moment of death, be fed vampire blood. (This is important to remember when investigating a "vampiric" homicide.)

Vampire Stages of Life

The vampire passes through several stages of life. These are the names and phases of growth a vampire may pass through.

- **Childe:** A new vampire. Has yet to be introduced to a Prince. Not yet a member of vampire society.
- **Neonate:** A young member of vampire society.
- **Anarch:** A rebellious young vampire, hated by the older vampires.
- **Ancilla:** Young, respected vampire. Follows rules of Camarilla.
- **Elder:** Older, mature vampire.
- **Methuselah:** Strong, ancient vampire.
- **Antediluvian:** Third-generation vampire, most powerful.

Clans

These are the races of vampires that exist in the Masquerade.

- **Brujah:** Rebellious questioners of Kindred traditions.
- **Gangrel:** Shapeshifters who can change into bats or wolves.
- **Malkavian:** Insane followers.
- **Nosferatu:** Grotesque creatures who can't mix with humans.
- **Toreador:** Artistic, they live to study and produce art.
- **Tremere:** Vampires not born from Cain. Born from Transylvanian mages who wanted to become vampires in order to work magick forever.
- **Ventrue:** These claim to be founders of the Kindred.

Other Terms of Note

- **Sects:** This is the classification of the orders within the vampire community.
- **Camarilla:** The large secret network of vampire groups.
- **Conclaves:** Political gatherings of vampires.
- **Inner Circle:** A meeting of the highest elders.
- **The Sabbat:** Enemies of the Camarilla, involved in black magick.

Investigative Notes

Murder victims suspected of involvement with the vampire movement should have the contents of their stomachs analyzed by a medical examiner for foreign blood traces.

The proliferation of vampire merchandise in the mass market is incredible. Some optical supplies groups now offer "vampiric lenses" that allow the wearer to appear to have red eyes, snake eyes, or any number of new designs for a demonic appearance. Investigators that find victims with "vampire" bite marks should be advised that a growing number of dentists are offering to cast fangs that will adhere to normal human teeth.

Investigators who find evidence of bodily injury on subjects in the form of cuttings and scarrings should note that sado-masochistic groups tend to cut and scar on places of the body where skin is not stretched tight, such as the buttocks, shoulder blades, and the front of the thighs. Skin is cut softly, so as not to scar. Evidence of rubbing alcohol, latex gloves, and other precautionary measures are usually found in structured "safer" S&M groups that practice these acts.

GOTHS

The term "Goth" comes from several sources and is very eclectic in its meaning. One meaning of Goth comes from the Germanic tribes that conquered the Roman Empire. By this definition, Goths are barbarians. Gothic is a term used to describe several types of ornate architecture of the High Middle Ages, or the dark, romantic literature that came out in the late 18th and early 19th century, such as Mary Shelley's *Frankenstein*.

The Goth lifestyle and subculture have been described as merely a new version or perhaps an offspring of the punk movement. When British punk bands began to experiment with electronic keyboards, it led to such bands as Bauhaus and Siouxsie and the Banshees. These were seen by many Goth historians as the originators of the modern scene.

One Goth calls defining the scene difficult, because it is "a subculture full of intelligent individuals." The contemporary Goth subculture is a lifestyle that is characterized by the wearing of dark clothing, the romanticizing of death, a creative yet rebellious attitude toward society, and cultural elements that embrace those things that frighten many in the mainstream.

Goth Religion?

The Goth movement is not a religion. This has been a mistake made by the popular media. The Goth movement is more of an expression or a lifestyle. Goths may subscribe to any religious philosophy; there are Goths who are Christians, Wiccans, Satanists, and agnostics.

There have been a number of high-profile Goth groups that do appear to mix occult reli-

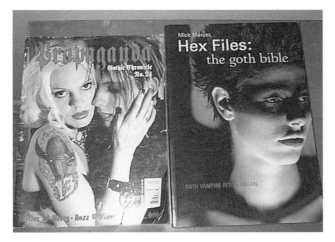 

Left: The Goth subculture has its own music, clothing, and literature. Although much of the material appears to be malevolent, the true subculture is not Satanic or violent.

Right: A member of the Goth subculture.

gions with their lifestyle. Some subscribe to the vampire lifestyles as well. Some Goths may wear religious jewelry such as crosses or pentagrams, but the jewelry may have no religious significance to the wearer.

Group Structure

There are many Goth youths who are alone in their practice. They usually feel comfortable being the only "dark" kid on the block. This identification with darkness may be a defense mechanism to avoid social rejection.

There are also those involved in the subcultures who exist within the structure of a group. These groups may hang out at clubs that feature Goth décor, at coffee shops, thrift stores, or graveyards. Many Goths attend raves, which are large-scale, audiovisually enhanced parties that evolved from the European "house" scene, and which originated as "acid house" parties. These were parties characterized by dance music with rhythmic beats that sometimes hit 150 beats per minute, which enhanced the effect of psychedelic drugs. Rave parties use intense electronic dance music played by disc jockeys with large video screens that show psychedelic and tracer-based images. Synthetic drugs such as ecstasy are popular at these events. Rave parties are usually secretly announced by groups anonymously passing out invitation cards. The invitation will usually not contain the location of

the event but will contain a number that can be called on the day of the event. Some claim that this is to foil any attempts by law enforcement to infiltrate such events.

Dangers?

It should be noted that active participation in the Goth lifestyle does not necessarily mean participation in harmful practices. The Goth movement received negative press after the Columbine shootings because the shooters wore black clothes, listened to what adults considered dark music, and exhibited extreme antisocial behavior. Gunmen Eric Harris and Dylan Klebold were not Goths, but nationwide, a number of Goth adherents were put under the microscope for fear of copycat violence.

Any dangerous behavior exhibited by members of the Goth subculture are not results of the lifestyle but are the same problems that may be had with any youths, whether they're in sports, cheerleading, or even band. The typical Goth will not present trouble for the law enforcement officer, with the normal teenage exceptions of loitering and maybe trespassing. Most Goths are nonviolent.

Goth Style

Goths are usually characterized by a number of physical indicators. The most obvious style of dress is the wearing of black clothing, though some Goths prefer blood red. Fishnet, silk, and even PVC material may be worn as outfits, along with black boots.

Hair is usually dyed black or an extreme color such as green or dark red. Facial makeup may be worn that gives a "death" appearance. Black or green lipstick may be worn by males and females.

Many Goths wear jewelry that features crosses, pentagrams, ankhs, coffins, and bats. Some Goths wear dog collars and spiked jewelry.

Goth Music

Goth music is characterized by its dark, moody sound. There are different subsections of Goth music such as Goth rock, ethereal Goth, and industrial Goth. Some of the more popular Goth music groups are these:

- Bauhaus
- Christian Death
- The Cure
- Dead Can Dance
- Fields of the Nephilim
- Joy Division
- Sisters of Mercy
- Siouxsie and the Banshees

There are hundreds of bands that are part of the Goth subculture. Many Goths order music off the Internet and from specialty music stores.

THEE TEMPLE OV PSYCHICK YOUTH

Created in 1981, the temple established its base in the Denver, Colorado, area. This particular group takes its name from a number of sources. The use of the word *Thee* is a salute to beat writer and philosopher William S. Burroughs. He made many comments in his writings about purposely misspelling words to fight against the traditionalists of society. The use of the word *ov*, however, requires deeper study. The group believes that ov is the word that stands for the bodily fluids man releases.

The group was started by Genesis P. Orridge, drummer for industrial band Throbbing Gristle. Orridge started a "propaganda band" for the temple called Psychick TV. The temple believes in preserving mankind through chaos magick, sex magick, Aleister Crowley's writings, and Satanism. Members are typically young men in their twenties, usually with shaven heads, ponytails, and several body piercings. There are several "sacred scars" that the group has its members wear, which are typically burns or cuts in parallel lines of one to three sections.

This group was extremely active in the late 1980s. In the early 1990s, the propaganda group Psychick TV had several of its concert tapes confiscated by Scotland Yard. The group had publicly shown many of the temple's recruitment tapes, including one that depicted a ritual murder. However, it was later proven that the tape was a fake.

Temple activities are not as publicized as they once were. There are only a few Web sites for the group; they advertise temples in California, Washington, and Oregon.

The group's literature includes several manifestos including *Thee Grey Book*. A manual of temple lifestyle, the book tells followers how to have a fantasy "magickally" fulfilled. The member is to take a sample of bodily fluids of blood, sperm, and saliva and put them on a piece of paper with their fantasy written on it and send it in to the temple. Temple officials assure the member that the sample will be kept for safekeeping in a locked vault in the temple's headquarters. The group also releases a monthly periodical, *Broadcasts*.

Chapter 9

CULTS

"So my opinion is that you be kind to children and be kind to seniors and take the potion like they used to take in ancient Greece and step over quietly because we are not committing suicide; it's a revolutionary act."
—Jim Jones, leader of the People's Temple

There are a growing number of groups in the United States that are labeled as cults. The word *cult* is a term that has many negative connotations. Some of the various meanings of the word refer to "deviant religious groups" or "those groups that are not Judeo-Christian." However, most standard dictionaries define a cult as a "sect that follows a common ideology, doctrine, or leader." Using this definition, most religious or philosophical groups of any nature can be called cults.

The focus of law enforcement should not be concentrated on groups simply because they follow nontraditional beliefs; it is not the beliefs but the behavior that should be of interest. An analysis of destructive cults is deemed more appropriate for protecting the well-being of society. A destructive cult can be defined as "a sect that follows a common ideology, doctrine, or leader that recruits followers through deceptive practices and keeps members through manipulation and coercion."

The cult is typically seen as a religious group, but this is a misnomer. There are several destructive cults that are not religious in nature. Coercion and manipulation are universally used by groups that espouse Christian ideologies, Buddhist teachings, and even self-improvement classes. The belief system associated with a destructive cult is merely a vehicle for the abuses that occur by the group.

IDENTIFYING DESTRUCTIVE GROUPS

The process of identifying destructive cults in our nation has become increasingly difficult. There are a number of deviant religious groups that resemble groups with destructive qualities but are a world away from being hazardous to society.

Another difficulty in identifying these groups is in gathering research and intelligence from watchdog groups. While these groups can be a valuable resource for law enforcement officers, they must be viewed with discretion because some of these agencies have agendas. Some groups exist only to monitor groups with differing ideologies. An existing bias may exist when disseminating materials to law enforcement.

On the other hand, some of the cults themselves have created phony watchdog groups to disseminate information that puts a positive spin on destructive group activities and publicly accuses critics of wrongdoing.

Some of these groups have surveillance teams and a never-ending source of income from group members. Officers should be advised that information from these groups may be slanted. To gain a balanced view of these groups, officers should gather information from a number of sources.

TYPES OF DESTRUCTIVE GROUPS

There are several types of groups that have characteristics that may pose a threat to members of the group or outside society. Some of the more common groups are the following.

Therapeutic Cults

These are groups that may use self-improvement programs to "increase human potential." Therapeutic cults may offer their programs through schools, businesses, and community organizations. The techniques used by the group may not be manipulative in them-

selves, but the group that sponsors the training may offer retreats that are vehicles used to recruit followers.

An example of this took place in the Southwest United States, where an elementary school teacher was recruited into a group. Through her school, the teacher attended a training session offered by a group of consultants that had been contracted by an outside company. The consultants offered a training program that was to help increase motivation among the teaching staff. The consultants offered an advanced program for those attendees who showed a continuing interest, and the teacher decided to attend. The group invited the teacher to a retreat that was to take place at a conference center.

The teacher called her roommate from the conference center and advised her that she was going to be leaving her job and moving into the desert with the program sponsors. She had received a "calling" by the group to join them in their spiritual endeavors. The roommate asked her how an educational group could also be a spiritual group. The teacher began to tell her how the group used natural energies, UFOs, and even angels in its spiritual work.

The teacher came home. She packed every material object she owned into her car and then went to the school where she had taught for several years and resigned. Lastly, she told her family that she was no longer part of it, but had a new spiritual family.

Subsequently, through correspondence and telephone conversations, the teacher has shown evidence of manipulation, coercion, and depression as a result of involvement in this group.

Political Cults

These groups have a twofold purpose. They use political philosophies to recruit members, and they use recruited members to build their political base. In April 1974 the daughter of millionaire William Randolph Hearst was caught on tape robbing a bank along with members of the notorious Symbionese Liberation Army. The SLA had kidnapped Patrica "Patty" Hearst to use her to gain ransom money and as a political statement against the "fascist regime" of the U.S. government.

The kidnapping of Hearst was to create World War III and to bring an end to the ruling class society through starvation and slavery. The "programming" that Hearst testified to, which included beatings and confinement, was very similar to the indoctrination techniques used on U.S. prisoners of war. The SLA had decided to take its political ideologies to an extreme. Most political cults today are not as extreme but do continue to use manipulative techniques to gain and keep members. Some of the more popular racial extremist groups are also political cults that endorse total dedication to the group and violence toward its enemies. Racist topics, economic philosophy, and social status are all used as bait for political cults.

Mystical Cults

These groups are distinctive in their use of "sacred sciences" to lure new members—they use age-old metaphysical practices placed in a contemporary package. An example of this is channeling, which is the act of a spirit taking over the expressions and consciousness of a person. The spirit speaks through the medium and gives advice from the spirit realm. Although this has been practiced in magickal religions for centuries, it is presented as a new science that the cult has discovered.

Society has seen a growth in these groups as more Americans are discovering occult religions. A group known as the Order of the Solar Temple was involved in two mass suicides and murders in the mountains of Switzerland in 1994 and in France in 1995. The group's doctrines were a mixture of quasi-Masonic Rosicrucian ideas and the Knights Templar ideologies.

The group members were found dead—several members had taken sleeping pills, many had plastic bags over their heads, and several were shot to death. The final attack by the group was a fire that burned the bodies of the members, which had been arranged in the shape of a star. The suicide was meant to send members to the star Sirius.

I received a call from a judge in a nearby large city who had lost his wife to a group that claimed to have spiritual powers. The group encouraged his wife to drain her family's assets and give them to the group. (In the end, the only magickal power that the group had was to make new members' money disappear!) The "sciences" that were used by the group were very ridiculous but were effective enough to fool a very intelligent wife and mother.

Doomsday Cults

The concept of a spiritual and physical armageddon is a common thread in many religious groups. In many religions, this is a spiritual showdown between the deity the group follows and the enemy of that deity. A battle between good and evil takes place, with the followers of the religion becoming victors. Doomsday cults take advantage of this concept by promising to be the only safe passage to surviving this war. Many of the most recognized cults in the news have been doomsday cults. The Aum Shinri Kyo (The Supreme Truth) cult in Japan was responsible for attacking Japanese citizens on a subway by gassing the facilities with Sarin gas, a very destructive and often deadly nerve agent. The leader, Shoko Asahara, ordered the "hit" that killed 12 and injured 5,000. The group was also responsible for a terrorist attack on an attorney who dared to speak out against the group. The group sent a few followers into the attorney's home, where they kidnapped and murdered his wife and child.

Charles Manson's Family was also considered a doomsday cult. The group tried to start Helter Skelter, an all-out race war. The murder of actress Sharon Tate was to be the springboard for this war. Manson and his group planned to survive the war in the desert.

There have been a number of doomsday cults in the United States and abroad. As I am writing this text, there is a report of a group known as the Movement for the Restoration of the Ten Commandments of God that has apparently committed suicide by setting itself on fire. Close to 1,000 bodies have been found in temples throughout the countryside of Uganda.

These groups pose a particular threat to society and law enforcement because of a tendency of inward and outward acts of violence. People who are prepared to die have no fear of physical force.

Messianic Cults

There are a number of messianic communities throughout the United States. Most of these groups are sociological experiments to bring together believers for a utopian society in preparation for the arrival of a messiah.

Problems arise when a manipulative individual or subgroup within the community uses destructive behaviors or criminal acts. Most messianic communities live in large communes, which makes the covering of negative acts very easy. Abuse and crimes may even be hidden from the rest of the community.

Religious Cults

The use or misuse of spiritual teachings of established religions is the focus of religious cults. This category of cult is the most popular in the United States. The religious cult uses concepts of Christianity, Islam, Buddhism, and other world religions, with the leader of the group typically adding to the sacred texts to include himself and the group as the object of the texts. The leader may claim a personal affiliation with the deity mentioned in the text. An example of this is the Branch Davidians' teachings regarding David Koresh. Teachings from the Bible are given personalized meanings by the group.

The verse found in Matthew 24:10 states: "And then shall many be offended, and shall betray one another, and shall hate one another."

The Davidians personalize this by saying:

Many former believers of the Seven Seals scroll (as revealed by David Koresh) betrayed their brethren to the Babylonian Beast. This betrayal by some former Branch Davidian believers caused the Mt. Carmel church to be attacked on February 28, 1993, by the latter day Babylonian Beast.

There are any number of these groups that use sacred texts as tools of manipulation in their groups.

ORIGINS AND LEADERSHIP

Most destructive cults are lead by a very charismatic individual. The personality profile of these individuals have several common characteristics, some of which are the following:

- **Claims a personal connection with deity.** The leader will usually claim to have had a personal revelation from the group's deity. This revelation may reveal the leader's connection with the deity (sibling or chosen one of the deity). The leader typically claims to have a personal relationship with the deity that cannot be attained by members of the group.
- **Does not tolerate other views.** The leader does not allow the views of others to be expressed. No open criticism is allowed by the leader.
- **Builds up their "kingdom."** The leader usually builds up the group and their activities.
- **Manipulates.** The leader of the group is usually very charming and, much like a typical abuser, has the ability to spot potential victims. The leader will begin to focus on making the new recruit feel wanted and needed. The leader will usually have excellent presentation skills. This helps in recruitment and the group's public relations. There are promises of spiritual and material goods to come. The members work and proselytize to see this promise manifest.
- **Builds paranoia.** The leader will build fear of the outside world among the members, causing them to fear other religions, but most of all instilling the fear of being unfaithful to the leader. Leaders often tell members that Satan will kill them if they leave the group.
- **Exploits.** Sexual exploitation of members is common in many destructive

cults. One ex-member shared with me how the leader would sexually fondle his members and later tell them they were trash for seducing him.

- **Creates a husband/father role.** One of the common roles that I have seen taken by cult leaders is that of the husband and father in a family. The leader usurps the husband's role, separating spouses and taking the position of male leader in the woman's life. Children may find that they have a new parent. I have seen instances in which the leader has told the child to call him "daddy" and to disregard his or her natural parents.
- **Demands possessions.** Leaders of groups typically call for all members to give up possessions. Many members are encouraged to steal or ask for money from parents. This money is given to the leader to show allegiance.
- **Is hard to please.** The leader will continually push for members to strive for acceptance by the leader. The leader may also put unrealistic requests on the members.
- **Demands harsh punishments.** Along with the difficult personality, the leader will use harsh punishments. These punishments usually exist to maintain the group's devotion. In one of the cases I worked on, the leader of the group punished a member who had left and then returned to the fold by making him walk around barefoot with shoes on his hands to show his humility. His wife, who abstained from pork for dietary reasons, was forced to eat a plate of ham, bacon, and sausage in front of the group. Harsher punishments exist in many groups such as beatings and acts of humiliation.

Because of his charm and leadership abilities, the leader will usually form a small group around himself in the early formation of the group. In most instances, the leader takes members from an established religious or political group and exploits their shortcomings in order to gain favor. From this core group of followers, the leader may begin to form his own sect.

GROUP DYNAMICS

Destructive cults usually have a number of characteristics that distinguish them from non-threatening groups. A popular litmus test that is used by researchers to gauge the threat assessment of a group is taken from a classic text on brainwashing and mental coercion. These criteria are taken from the book *Thought Reform and the Psychology of Totalism.* Written by psychiatrist and psychologist Robert Jay Lifton, the book is a study of the brainwashing techniques used on Americans in Chinese prisons.

This test is commonly known as Lifton's criteria for thought reform. His criteria and explanations are as follows:

- **Milieu control.** This is control over communication in the environment. This limits communication within and outside the group. This is also control over criticism within the group.
- **Mystical manipulation.** Experiences and natural events are presented as being "expected miracles." Natural events are viewed as spiritual events that are for the group. (One of the leaders I dealt with would stand outside during thunderstorms and tell members that it was a show for the cult.)
- **Confession.** This is the destruction of privacy. Confession lowers the member's guard and makes him or her vulnerable. The act of confession also gives the leader blackmail material to use against members who try to leave.
- **Self-sanctification through purity.** Members may have to strive for perfection in the leader and group's sight. This self-discipline creates an atmosphere of being spiritual. An abstinence from certain foods, thoughts, and activities may also be required by the group. Some group members have gone so far as to

whip themselves when they feel tempted to do things that conflict with group ideology. Confession may also be part of this purification process.

- **Aura of sacred science.** The ideas and laws surrounding the group are accepted as the only truth. There are sacred principles that cannot be questioned by members of the group.

- **Loading the language.** Words used in the group may replace words used outside the group. For instance the word father may be redefined from meaning a natural parent to referring to the group's leader. When the member is outside of the group, this term always reverts back to the group's definition. This "loading" of the language can taint the thought processes of members who try to leave. When cult words are used in society, the ex-member is taught, "See, we are everywhere." New meanings for old words also give members the feeling of having their own language.

- **Doctrine over person.** Dogma overrules human needs and wants. No amount of human suffering can change the rigid rules of the group. Every aspect and experience in a member's life can be reduced to a basic set of rules and laws. These laws are used when a member may dispute or question the leader's actions.

- **Dispensing of evidence.** Membership in the group makes one exist. Outside of the cult, a person does not exist or matter. The leader of the group reserves the right to announce who is of worth and who is not. The leader can dictate good and evil to the world. (An ex-member of a messianic cult told how the group's leader announced to the group that "our house" is of "God" and those outside the group "are of Satan.")

RECRUITMENT

As the group seeks to spread its message to the world, it relies on the recruitment activities of the group to gain members. Members recruit in a number of places. Recruiters have been found on street corners, schools, businesses, airports, Alcoholics Anonymous meetings, community gatherings, and just about anywhere that people are at a crossroads in life. Recruitment focuses on finding people at their weakest point.

Recruitment may be performed by simple proselytizing and preaching to gain recruits. Recruitment may also be performed by the recruiter selling literature, videos, and crafts created by the cult. Recruiters are usually those members who have advanced in their faith so far that the group feels no fear in letting them go out in public. Recruiters may be male or female. Female recruiters may be picked from the most attractive of the female members. One infamous cult used to have females prostitute themselves in an act known as "hooking for Jesus."

Recruiters are usually trained in logic and rhetoric. Many are experts in questioning potential recruits. Have you ever wanted to know the meaning of life? Do you ever get spiritually hungry? Did you ever think that there is something more than working 9 to 5 every day? Questions and inquiries are meant to open up prospective members.

The Path to Enlightenment

Once a prospect is invited to visit the group, a slow but steady stream of indoctrination begins. The prospect is typically given a tour of the "utopian community" that the cult purports to be. All of the wonderful pluses of membership in the group are accented to the prospect.

Many groups engage in a manipulative technique called "love bombing," which is essentially mass affection focused on the prospect by the group. Prospects are hugged, kissed, and touched by total strangers to make them drop their guard and become vulnerable.

Many groups encourage the prospect to stay the evening. During this time the prospect typically endures a bombardment of the group's ideology. The leader may speak or tapes may be continuously played of the leader's speeches.

Group members may read the group's sacred texts to the prospect.

Prospects are generally not left alone to engage in any kind of thought process. By always staying with the prospects, they are constantly reminding the prospects of the fellowship available in the group.

A degree of sleep and food deprivation may begin to break down the prospect. Junk foods and sodas may be given as meals. This lowers protein intake and makes the brain and immune system weak.

Games and "group sessions" may be performed with the intent of drawing confessions from the prospect. These confessions bind the group together through admissions of weakness and also provide material to be used against the member if he or she decides to leave.

Snapping

The ultimate goal of the indoctrination is an eventual "snapping" of the prospect's mind to replace the member's identity with a cult identity. The member will usually take on a new name given by the group; many times this is a name having to do with the group's ideology. Members of a pseudo-Christian cult may have Biblical names, and members of a mysticism-based cult may have names taken from metaphysical texts or even names of spirits.

The dress and overall appearance of the member typically becomes unrecognizable by loved ones. The member who has given up total control of his or her decision-making process will many times appear in a zombie-like state. Officers who run into members in this state may think they are on drugs from their appearance.

Those groups that do not commit criminal acts but do coerce and perform mental manipulation have an awesome power to control and direct members. Although unethical, these groups do not break any law by exerting this power over members. Members in such groups usually serve their time in the group by working and recruiting for the group.

There are a number of groups that *do*, however, involve themselves in illegal prac-

tices. These groups can use their membership to carry out illegal acts. Some of the criminal acts committed by these cults include theft, charity fraud, weapon stockpiling, arson, assault, and murder.

Child Abuse

There are a number of destructive cults that believe in disciplining children through harsh means. One infamous group was accused of using thin wooden sticks dipped into a solvent that hardened them. The members would beat children on the legs and buttocks with the sticks.

One of the cases I assisted on resulted in a fierce custody battle between a man who was a member of the group and his wife, who was not a member. The two shared custody of three children, who were allowed to visit the cult's commune.

The mother gathered information about the unsafe conditions at the cult's commune. One weekend she was allowed to visit and pick up the children, so she brought a video camera and documented the living conditions. The footage showed live electrical wires lying around in reach of children, raw sewage buildup, and even a hypodermic needle lying in the grass. She was also able to videotape the condition of her children, who were dirty and neglected. She took this video into court and gained temporary custody.

The same group was documented as having a "discipline session" with a young girl who had gotten out of hand. A female member of the group beat the child across her back with a plank of wood. The woman was fined and given a light sentence.

The abuse of children by cult members may fall in with the group's ideology. One particular cult has an act called the "holy kiss," in which the adult men in the group kiss young girls on the mouth.

There are several recorded incidents of child abuse by cult groups. Investigating officers should question members' theology regarding children and physical or sexual acts. If investigators can find sacred texts or group documents that point to this kind of theology, they can provide helpful evidence to use in prosecution.

Some groups that have views on exorcism or deliverance of spirits may actually attempt to beat the spirits out of their children. These acts have been documented in a number of cases.

LAW ENFORCEMENT AND CULTS

The presence of a cult in your community may cause a number of problems for your agency and population. However, if the group is not committing criminal acts, it is allowed to freely practice its beliefs. If the group is a source of annoyance, agencies will receive complaint calls; it is suggested that a member of the agency create a condensed report on the group to serve as a reference when citizens question the activities of a group. The agency should conduct a meeting with the group to gain a picture of the group's directives, meaning, and presence.

Officers should open and maintain a line of communication with the group's leader. This may prevent the group from feeling isolated from society and discourage the negative behaviors that could result from isolation.

Although the group may not present criminal problems, it may cause trouble by proselytizing on private property; local solicitation laws should apply to this type of activity.

Another problem that usually follows these groups is the harassment and threats that citizens of the community may offer. A community lynch mob will not help the peace in your community, regardless of its good intentions. In one jurisdiction, a cult was vandalized when citizens dumped several dead animals and piles of manure on cult property. Threats became more serious as citizens began to arm themselves when traveling near the cult's property.

People worried about family members who have joined the cult may seek the help of law enforcement in hopes of "rescuing" them. Families who inquire about minors within the group can seek legal assistance for child custody, and those with adult members in the group may seek to hire someone to remove their relatives. Officers should show concern and empathy for the parents but should remind them that adults enjoy the freedom to choose their beliefs. Taking away this freedom is a serious violation of civil rights, and a charge of kidnapping could result.

If possible, officers should advise families to seek assistance from clergy and mental health professionals.

Gathering Intelligence

Agencies investigating a new cult may be accused of harassment of a minority group. But officers don't have to perform surveillance on a group to obtain intelligence on them; there are several sources of data that can be consulted to gain insight into the group.

The Internet is a wonderful investigative tool. (More on this in Chapter 11.) Many groups now have online propaganda. This can give officers an idea of what the cult believes and if they have branches established in other areas. The Internet is also great because it offers freedom of speech to ex-members who want to post information and warnings about the group. This can serve as a good resource tool for officers.

The group may produce books and pamphlets that it makes available to the public. If officers can obtain these books, they can find out some of the basic ideologies of the group as well as information about the group's leadership.

Officers investigating cults should check the background of the group's leader.

Ex-members of these groups are good sources of information, but officers must be discreet. Many ex-members are very vulnerable to rejoining the group (researchers call this "floating") and may take information on your investigation back to their leader.

Officers may also consult agencies that assist families in cult-related issues. There are a number of these agencies on the Internet. Officers should be cautious when choosing a reference point because some agencies have been found to actually be fronts for cults themselves.

Officers may find that the cult has a business front. One case involved a large cult that had several business fronts ranging from craft shops and art supplies to automotive repair and landscaping. These groups placed their income into a community pot for the cult. The pot was actually a nice account for the leader of the group to live off while his members dove in Dumpsters for food. Investigators may also find evidence of unreported tax income and charity fraud among these groups.

SPECIAL ISSUES

GANGS AND THE OCCULT

The issue of occult-related gangs has been a somewhat curious subject among some sociologists and law enforcement officials. A Texas newspaper reported the findings of one local department.

The Donna, Texas, police department's antigang efforts have identified 23 gangs in the area, including three whose rituals have been labeled Satanic. Gang members have been known to flash gang symbols they say symbolize the devil. Some buildings in town are tagged with graffiti featuring the number 666 and pentagrams.

Detective David Fuentes, the department's resident gang expert, has been studying gangs with ties to the occult during his 2 1/2 years on the force. In his office, among the pictures of graffiti and incantations to demons, he has pictures of a skinned dog that was found earlier this year, its limbs and tail missing. The dog was on ice, apparently waiting to be used in a ritual. Symbols found with the dog were deciphered by police to mean that the dog was part of a magick spell intended to kill someone.

The dog was not the first to be found mutilated in Donna, Fuentes said. Another one was found gutted

with its head and paws cut off. Meanwhile, an increasing number of "lost dog" posters keep popping up around town. Fuentes said most of the department's information on gangs that are linked to the occult comes from gang members themselves. "They'll come right out and let you know," he said."[1]

A more conservative description of gang involvement in the occult comes from gang expert Al Valdez:

> A number of gang members accept the philosophies of these occult belief systems. Individual gang members or small groups can practice personalized forms of these religions. In fact, in some cases it appears that the activity of some small occult type gangs is based solely on these belief systems.[2]

OCCULT IDENTITY

Many street gangs will use an existing belief system—such as black nationalism, militant Islam, or Christian identity—to structure their criminal enterprise. Some groups use the structure and beliefs of the occult as tools to both empower and control their gang. Groups like the Satanic Gangster Disciples or the Triple 6 Crips have combined traditional street gang movements with occult elements in their behavior and graffiti. This element is particularly useful to create an atmosphere of fear in neighborhoods where superstition is high.

An example of this comes from a federal agent who told me the story of a street gang that would cut a finger off anyone they had a fight with. Members of this group would wear the fingers or display them to show their "allegiance to evil." The agent recalled how scared an informant of his was when encountering this group. "They worship the devil, don't mess with them!" he pleaded.

The use of demonic imagery is even becoming more prevalent in the gangster rap industry. Musicians like Triple Six Mafia and the Ghetto Boys have produced lyrics involving the mystical world of Satan and demons. To those self-styled gang members who create their lifestyle according to what they see on television or hear on the radio, this is a new genre to indulge in.

Latino groups known as Stoners have been legendary in using Satanic artwork and rituals in their practices. The groups usually wear black, listen to death metal music, and perform rites similar to those of traditional Satanists. The Stoners were very active in the 1980s but are not as visible as they once were.

Many racist gangs, such as skinheads, employ occult belief systems such as Norse Paganism and European Satanism in their practices and behaviors. Some of these groups use Satanism because of its philosophy of self-indulgence and belief that "only the strong will survive." Pentagrams, devils, and Satanic imagery have been found in artwork, tattoos, and graffiti of hate gangs.

Officers who monitor gang activity may find occult symbolism in graffiti and tattoos. Traditional street gangs like the Gangster Disciples and Vice Lords use a number of five- and six-pointed stars. Latin Kings and some Mexican mafia groups use pictures of devils and pitchforks. However, these traditional street gangs have nothing to do with the occult. Officers may be following a red herring if searching for the meanings of gang graffiti in the books and writings of occult lore.

The occult may offer an identity to groups that have no ethnic culture of their own. To quote one youth: "The black kids had Crips to belong to, the Hispanic kids have the Latin Kings, poor white boys got nothin'! That's why we use the devil!"

To reiterate, the degree of sophistication in rituals and religious knowledge among occult gangs will usually be very low because the occult is used for its trappings, not its spiritual aspects.

OCCULT GROUPS IN CORRECTIONAL SETTINGS

Correctional settings are a challenge to occultists as well as administrators who are responsible for preserving prisoners' religious rights. Prisoners can follow any religion, but sometimes inmates request special religious services and materials that stretch the boundaries of prisoners' rights.

Requests for special treatment are nothing new to corrections administrators. While some inmates sincerely need religious paraphernalia, others are just using the system for personal gain. In one case, an inmate said his religion required that he be served steak and burgundy wine for his sacrament. In another case, an occultist identified his religion as being a "sex magick" group; his request to have ritual sex with his girlfriend was denied.

Many requests are denied after the administrators obtain good working knowledge of the religious belief system they are dealing with. An example of this is in the case of a Wiccan who said he needed a ceremonial knife for use in his rituals, and that it must be sharp. His case actually looked good until personnel researched Wicca and found out that a sharp object is really not needed to perform such ritual tasks as "casting the circle." In fact, the athame in Wicca is never used to actually cut anything physical. The use of a paper knife or even a piece of plastic would suffice, as well as preserve safety.

In a 1983 court decision (*Childs v. Duckworth*), an inmate at an Indiana state prison was denied the right to start a Satanist church while in prison.

He requested that his church, "The Satanic Brotherhood," be allowed to have books available to inmates in the prison library. He also requested that a special meeting area, complete with candles and incense, be made available to prisoners within his group. The prison board turned his request down, citing that he had no recognized religious group as a sponsor and there were no other inmates who requested to be in this group. The prisoner did not appear to be sincere about his beliefs. Finally, the board declared the practice of Satanism as being counterproductive to the inmate's rehabilitation.

The case was taken to state court, where the state proclaimed that while it was the inmate's right to believe in any religion he chose, he was not necessarily free to exercise that right. The court also added that the prison system has the right to prohibit and restrict any activities they feel are counterproductive to rehabilitation or a threat to prisoner safety.

Another such case was *Dettmer v. Landon*, which took place in a Virginia prison. A Wiccan inmate requested candles, a statue, a white hooded robe, incense, and either sulfur, sea salt, or uniodized salt for his rituals. The officials told the inmate that the items were not safe for him to have and that Wicca was not a recognized religious belief system.

Corrections officials told the inmate that they felt he could use the robe's hood to cover his face during an escape; hit someone with the statue; make gunpowder with the sulfur; and mask the scent of drugs in his cell with the incense. The inmate countered that he could use salt instead of sulfur, a robe without a hood, and a plastic statue.

In 1985 a district court allowed the inmate to have the items for his religious rituals. However, an appeal filed by the prison in 1986 reversed the previous decision. The 1985 case did contain the announcement that "Wicca is a religion for First Amendment purposes," giving the religion some legal basis in later cases.

A similar case involving the right to use incense in a neo-Pagan ritual by an inmate was the subject of a 1983 lawsuit against the Michigan Department of Corrections. The prison concluded that the incense was not necessary to practice the religion.

One of the easiest ways for a prison study group to find a sponsor is to go through the Church of All Worlds, a blanket organization that supports and sponsors religious bodies that seek to improve Earth-based spirituality. Many occult groups outside of prison join the church as "branches" or "nests." These groups enjoy tax-free status under the IRS church exemption and have several networking capabilities available to them. The church sponsors Pagans in prison through prison "study groups" and helps prisoners arrange for meeting areas and literature. The popular neo-Pagan magazine *Green Egg* is the official magazine of the church and contains advertisements from active neo-Pagan groups as well as incarcerated Pagans. Groups sponsored by organizations like these are probably safer than "roll your own" groups because a higher office is setting rules and boundaries.

One of the issues facing corrections personnel is that many subversive groups are recruiting and unifying members. Many of the white supremacist groups use meetings for Christian and Norse Pagan groups to recruit members. At meetings unattended by prison officials, the groups hand out hate literature and offer protective services. Another example is the number of Islamic groups that are being used by traditional street gangs such as the Vice Lords and the Gangster Disciples.

Many corrections officials who monitor security threat groups in their facilities have discovered intelligence being passed back and forth between members of these groups using occult writings. A recent discovery turned up a group of gang members in Chicago using Norse runes to secretly communicate with each other.

DRUGS AND THE OCCULT

Since the days of noted occultist Aleister Crowley, drugs have had a major influence in the occult realm. Drugs themselves have always been viewed as somewhat magickal. They can take users into other spiritual realms, as well as enhance spiritual visions. Many world religions use drugs as part of a sacrament, such as the Native Americans' peyote.

Psychoactive drugs are used to enhance rituals and, many times, to lower inhibitions. To quote one counselor, "You've got to have your inhibitions lowered to practice some of the more bizarre rituals, especially those involving bloodletting and animal sacrifice." One particular juvenile occult group used over-the-counter "white crosses," a legal form of speed, to enhance rituals. Many local occult groups use tea made from psychoactive mushrooms to assist in visions.

Drug sales make an excellent source of income for the criminal occult group. The dealer not only has an income but also, access to new recruits.

Drugs are an excellent control tool. In one particular abuse case, a photograph was discovered of a child with a strange-looking herb sticking out of his nose. Further examination of the photo concluded that the child was given belladonna to induce a zombielike state. The child's eyes were bulging, a characteristic of belladonna use.

Because drugs are used as controllers in many circles, occult-related homicide victims should be examined for drugs in the system.

I received a letter from a former criminal Satanist who was a recruiter for a Satanist group. His methodology for gaining new members was to throw a party involving drinking. Guests were invited to a second party that distributed drugs and encouraged group sex. This party was used to introduce occult philosophies and concepts to possible recruits.

Many drug dealers have sought protection from occult groups to safely practice their dealings. The Santeria orisha Eleggua, who controls roads, is invoked by many in the trade to protect drug-running activities. Dirt taken from police departments is sometimes inserted into the bottom of the statue of Eleggua to exert spiritual control over that particular precinct. Officers in Texas have found Santeria priests blessing large quantities of cocaine and other narcotics to protect them from being discovered by authorities.

I interviewed a Pagan from the Midwest who told me the story of a drug-related case she assisted police with. The officers found a male suicide victim who appeared to have bled to death after removing his genitals with a piece of glass. Candles were burning around his body and all the mirrors in the house had been covered with black cloth. A bowl containing cocaine was found at the scene, as well as a bowl containing an unknown resin that was discovered to be the remains of a ground-up Sonoran desert toad (*Bufo alvarius*). This toad contains high doses of a hallucinogen called Tryptamine 5 MeO-DMT and is used by South American Indians to induce spiritual states. The victim had ingested the toad resin in some kind of neo-Aztec ritual.

Undercover agents trying to infiltrate drug-running groups should be aware of any occult links to the group. Unless the officer is very familiar with the occult practices and norms, however, trying to mimic occult practices is highly discouraged. Because there are so many varying traditions and practices, it would be very difficult to use a specific practice to persuade others of the agent's authenticity. An incident involving an undercover officer who had infiltrated a street gang resulted in the officer's death when he tried to mimic other gang members' style of clothing and practices. He had inadvertently "disrespected" the group by performing the wrong practice.

CONSPIRACY THEORIES

It is easy for officers to fall into the trap of conspiratorial thinking when they are working with investigations into occult groups. Because of the bizarre and secretive nature of many of these groups, a newfound interest in this area of study can open a Pandora's box of overactive imagination.

I must admit that in the beginning of my research of these groups, it became very easy to make some wild deductions. I think it is easy to fall into this trap simply because the factual aspects of the occult are so unbelievable that once the untrained eye and mind are open to them, one can become *too* open-minded. It is fantastic to imagine people who call upon spirits, fight off evil demons, and even become possessed by spirits of the dead. It is even more fantastic to know that many of these believers are educators, doctors, police officers, and other prominent figures in society. Those who sincerely practice these beliefs are not primitives living in a fantasy world but are some of the most brilliant and educated people in the world.

The fact that a businessman can appear in public in a three-piece suit and then secretly wear a robe to Pagan rituals seems rather like menacing, clandestine behavior; however, practicing a religion in secret does not necessarily denote illegal activity. But this secrecy does become a propellant for rumor and innuendo. To add to the problem faced by innocent practitioners, there have been cases of criminal occultists performing a very good masquerade as normal businessmen. Officers must walk a fine line in assessing these individuals.

The conspiracy mind-set is easily fueled by the many people who have claimed a connection to a vast network of millions of Satanists who exchange child pornography and sex slaves through the U.S. government. These figures tie stories of government mind-control experiments, occult groups, and presidential figures into a tangled web of sex and sorcery. While these stories may sell books and seminars, they only muddy the waters for those sincerely seeking the truth of the phenomena surrounding these groups.

Officers who investigate the occult will find that they not only need to maintain a working knowledge of what the occult actually is but also inform themselves on what the occult is not. The theories with no substantiating evidence will only serve as stumbling blocks to those officers seeking to maintain credibility.

Another aspect of the conspiracy issue that can hurt an officer is the fact that some of the groups that push the government-and-occult theories have been documented as hate groups. Many militia and patriot groups that have racist agendas use these conspiracies to join the government and minorities in a Satanic system. Officers do *not* want any connections with these groups or their output.

One of the most important aspects to researching or investigating such groups is proper documentation. Any evidence relating to the presence of these groups can serve to assist in any investigation. However, it is very hard to accept testimony from subjects when there is no evidence whatsoever of the presence of the groups. Many of the wilder conspiracy theories have very little evidence to back them up.

Some of the conspiracy theories include these claims:

- Large companies have sold their souls to Satan for success.
- Every Halloween a group of Satanists

gather and hunt down a blonde, blue-eyed child.

- Government agencies are using mind control to program sex slaves to be used by Hollywood actors and actresses. Occult groups provide the "magick."

ABSOLUTES

The only thing worse than a wild conspiracy theory is thinking that all groups behave in the same way. Looking at occult religions as recognized spiritual movements, it is only natural that interpretations of rituals, beliefs, and use of religious icons will differ among so many groups.

We can safely assess a universal approach to some aspects of occult religions, such as the widely recognized interpretation of some colors used in magick, elements of nature, and others. However, it is not safe to assume that an occult group will use the same calendar of sacred days or attach the same meanings to the color of a robe. Many previous texts on occult-related criminal groups have tried to establish absolutes for some occult aspects. This is not fair or safe to do because of the number of changing interpretations and inclusions in these religions.

SERIAL KILLERS AND THE OCCULT

There are several other factors in the making of a serial killer, but the number of killers with occult connections is quite interesting. Here are a few of the more notorious killers and their ties or alleged ties to the occult.

Charles Manson

Charles Manson is viewed by many as Satan himself, and his ties to criminal occult groups can help us understand his reign of power and use of occult ritual and philosophy. Many modern-day Satanists, like Nicholas Shreck of the Werewolf Order, view Manson as a prophet of sorts. Manson's philosophy of Helter Skelter is very similar to the agenda that many of today's racist occult groups follow. Helter Skelter was intended to be a series of murders that triggered an all-out race war, leaving only an elite group behind.

Manson's possible connections to the Process Church of Final Judgement have been suspected by some writers. Manson used the combination of God and Satan in a way very similar to what the Process taught. He also dealt with a Satanist group known as the Kirke Order of Dog Blood. He was known to hire out "mercenaries" from the prison gang called the Aryan Brotherhood.

Night Stalker

In 1984 police discovered the body of a 79-year-old woman who had been murdered in Glassell Park, California. This would become the first of a series of victims that Night Stalker Richard Ramirez claimed. Ramirez is legendary as *the* Satanic killer. Ramirez left the Satanists' inverted pentagram at the scene of his crimes, whether it was on the body of a victim or on the wall of his crime scene. Many victims were raped and forced to pray to Satan.

For several months Ramirez kept the residents of California in constant fear. It was only after he was recognized and attacked by a group of California residents that he was apprehended. Even while he was captured, Ramirez still proudly displayed his faith in Satanic occultism by shouting "Hail Satan!" to the courtroom. Ramirez's fondness for heavy metal music, violence, and Satanism was laid out during his trial. However, the ferocity of his crimes could not be comprehended by the public. It was only in his own words that Ramirez shared the dark truth about himself.

"You don't understand me. You are not expected to. You are not capable of it. I am beyond your experience. I am beyond good and evil. Legions of the night, night breed, repeat not the errors of the night prowler and show no mercy. I will be avenged, Lucifer dwells within us all."

Since his imprisonment, Ramirez has acquired quite a following of groupies, including several young women. He was also visited by a group from the San Francisco-based Church of Satan.

Henry Lee Lucas

Henry Lucas was arrested in 1983 on a misdemeanor charge of possessing a firearm. During his short stint in a Texas jail, Lucas confessed to the murder of an 80-year-old Texas woman. After taking officers to the crime scenes and showing them the evidence, Lucas began confessing about a murder spree that spanned North America and allegedly included more than 300 victims. By 1985 Lucas and his pervert sidekick, Otis Toole, were implicated in 12 slayings across the United States. Lucas and Toole are reported to have kidnapped, raped, and murdered hitchhikers, runaways, and homeless victims.

During his confession sessions, Lucas started rambling about his participation in a criminal Satanist group known as the Hand of Death. This was reported to be a nationwide network of those who served the Prince of Darkness through murder and drug running. The group was involved in child pornography and the making of snuff films. Group locations in Florida, Texas, and Mexico were identified. Law enforcement agencies created a nationwide task force to identify and uncover this clandestine group, but, even though the description of many of the sites and members were identified correctly by Lucas, there was little evidence that the group actually existed. Lucas claimed that the group went underground when it was being investigated.

Lucas recanted his story about the group and later recanted his denial of the group's existence.

Skid Row Slasher

Serial killer Vaughn Greenwood was convicted on nine counts of first degree murder in 1976 for crimes heavily laden with occult overtones. Greenwood would slash a victim and allow the victim's heart to pump blood out for his drinking. After he killed his victim, he would pose the body in symbolic fashion. He would then surround the corpse in a salt circle and empty its blood into cups. He also painted mystical symbols at his scenes.

Greenwood's exploits were duplicated by Tennessee-born Bobby Joe Maxwell. In 1978 Maxwell murdered nine homeless people and used their blood to write names used for Satan.

While imprisoned, Maxwell told fellow inmates he had killed to "obtain souls for Satan."

Son of Sam

Responsible for a string of murders in the New York City area in 1976–1977, David Berkowitz became notorious as the "Son of Sam" killer from letters he had left at crime scenes referring to the name. Initial references to demons, Beelzebub, and drawings of summoning seals became indicators of an occult connection. After his arrest, Berkowitz began telling tales of a demon-possessed dog that told him to murder. This, combined with his claim to have set more than 2,000 fires in the New York area, did not help his credibility. Berkowitz also opened up to police about his involvement with a criminal occult group that intermingled with the Process Church and a Scientology group. Berkowitz has shared numerous pages of testimony about these groups, and much of the data has been confirmed. Berkowitz has had several attempts on his life as a result of his testimony involving these groups.

THREATS

Officers taking reports about harassment of or assaults on ex-members of nontraditional groups may find intense threats directed toward the defector. Investigating officers may even find threats in the form of curses aimed at the individual. Threats may appear in the form of phone harassment, vandalism, death threats by letter, or items left on the property to intimidate the defector. Officers should encourage victims to document all harassment.

LEGAL ASPECTS

When do the customs and traditions of a cultural group guide the practices of law enforcement? There are many situations in which a proper assessment of a group's norms and folkways are not only the key to effectively communicating with the group, but also key to the way officers approach a situation.

In 1986 a raid on the home of a group of Roma (gypsies) in Spokane, Washington, caused a national stir. During the raid officers found a large amount of cash, which was confiscated by the officers without the support of a proper search warrant. Officers also broke items considered sacred and unknowingly broke sacred rules by touching the female Roma. This resulted in the gypsy group being ostracized by the rest of their community. These mistakes resulted in a $1 million lawsuit and a tremendous amount of negative press for the city.

Could another approach have been taken? Did officers have other options that would have changed this case? Only the officers involved know what happened that day, but it is certainly a lesson for us all.

I must reiterate, the focus of this manual is not to cater to those groups and individuals who use religious freedoms as a shield and a crutch for illegal activities. It is to help officers focus on doing their jobs to the best of their ability. It is to act as a guide to keeping officers out of trouble with liability issues and to be accurate when dealing with issues relating to these groups.

Cases involving nontraditional groups can give officers an idea as to how to handle these groups, as well as provide some legal decisions to back up court actions.

OCCULT PRACTICES AND THE LAW

The First Amendment states that "Congress shall make no law respecting an establishment of religion, or prohibiting the free exercise thereof; or abridging the freedom of speech, or of the press; or the right of the people peaceably to assemble, and to petition the government for a redress of grievances." The following rulings all touch on aspects of occult religious practices.

Animal Sacrifice
Church of Lukumi Babalu Aye v. Hialeah, 508 U.S. 520 (1993)
This ruling said ritualistic animal sacrifices are an important part of the Santeria religion. The sacrifice of animals is allowed but must be performed without any cruelty to the animal.

Child Custody
Pater v. Pater–588 N.E.2d 794 (Ohio 1992)
This decision says a court may violate a parent's constitutional rights if a custody decision is improperly made based on a parent's religious beliefs.

A court may not remove a child because of the parent's beliefs unless these beliefs prove evident to harm the child. A court may also not restrict the beliefs and teachings of a custodial parent unless these cause a conflict between parents that can be proven to be harmful to the child.

Drug Use as a Sacrament
Employment Division v. Smith 494 U.S. 872 (1990)
This rules that the free exercise clause cannot exempt one from drug laws. The two defendants were members of the Native American Church and had ingested peyote, a hallucinogenic drug. The high court stated a new rule: No religious actions may violate general laws, but laws aimed specifically at religions or a particular religious practice will be held unconstitutional.

Occult Beliefs as a Mental Illness
Genius v. State (986 F. Supp. 668 D.Mass. 1997)
A woman and her lover, a married man, had a fight in which the woman attempted to shoot the man. The gun misfired. The man stabbed the woman repeatedly in the face and upper body. When authorities confronted the perpetrator, he claimed he was only acting out of a magickal spell that his wife had put on him. She was a practitioner of Voodoo and had used Voodoo in his presence to make him fear her. The defendant claimed that he had been the victim of a curse that left him no choice—either he was to kill his lover, or his wife would magickally kill him.

He was convicted of first-degree murder. During his appeal, the husband consulted a psychiatrist who spoke on his behalf in court. The psychiatrist stated that he believed that the man acted out during a "trance" state. Because of this, he felt that the man was not responsible for the murder. The defense was equating belief in

Voodoo with mental illness. The conviction stood after the court concluded that a belief in Voodoo does not constitute insanity or any sort of mental illness.

Wicca as a Religion
Dettmer v. Landon, 617 F Supp. 592 (Virginia, 1985)

The District Court of Virginia declared in 1985 that Wicca is clearly a religion for First Amendment purposes because members sincerely adhere to a fairly complex set of doctrines relating to the spiritual aspect of their lives, and in doing so they have "ultimate concerns" in much the same way as followers of more accepted religions. Their ceremonies and leadership structure, their rather elaborate set of articulated doctrine, their belief in the concept of another world, and their broad concern for improving the quality of life for others gives them at least some similarity to other more widely recognized religions.

Judge J. Butzner of the Fourth Circuit Federal Appeals Court confirmed the *Dettmer v. Landon* decision (799F 2nd 929) in 1986. He said: "We agree with the District Court that the doctrine taught by the Church of Wicca is a religion."

ENDNOTES

1. Madeline Baro, "Donna police keep tabs on gang involvement in the occult." Associated Press, Donna, Texas, June 15, 1998.

2. Al Valdez, *A Guide to Understanding Street Gangs* (LawTech Publishing: 1997), p. 189.

Chapter 11

INVESTIGATIONS

IDENTIFYING OCCULT PRACTITIONERS

When dealing with subjects who partici-pate in occult religions, officers may see several physical indicators that identify them with a particular group or religion. While these indicators do not necessarily denote criminal activity, they are help-ful in assisting officers in recognizing a suspect or vic-tim's ties to a group. The following are a few of the very visible indicators.

Tattoos

When analyzing tattoos of different subcultures, whether it is a hate group, street gang, or motorcycle gang, occult symbols frequently appear. The Aryan Brotherhood uses symbols such as a 666 tattoo as its

Investigating officers should be prepared to use biohazard procedures when handling evidence from magico-religious scenes. The blood used in many practices can carry a number of diseases.

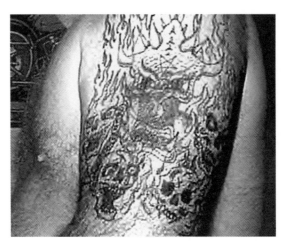

identifier. Another popular prison tattoo is that of a nude woman sitting on a devil's tongue. Many of these groups borrow occult imagery but do not necessarily follow occult religions.

Tattoos are worn by these groups for many reasons, the most common being that members can identify themselves to one another by showing the tattoos. Some may wear a tattoo because they simply identify with a religion or deity. One particular Satanist group requires new members to get a tattoo of an inverted pentagram without its bottom horizontal line. After the new recruit has committed several criminal acts, the bottom line of the tattoo is added.

Some members of neo-Pagan groups are tattooed with images of magickal creatures such as fairies, unicorns, or angels. God and Goddess images, such as the Green Man or Pan, are sometimes pictured. Some members may have their coven name or personal magickal symbol tattooed on them. The use of Celtic knotwork has become very popular among members of Celtic neo-Pagan groups, but this style of tattoo has also become popular outside the occult community.

Afro-Caribbean Groups

Members of Afro-Caribbean groups often have tattoos of the saints or even images of the African gods themselves. Some members of Cuban criminal groups that arrived in the Mariel boatlift may have identifying tattoos on the web

of their hand. In the late 1980s many agencies were instructed to look for these tattoos.

However, the meaning of these tattoos differs according to the wearer. Some claim that a cross figure in the hand represents an executioner, but there are many that simply wear it to stand for the cross of Christianity. Officers should be cautious not to paint too broad a stroke with meanings behind tattoos.

Ritual Body Art

There are a number of magick-based religions that have always used body paint in a ritualistic context. Many early hunting and gathering Pagan cultures used paint to help in hunting and even to identify the spiritual leaders of the community. Afro-Caribbean religions use paint to cover the head in the colors of the deity in many of their traditions. There are a number of neo-Pagan traditions that use body paint to identify a particular sect. This practice is similar to the Native American use of paint to show affiliation with a specific cultural group.

Some groups use paint for ritual purposes. A level of initiation may be indicated by the presence of body paint on the practitioner. The paint may be used to perform magick, acting as a "transformer" to make a spiritual change from the physical realm. The paint can act as protection from harmful energies or powers. Some groups use paint as a symbol of a rite of passage. Pregnancies, marriages, puberty, and many

A Cop's Guide to Occult Investigations

other stages of life can be marked by the use of ritual body paintings.

The color of paint may represent an emotion or an idea. In some groups red body paint stands for blood. This may be of use in a rite of passage to represent life. Red may also stand for lust and can be found in love-based rites. White paint represents the spirit world and may be used on a body to communicate with spirits or to represent someone who talks to spirits. Some groups also use white to represent the milk of a mother, and it is also found in pregnancy rituals. Black stands for power and death; it may be used to repel negative energies or to represent mourning or sadness in a person's life.

Green paint is used to represent fertility and birth; women may be found with this color painted on their stomach. Blue paint may be used in healing rites, since it represents the healing power of the water element. Pink paint may represent love.

There are a number of symbols that are used in body paint. Triangles, circles, arrows, and other geometric symbols are used to represent emotions and actions. The runic alphabet symbols may be used, as well.

Ritual Scarring

Ritual scourging is used by many different occult religions and may leave temporary or permanent marks on the member. This act is usually performed with a cat-o'-nine-tails.

While some may use the scourge in a sexual context, the religious symbolism in some groups may pertain to female gender domination in Goddess-based religions.

Followers may also have scars from self-mutilation rituals. If the member has been involved in a vampire-based or blood fetish group, there may be marks on a number of places on the body where blood has been taken.

There is a ritual cutting in the Congo tradition of Palo Mayombe called rayado, which is called being "scratched" into Palo. The areas where the initiate is cut are kept secret and are filled with herbs and other items. This cutting is also practiced in Santeria, where the initiate's head is cut and the saint is "crowned" onto the initiate's head.

Self-mutilation for religious purposes may be performed to achieve a state of ecstasy. In this state, the user may faint or go into a trance to do spiritual work.

Genital Mutilation

Some magick-based belief systems embrace the concept of genital mutilation. Some African and Egyptian practitioners will perform a cutting of the labia and clitoris. This controversial practice is typically used as a rite into adulthood.

Some blood fetish groups use a technique in which they pierce the labia with blades to make the labia look like it has fangs.

The Psychick Youth movement also uses genital mutilation in its practices. Internet sites by the group show pictures of male genitals with tattoos and piercings.

One case that I assisted on involved a woman who used blood in magick rituals. To obtain it, she would meet men in bars and invite them to her home for sex. Before the man would have an orgasm, she would cut his thigh area below his genitals with a small blade. She would then take the blood into a cup and use it in rituals.

Jewelry

Some occult groups give members select pieces of jewelry to indicate involvement or status in the group. The high priestess in Wicca many times wears a special garter that contains small bells or ribbons. The number of bells or ribbons indicates the number of covens that she has started. Some pieces of jewelry, such as talismans or power charms, will be given spiritual energy during a ritual. This object, once charged with spiritual powers, may be used to focus power or protect the wearer from harm. Some feel that if an outsider touches this object, it will lose its power. Followers of Santeria will wear multicolored beaded necklaces to identify their personal orishas.

Some jewelry and other physical indicators can be used as associative evidence to link members of a group to the scene or scenes of a crime. Physical indicators can also serve to link a victim to a crime scene.

COMPUTER INVESTIGATIONS

As in the case of child molesters, the Internet is providing a massive network for hate groups, deviant movements, and criminal occultists. Web pages and news forums that many can hide behind anonymously have replaced the use of computer bulletin boards (BBS). Many groups still use freestanding dial-up BBS.

On May 28, 1999, police officers in Florida responded to a call regarding a vicious attack on a 22-year-old man. The victim had met his attacker, a 17-year-old male, on the Internet. The victim was lured to a wooded area to take part in a ritual in which the men slit their wrists and mixed blood and dirt to form a pentagram on the ground. The attacker then turned to the victim and sliced him across the neck. The victim managed to flee and call for help but nearly died from loss of blood.

Computer Bulletin Boards

Investigators may find a BBS that acts as a virtual meeting place for members. Evidence of criminal acts as well as intelligence on group members can be found here. When dialing into these boards, investigators are advised to exercise caution. Many use Caller ID to keep track of callers.

Investigators should find out if there is an Internet access point to this board. If it is available through services such as Telnet, investigators can enter through other BBS doors. However, if a BBS is being monitored by its system operator, your identity may still be traced through your Internet service provider (ISP).

Once inside a BBS, an investigator must log in. Some systems allow guest access; however, it is usually limited. Password information can be located through informants, or through analyzing evidence such as personal papers and computer diskettes of a subject. Once logged in, the investigator may be questioned about his affiliation. One particular board I looked at asked questions such as these:

- What tradition do you follow?
- Who is your priest/priestess?
- What is the name of your group?
- Who referred you?
- What is your definition of Satanism?
- Are you an official grotto?

You get the idea: The BBS are usually very secure. However, one element I did find was that some criminal-based groups will ride on the coattails of legitimate noncriminal group BBS. A metaphysical board that talked of herbs, healing, and UFOs also contained hidden forums for some very deviant practitioners of dark religions.

Once inside, the investigator may find text files of rituals, spells, and contact points for the group. Also, images in the form of jpg, gif, or bmp files may be found. Many of these photos make good intelligence for investigators gathering evidence.

Web Pages

Many groups use the Internet to communicate and recruit. Most of the pages are open to any viewer, but this doesn't mean investigators can forget about safety precautions. A training officer from Florida told the story of some fellow officers who had visited a gang-related Web page and downloaded images and files. The owners of the site traced their address and sent a computer virus to the officers that killed their hard drive.

Some Web pages have restricted access and require a password. Many pages seem quite open to the public but have secret areas. One particular Satanist's page contained a small graphic placed on the page that would only provide access to it if you knew its location.

FTP sites/Newsgroups

Some experienced computer users employ FTP, which stands for file transfer protocol. This is an area where users can log in to access files directly from a drive or directory. With FTP, a user can make a batch of files available in a secret location where users can anonymously log in and remove and trade files easily. FTP files can be quickly removed and swapped in seconds as opposed to lengthy Web page downloads.

Newsgroups are another important method of communication among many deviant groups. A newsgroup is somewhat like "computer graffiti." Users can choose a subject such as "Satanism," "white identity," or "blood drinkers" and read and post ideas and articles pertaining to the subject. This area provides a powerful recruiting tool for such groups. Monitoring these groups will give the investigator an insight into current groups, publications, and Web sites they are using. Many groups will post notices of meetings in local areas. Photographs of local activities are also posted.

Internet Relay Chat

Internet relay chat (IRC) is a very popular outlet on the Internet that can be thought of as a computerized CB radio. Users can type messages and send them immediately to other users. Users can also send pictures and files to other members in seconds. To use IRC, you must first get the software for the application. Most ISPs include this in the basic software package. Once inside, users can choose from thousands of categories to discuss. These categories will have the user listed so that new users can choose a partner to chat with.

Users who chat on IRC can be traced by looking up their DNS numbers, which identify their names and systems. There are several search engines on the Web that can identify their names and ISP, which is the provider they are using.

Security

There are several commercially based security programs that can be used to protect the privacy of investigators who do choose to explore the Web. Using computer firewalls and a false screen name are good methods to use. Another area that needs to be protected is the user's e-mail account and any communication sent to other officers. Encryption programs such as PGP (Pretty Good Privacy) are very useful in scrambling messages and making them available only to those with the proper keys to decipher them.

Investigators should use caution in creating Web pages and should guard against using any sensitive information in their Web site. Some hacking programs make it possible to crack Web pages and enter the background to change, manipulate, and even remove information. There are several law enforcement Web sites that publish specific pages on gangs, hate groups, and security threat groups. Sites should be monitored regularly for possible weak spots. If the site is using a public guest book, officers are cautioned not to leave private messages or e-mails. It is safe to say that anything that is printed on the 'Net is available to anyone!

Raids and Search Warrants

The computer has allowed deviant groups to warehouse thousands of pages of materials onto disks and hard drives. Membership rosters, meeting notes, photographs, and recruitment tools can be found among the computer storage areas. If there is evidence that a group under investigation is using computers, investigators

Some magico-religious groups may leave behind small clues that they were there. These traces of candle wax were left behind by a neo-Pagan group.

should carefully articulate their probable cause and add computers and disks to the search warrant. If you are seizing these items, be aware of exactly what you are taking.

While confiscating a member's computer may seem like a good idea, there may also be information on floppy disks and other storage media relating to a crime. If a computer is running and has a network or modem connection, pull the plugs that connect it to the outside world first. Other users can erase and corrupt files that are being taken as evidence. Have a computer expert analyze the files before running them. Some computer programs can be booby traps to erase the contents of the hard drive. Exercise caution in tampering with files you're unsure of.

INTERVIEWING

Your field interview with an occultist may be conducted in several different formats. You may initially be conducting a traffic stop, taking an incident report, questioning a suspect, or investigating an occult-related complaint.

When arriving at the scene of a ritual, locate the leader(s) of the group. Many groups have a spokesperson who will be glad to talk with you. When possible, ask the person to leave the group for questioning to avoid any group hostility. The last thing an officer may be worrying about when arriving at a ritual site is how to make his subjects feel comfortable; however, effective communication between the subject and the officer is needed to properly assess a call. While an officer may be asking himself, "Who are these weirdos?" on the inside, it is necessary to maintain a professional demeanor. The officer who decides to preach to or lecture

his subject will quickly experience loss of communication. Allowing the subjects to speak freely while maintaining officer safety is of paramount importance.

Understand that although you may disagree with the practices and beliefs of these groups, if they are engaging in noncriminal acts, they have the right. It is important to remember that many of these groups are constantly harassed and chastised. An officer showing a little courtesy is refreshing and helpful to many of these people. They will remember your courtesy and will be much easier to deal with in the future. Last, it is easy to get caught up in what some officers call "all that mumbo jumbo stuff" in reference to the occult aspects. If a crime has been committed, focus the investigation and your directed interviews to the crime, not your personal feelings about their belief system.

RITUAL SITES

Officers may encounter a ritual site when answering a call or just by discovering its presence while on patrol. Ritual sites may be found in homes, abandoned buildings, graveyards, wooded areas, or other secluded areas.

Because the practice of magick is viewed by mainstream society as strange, noncriminal occult groups may choose hidden areas to perform rituals and religious ceremonies for the sake of privacy.

An initial question a responding officer should resolve regarding the location of the site is whether the site is on private or public property. If the site is on private property and it does not contain elements that could be considered criminal evidence, nor does it pose an apparent threat to the public, officers should leave it alone. Many occult groups own private farms and buildings that are used specifically for religious rituals. Officers may receive calls regarding these areas from concerned citizens.

Officers may also receive calls from occult groups that have outsiders trespassing on their property. There have been neo-Pagan groups whose sacred sites and ritual areas were disturbed by vandals.

An officer who comes upon a ceremony in progress should exercise caution. Although the majority of American occultists are not violent criminals, officers should approach the site with the mind-set that danger could be present. Officers should be mindful that the disturbance of a ritual might create a negative atmosphere for the group. Some may feel that the sanctity of the ceremony has been disturbed, and some may automatically become defensive because they feel they are being hassled by police.

An immediate assessment of the area should be made. When approaching subjects, officers should use the "plus one" rule. This is the rule of mentally counting on at least one extra subject being present at the scene.

A training officer once said, "Movies and television tell us to 'watch their eyes,' but it's not what's in their eyes that will kill you." As in approaching all subjects, officers should immediately take note of where subjects' hands are and if they are holding any objects.

If subjects are wearing robes or baggy outfits, palming or otherwise concealing a knife or firearm may be easy. Officers should also be prepared for "watchers," or any outside security for the group. Some groups have someone to monitor perimeter areas. This security may very well consist of unarmed and benevolent believers, but officers should not presume anything until confident of the situation.

When approaching multiple suspects, officers should always call for backup before initiating contact.

Officers should also follow standard stances, with firearm side away from subjects when interviewing. If victims are present at the scene, the officer should give any emergency care necessary and call for assistance.

An officer encountering a ritual site may be puzzled at what is discovered. Strange symbols, candles, decapitated animals, or many other implements may be at the locale. Some of these areas may be used by groups regularly. If a group finds a "natural" altar area such as a large stone surface, it may frequent this particular site.

Remember that not every ritual site is used for criminal activities or for occult rituals. I have a report from a department where its officers stumbled upon a Buddhist ritual site. There were elaborate statues, pyramids, gold coins, and burned candles. The initial reaction by many was that a "Satanist" group was at work, but after an analysis of the ritual implements and ritual layout, it was proven to be otherwise.

Officer Safety

Officer safety cannot be overemphasized. An officer encountering an active ritual site should take the same precautions as when dealing with a crime scene. *Secure the site!* It is not uncommon to find an armed member working security for the group. If an officer encounters such a site, it is wise to call for backup. Officers should set up a secure perimeter to work in.

Booby Traps

There have been instances in which booby traps have been set for intruders. Look for trip wires, foxholes, and other assorted "goodies" designed to alert and aggravate. One particular officer shared with me his experience with booby traps. He was investigating a ritual area inside an abandoned old house. He discovered that the front porch area was set to collapse unless you stepped in a particular pattern. He found several trip wires around the house. One room in the house had a large jar filled with shards of glass and nails set up above a doorway to fall on intruders.

Circles

One of the first visible discoveries at ritual sites is a circle. The circle is traditionally where magick takes place. The traditional Wiccan circle is usually 9 feet in diameter and may be formed with rocks or leaves or be drawn in chalk. Because most Wiccan groups honor nature, it is uncommon to find any kind of vandalism such as a painted circle in an outdoor setting. There may be footprints found in the circle, and these may be in a clockwise or counterclockwise pattern. It should be noted that a counterclockwise pattern (widdershins) may be evidence of a negative ritual, or just a group's way of closing the circle.

The discovery of double- or triple-walled circles may be the evidence of a ceremonial or Satanist group. The walls may contain names of spirits, demons, or angels.

Pentagrams

The symbol of the pentagram is found at many ritual sites. The officer should view the direction from its south end. The pentagram with its point facing up is used by Wiccan groups. Black magick groups use the point going down. There are some Wiccan groups that will use the inverted pentagram as a degree symbol, but it would be uncommon to see it on the ground.

Investigators can use a compass to find true north, as do many occult groups.

Cemetery Desecrations

Many times graveyards will be found desecrated by criminal occult groups. Some rob graves for bones and jewelry, frequently leaving occult symbols and anti-Christian symbols painted on mausoleums and tombstones. The presence of graffiti is usually the work of juvenile occultists. The presence of ritual implements like candles, altar cloths, and the like may be left behind by a sloppy adult group.

If a grave is broken into, the body parts may be used in rituals. The skull may be used in Satanic and in some Afro-Caribbean religions. It may be used as an altar piece or as a chalice to drink from during rituals. In Palo it may go inside the nganga. Bones like the tibia may be ground to produce a powder used in spells. The bones may be used to represent the dead in rituals or on shrines. A bone is wrapped in a ribbon to "rule over the dead" in Palo. Group members may wear bones as charms on necklaces and bracelets.

Investigators should look for evidence of necromantic rituals, which call on the dead. Candle wax, oils, and powders may be found in graves. There are groups that take part in necrophiliac rites, which are rituals in which someone has sex with the dead. Look for evidence of semen on the corpse when investigating these types of sites.

If officers encounter a specific disturbed gravesite, they should check on the family of the buried. Retaliation rituals, as well as rituals performed to frighten enemies of the group, may be performed on deceased relatives. The deceased may have also been a relative to a traitor of the group.

In all cases of disturbed gravesites, the coroner or medical examiner should be called in to conduct a forensic examination. Officers should also exercise biohazard procedures in handling any human or animal remains.

Some Afro-Caribbean groups believe in appeasing the dead with food and gifts. It is not uncommon to find rum, cigars, cakes, and animals left for the dead in graveyards in areas where there is a large Cuban or Haitian population. One officer shared a report of finding a dead duck laid on a tombstone. It was found wearing a red and black tie and had cigars next to it. This was left for the Santeria orisha Eleggua.

Homicide Scene

Victims of occult-related homicides may be chosen for a particular purpose. One incident in West Tennessee involved suspects faking car trouble to draw a "good Samaritan" offering assistance. A young man stopped and was quickly overpowered. He was stabbed and dismembered, and his heart was sucked on. Victims may be chosen because they are traitors to a group, or enemies of the group. But victims may also be randomly picked because of convenience and location. Hitchhikers, transients, and the homeless are easily taken and often will not be missed. Criminal occultists may use a human body as a source of blood in certain rituals.

The blood is considered an energy, or life force. To eat or drink someone's blood gives energy and power to the partaker.

As mentioned before, bones are used in necromantic rituals, "working with the spirits of the dead." Powdered bones may also be used to bring energy and power from the dead. Some groups may use bones as altar decorations. Skulls have a number of functions in the occult. The most basic is that of an altarpiece. Many ancient occult traditions believed that the skull contained the intelligence of the dead. A skull may also be used to represent ancestral spirits or may be used by Satanists as chalices to drink from.

The location and positioning of the victim's body can indicate an occult-related crime. If the body is tied down or tied to a cross or structure, there may be a religious significance to the death. If it is found within a magickal circle or sigil, look for ritualistic overtones. Absence of blood or body parts may also be indicators of an occult ritualistic killing. The presence of oil or candle wax on the body is also a good indicator of ritual activity. The body should be examined for evidence of the ingestion of blood, wine, urine, or ritualistic liquids. Look for evidence of occult symbols branded, tattooed, or cut into the flesh. Note the location, on the right or left side of the body.

Check for the presence of ritual tools that may have been used in the act. If the tools are in the hand of the victim, the victim may have been part of a ceremony with other members.

A victim who is a known occultist and who is found nude ("skyclad") may have been participating in religious rites. Knowing this can help investigators determine the time of death and identify details of the crime.

Ritual Scene Assessment

The call:
How and when was the report received?
What is the name and relation of caller?

Arrival:
What time did responder arrive at scene?
Immediate arrests?
Did you assist any injured?
Any witnesses? Testimony?

The scene:
What was required to secure the area?
How large a perimeter was set up?
What made the scene the center of the perimeter?
What direction to true north was ritual area?
What were your initial observations of the scene?
What are the obvious access points to the scene?

The Body:
If a body is present, what was its position?
Was the body in a form or shape, spread-eagled, or slumped?
Are there any obvious secretions such as blood, urine, vomit, or spittle?
What is the apparent cause of death or injury? Is there a weapon present?
Is the body dressed? What type of clothes? Robed? Nude?
Any apparent brands, tattoos, or burns? Location?
Is there any paint visible on body?
Does any strange jewelry appear on body?
Are there any apparent scents in the air? Incense? Drugs?
Is there an absence of blood?
(Forensic) Was there any evidence of blood, urine, feces, semen, wine, or herbs in victim's stomach?

Animals:
Are there any animals present? What color are they?
How did the animal die?
Any cloths, beads, coins, or herbs on the animal's body?

Symbolism:
Is there a circle present? Describe the size,

material used to create it, and other symbols in or around circle.

Are there any fires or candles burning? Any objects in the candle or under it? Any objects in the fire or ashes?

Are there four corners marked off?

List any symbols, ritual tools, or other evidence found at the scene.

Moon Phases and Magick

Many occult groups use the moon to aid in spell workings. The following is a guide to the phases of the moon and what they mean to the occultist.

- **New moon:** This marks the beginning of growth. Rituals can begin at this phase. The moon is not visible.
- **Waxing moon:** Positive magick is practiced during this moon. The moon is getting larger. (A handy mnemonic for determining if you're looking at a waxing or waning moon is "DOC." The waxing moon is a D-shaped crescent, followed by the full moon, "O," followed by a C-shaped crescent.)
- **Full moon:** This marks the peak of power. Energies are high on this night. You can see a full, round moon.
- **Waning moon:** Negative forces can be conjured on this moon. The moon is getting smaller.

Correspondences

Occultists believe that planets and the movement of the Earth affect the spell. There are months, days, and hours in which a successful magickal operation should take place.

- **Jupiter:** Gaining wealth and good health; corresponds with Thursday
- **Mars:** Destruction, hatred, raising the dead, curses, overthrowing enemies; corresponds with Tuesday
- **Mercury:** Obtaining knowledge, revealing the future, theft; corresponds with Wednesday
- **Moon:** Raising the dead, love, becoming invisible, movement by water; corresponds with Monday

- **Saturn:** Death, destruction; corresponds with Saturday
- **Sun:** Gaining money, finding buried treasure, love, kindness; corresponds with Sunday
- **Venus:** Love, lust, pleasure, friendship, madness; corresponds with Friday

Evidence Collection

Prior to collecting any evidence, officers should photograph and videotape the entire scene and surroundings. In this manner, the integrity of the crime scene is preserved.

Officers should keep in mind that tools and ritual implements may have blood or hair on them; these tools can carry diseases and pathogens. Use universal biohazard precautions. Luminol can be used to detect the presence of blood on these materials or at the crime scene.

Tools that are gathered should not be handled or packaged in the same container. Dried blood or other evidence from one object can contaminate another.

If the tool is wet, it should be wrapped in clean paper and placed in a bag.

Such ritual implements as an incense burner, candles, swords, daggers, and wands may hold bits of trace evidence such as fingerprints or hairs that may have been used in a ritual context. Officers should note and preserve any incense or candles. If there are any spells or writings in an open book, officers should note what pages are open and photograph the particular sections.

INFORMANTS

The use of informants in criminal occult groups is effective but risky. Occult groups are very careful about opening their doors to just anyone. Informants may be asked to take part in criminal activities to prove their allegiance to the group or deity.

Many agencies have used people involved in noncriminal occult groups to give information on other groups. This can be fruitful; however, I have heard of experiences where information from an occultist was

Officers may encounter defectors from deviant groups who are being harassed. Some groups have even killed ex-members for revealing information about the group.

"tainted" because he wanted to protect the occult community.

The amount of confidential knowledge shared with the informant should be carefully limited. Many affiliates believe that the other members will identify them as "traitors" by magickally watching them. This fear factor may be a hurdle to the operation. "Magickal thinking" sometimes overrides common sense and reason.

There are also those who have hoped to infiltrate the law enforcement community by sharing information about fellow occultists.

One particular occultist has attempted to ride the fence between law enforcement and the criminal occult community and share information about both sides. Regarding the law enforcement community, at worst this man could end up ignored; at the worst in the criminal occult community, he could end up dead. Use caution when using informants.

RITUAL ABUSE

The subject of ritual abuse is one of the most controversial aspects of occult crime. It is a very complex crime to prosecute and identify, and its existence is also denied by many in the law enforcement community. Ritual abuse is best described as an extreme, sadistic form of abuse that is methodical and systematic in nature. It can include physical, spiritual, and emotional abuse, with the element of sexual abuse as a paramount theme. The abuse is justified by religious or political trappings. It is also used to instill religious or political ideologies.

Officers may come in contact with ritual abuse victims when answering a call about mistreated children or actual allegations of ritual child abuse. It is important to note that not all ritualized abuse is occult related; it can occur in a Christian, Pagan, white supremacist, or even Voudon setting.

The ritual abuse is not always the basis for prosecution; however, the aspects of this abuse are the grounds for criminal activity. Sexual abuse, cruelty to animals, or desecration of a venerated object (e.g., church, cemetery) are usually the individual aspects used in prosecuting these particular types of cases. All the same, there are states that do provide additional penalties if it can be proved that the crimes were committed in a ritual abuse context.

Chapter 12

REFERENCE GUIDE

This reference guide defines and explains the significance of certain objects commonly used in occult rituals. The presence of incense, candles, or other items at an occult scene may not seem important at first glance; however, when examined carefully they may shed light on the meaning and intent of the ritual being investigated. Deciphering cryptic alphabets may attach new meaning to writings found.

CANDLES

An investigator may learn what type of ritual has taken place at a crime scene by looking at some of the common tools found at the scene. Colors play a significant role in the occult, with each color corresponding with an emotion or a spiritual purpose. The following are common colors of candles and the type of rituals in which they are commonly used.

Black: Evil, protection, adversity
Blue: Moodiness, peace, tranquility, health
Brown: Neutrality, uncertainty, doubt, balance
Green: Money, success, fertility, luck
Orange: Encouragement, attraction, joy
Pink: Love, honor, femininity

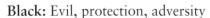

Purple: Power, tension, ambition
Red: Strength, love, passion, sex, vitality
White: Purity, truth, god, spirituality, clairvoyance
Yellow: Charm, confidence, creativity

There are a number of candles on the market that may be used in rituals. The most common candle used is one in a tall glass, found in many supermarkets and convenience stores; many have inscriptions and pictures on the glass. Everything from "Stay Away Evil" to "Lottery Winner Spirit Candle" are found inscribed on the sides of these candle glasses.

Many Wiccan groups will use candles shaped like a nude man and woman to represent the Horned God and Goddess of witchcraft. Some are found joined in a tux and dress to represent married couples. There is also a candle called the seven knots. It is seven small balls of wax on top of each other. The candle is burned at a rate of one ball per day, each day of the week.

There are crucifix candles representing the cross of Christianity that are used in many interpretations. It may be burned either to blaspheme or to honor the cross. It may also be used to represent the crossroads.

Candles in the image of a winged Satan or a tall, skinny Satan are used in black magick, usually to place a curse or hex on someone. A skull-shaped candle may be used in healing, cursing, or persuasion.

Usually the color of the candle denotes its purpose. Candles may be formed by the occultist themselves, and many times a wax image is found with a piece of jewelry or hair embedded in it. This is to perform "sympathetic magick" and affect the person who owns the jewelry or hair.

Many of the candles you find at scenes will be covered in scented oil. Oils are used to anoint or "dress" candles. The oil is rubbed on the candle, starting in the middle, rubbing upward, or down. It is used to add power and increase energy. While rubbing the candle with the oil, the user is encouraged to envision the result of the spell to make it happen.

Candle magick is likened to the common use of the birthday candle. The candle is lit, a wish is uttered, and then the candle is extinguished.

Herbs and gemstones may be found embedded or carved into the candle.

GEMSTONES AND MINERALS

Many magickal traditions use the powers of gemstones for spellwork. Some members of magickal traditions have personal stones that they believe were specifically designated for them. Occult lore says that if you find a stone for you, it may give off vibrations in your hand if you hold it in your palm.

Some believe that someone touching your stones may leave negative energies. The stone can be cleansed with sea salt to remove negative energies.

In healing, the stones may be placed on any of seven energy points of the body called *chakras*.

- **The root chakra** is the line of energy that runs from the feet to the lowest part of the abdomen. This is the energy area that provides survival and grounding powers.
- **The navel chakra** is found in the area of sexual reproduction and embodies creativity.
- **The solar plexus chakra** is located exactly where it indicates and deals with the will, energy, and power.
- **The heart chakra** covers the heart and lung area and encompasses the realms of love and lust.
- **The throat chakra** covers the throat and larynx area as well as the glands around them and covers communication.
- **The third-eye chakra** is located between the eyes and involves mental energy and focus.
- **The crown chakra** is found at the top of the head and protects against negative forces.

The following are some of the stones and their powers that are used in spellwork.

Agate: Calming, comforting, useful for relieving pain.

Amber: Electrifying. Relieves fear and problems, depression, tiredness, asthma, and infections. Soothing.

Amethyst: Protects against excesses in all forms. Powerful blood cleanser. Excellent for meditation. Calming.

Aquamarine: Keeps one young and happy. Calms nerves, helps banish fear and phobia. Excellent for meditation. Good luck for travelers.

Bloodstone: Balances and calms the uneasy mind. Develops courage and caution. Augments mental and physical vitality. Powerful physical healer.

Calcium: Alleviates fear and reduces stress. Valued as a thought amplifier, increases capacity for astral projection. Aids kidneys, pancreas, and spleen.

Carnelian: Energizes blood. Aids kidneys, lungs, gallbladder, and pancreas. Increases faith and repels fear. Alleviates bad temper and brings contentment.

Citrine: Relieves tiredness, brings happiness, and strengthens nerves. Good for heart, kidneys, and liver. Enhances body healing energy and tissue regeneration.

Copper: Influences blood flow, aids metabolism. Balances emotions. Alleviates poor memory. Eases arthritic pain.

Diamond: A master healer. Enhances brain function. Draws toxicity from the body. Useful for anxiety, insecurity, and low self-esteem. Thought amplifier.

Emerald: Calms the troubled mind and increases psychic clairvoyance. Makes one more mentally alert.

Fluorite: Strengthens bone tissue, especially teeth. Eases bone tissue and dental disease. Alleviates anxiety and sexual frustration.

Garnet: Enhances willpower and perseverance. Comforts depression, strengthens heart. Eases bad dreams.

Gold: Balances brain hemispheres. Aids tissue regeneration. Eases depression and

suicidal tendencies. Amplifies thought and aids thought retention.

Jasper: Helps morning sickness, relieves stomach and liver and kidney diseases. Calms uneasy minds and induces caution.

Moonstone: Brings success and contentment. Protects against accidents. Benefits pregnancy and menstrual problems and stimulates lactation.

Obsidian: Balances stomach, intestines, and muscle tissue. Alleviates inflammation and reduces stress. Protects soft-hearted and gentle people.

Opal: Emotional balancer used for radiating sex appeal. Amplifies thought, eases sexual depression. The friendship stone.

Peridot: Strengthens heart and eyes. Aids tissue regeneration, reduces stress, and helps personal disorders.

Quartz, clear: Conquers fear, protects against loss of balance and motion sickness. Balances emotions and stimulates the brain. Excellent for meditation.

Quartz, rose: The love stone. Aids creative thinking, stimulates creative ability. Eases sexual and emotional unbalances. Reduces stress, enhances forgiveness, and relaxation.

Quartz, smoky: Increases fertility, eases heart disease and neurological disorders. Aids depression, good for meditation.

Tiger eye: Assists thought, mental faculties, and literacy. Balances emotions and eases stubbornness.

Tourmaline: Builds self-confidence and concentration. Good for nervousness and sadness. Vitalizes and gives inspiration.

HERBS

There are a number of magick groups that use herbs in their practices. Officers may find herbs at a crime scene or while patting down a subject. Many of these herbs appear at first to be drugs.

Many herbs used in magick have strange-sounding names. Officers finding labeled herbs may see such strange names as dragon's blood or five-finger grass. The following are some of the more popular herbs that may be found among magick groups. Afro-Caribbean groups may use many of the same herbs, but the herbs may have different folk names.

Herbs are believed to emit energies. Each herb has a planet, an element, and sometimes a deity that it corresponds to. They may be charged with energy or blessed by a deity and can be used as sacred incense in rituals. Herbs can also be used to cover candles or be mixed with oils for rituals. Herbs may also be found in satchels or bags, giving the owner specific powers and energies.

In spellwork, herbs may be used as amplifiers to give spells an added kick.

The following are some herbal amulets found in the classic herb manual *Magical Herbalism* by the late neo-Pagan writer Scott Cunningham.

To see ghosts: Carry lavender and inhale its scent.

To allay fears: Carry a mixture of nettle and yarrow.

To detect witches: Carry a sachet of rue, maidenhair, agrimony, broom-straw, and ground ivy.

To be courageous: Wear a fresh borage flower, or carry mullein.

To avoid military service: Wear the four-leafed clover.

To ensure safety and protection on a journey: Comfrey worn or carried will safeguard you.

To prevent storms and wreckage while at sea: Put a clove of garlic in your purse or in your pocket. In the South Pacific or in Hawaii wear a garland of ti leaves.

To guard against rape: Wear the heather to avoid all acts of passion.

To keep one from dreaming: Hang a sprig of lemon verbena around the neck.

To conceive: Wear the mistletoe, the cyclamen, or the bistort.

To prevent weariness while walking: Put mugwort in the shoe.

To keep venomous beasts and wild animals afar: Wear avens or mullein.

To keep others from deceiving you: Wear the pimpernel or snapdragon.

To keep disease afar: Wear a sprig of rue around the neck.

To enable a soldier to escape his enemies: Wear the vervain.

To avoid being sent to the gallows: Wear or carry a carnation.

To ensure victory: Wear woodruff to win.

To ensure that friendly words are spoken to you: Wear the heliotrope.

To enter the underworld: Carry an apple, or the branch of an apple tree that bears buds, flowers, and fully ripened fruit.

To regain lost manhood: Carry an acorn or mandrake root.

To remain youthful: Carry an acorn.

To prevent drunkenness: Wear a chaplet of saffron, crocus, parsley, or rue to prolong your enjoyment.

To see fairies: Gather wild thyme and carry it with you, or put it on the eyelids (with your eyes closed) and sleep on a fairy hill.

To be a successful fisherman: Carry a bit of the hawthorn.

To see a unicorn: As this beast usually lives among the ash trees, carry a bit of the wood or leaves, and you may see one. Or lie down among ashes and place one of its leaves on your chest and wait for one to make itself known.

INCENSE

Officers are normally familiar with incense when dealing with suspects who burn it to cover marijuana scents, but they may find an occultist who uses incense for religious purposes. Incense is used almost universally by magick religions to set a spiritual atmosphere and to call upon various deities and spirits.

Some of the more common corresponding energies associated with incense are:

Blueberry: Burn to keep unwanted influences away from your home and property.

Blue rose: Specially crafted to honor the Goddess in all her aspects. Used in some Wiccan circles.

Carnation: A sweet floral scent traditionally used for healing.

Cherry: Sacred to the planet and deity Venus, this blend will attract and stimulate love.

Cinnamon: Used to gain wealth and success.

Coconut: Burn for protection and purification.

Frangipani: Burn to brighten your home with friendship and love.

Frankincense: Draw upon the energy of the sun to create a sacred space, consecrate objects, and stimulate positive vibrations.

Honeysuckle: Burn for good health, luck, and psychic powers.

Jasmine: For luck in general, especially matters relating to love.

Lotus: For inner peace and outer harmony, to aid in meditation and open the mind's eyes.

Musk: Burn for courage and vitality or to heighten sensual passion.

Myrrh: An ancient incense for protection, healing, purification, and spirituality.

Passion flower: For peace of mind, this sweet scent soothes troubles and aids in sleep.

Patchouli: An earthy scent used in money, luck, and attraction spells.

Pine: Burn for strength and to reverse negative energies.

Rose: For love magick and to return calm

Sandalwood: A delicious all-purpose scent used for healing and protection.

Spice: A fiery scent to be charged for any magick.

Spirit: Raise your personal vibrations, attract spirit guides, and honor your personal deity.

Strawberry: For love, luck, and friendship.

Tangerine: A solar aroma used to attract prosperity.

Temple: A devotional incense used for the altar during rituals.

Vanilla: Stimulates amorous appetites and enhances memory; also a good scent for those nights spent alone with the one you love.

Sage: Used to cleanse, protect from negative energies and negative spirits/entities, and to purify.

Vision spell: Used during meditations, scrying, or any other types of clairvoyant works. Also light it before you go to bed and take in the scent for pleasant dreams.

Dragon's blood: For love, protection, exorcism, potency.

Aloe: For protection and luck.

Apple: Used for love, healing, and garden magick

Angelica: For exorcism, protection, healing, and vision.

Aster: Used for love.

Belladonna: Used for astral projection.

Ginseng: Used for love, wishes, healing, beauty, protection, and lust.

Iris: Used for purification and wisdom.

Lavender: For love, protection, sleep, chastity, and longevity.

Earth: Used to invoke the element of earth.

KABBALAH

Sometimes spelled *quabala* or *kabala,* this is a magickal system used in many groups. The history of the *kabbalah* is disputed among occult scholars. Some claim this system of magick has its origins among the Israelites during their captivity in ancient Babylon. Among several other theories, some believe that it was created in the Jewish ghettos in cities like New York as Judaism met with occultism.

The kabbalah is a process in which the occultist may "climb" steps of magickal theory in order to attain a oneship with God. The beliefs and philosophies surround a diagram known as the tree of life.

Without going into the theology surrounding this process, it is simply important that officers at least be able to recognize the significance of the kabbalah to some occultists. Most occultists who do utilize this process are not involved in criminal activities; however, there have been a number of criminal cases in which the kabbalah was found in a peripheral context.

OILS

Oils are used in occult religions for a number of reasons. The common use of oil is to stimulate the sense of smell. It is also helpful to the occultist to use oil in anointing an object because it helps the practitioner to concentrate and meditate on the type of spell work to be performed. Candles are "dressed" with oils because some believe that the occultist develops a bond with the candle through the anointing process.

The candle is rubbed with the oil that best symbolizes the purpose of the spell being performed. Some seals and charms are anointed with oils to consecrate them to a particular deity or purpose. The object being anointed is doused with the oil, and the occultist moves his or her fingers toward the object, building energy. Sometimes oil is used to anoint a person's body. The oil may be used to consecrate or to bring good energies to the occultist. The spreading of the oil is important: inward spreading is for attracting energies and people, outward spreading is for repelling or sending energies outwardly.

The following are some of the commonly used oils:

Adrel: This oil brings happiness. Use it as a perfume or as an anointing oil.
Against harm: This oil will give you protection from your enemies.
All Saints: This oil assures success in work and endeavors.
Amber: This brings success and good fortune.
Ambrosia: Attracts love.
Anise: Brings peaceful sleep.
Apricot: An aphrodisiac.
Banana: Use this oil to get rid of a situation that is holding you down.
Basil: Put a few drops in the doorway of

your business to bring prosperity.
Bayberry: A money-attracting oil.
Beneficial dream: For a good night's sleep. (If you want to remember your dreams, put this oil on your temples before going to sleep.)
Bergamot: Brings money and success.
Blue cohosh: Eases emotional pain.
Canola: Cleanses your home of negativity if you sprinkle the oil in corners of the house.
Cashew: Helps get rid of stress when rubbed on the throat or wrists.
Cherry blossom: Opens opportunities for you. (When looking for a job, rub this oil on the soles of your feet and behind the ears.)
Cinnamon: An uncrossing oil.
Desire: An aphrodisiac.
Double luck: Gambling. (Rub it on your palms before playing any games of chance.)
Easy: Helps a situation to go smoothly.
Eucalyptus: A healing oil. (Great for headaches and colds.)
Evil eye: Protects you from curses and negative energies sent to you.
Eyebright: Enhances your psychic power.
Fairy: Calls on the aid of a fairy. (Anoint your palms, heart, and the middle of your forehead.)
Fast money: Self-explanatory.
Ginger: This is a good oil to use for workings in rituals or magick.
Goddess: Enhances respect and admiration from others when worn by a woman.
Hazelnut: To gain wisdom, anoint your third eye. This oil is also connected with the deities Diana and Thor.
Heart: Anoint your heart with this oil for your wishes to come true.
Irresistible: Wear this oil to attract the opposite sex.
Isis: Heighten a relationship that is dying or start a new one by wearing this oil. (Isis is the goddess of love in ancient Egypt.)
Jasmine: An all-purpose oil. Use it to bring love, sex, and money.

Job: Wear this oil to get a job or to keep the one you have.

Keep away evil: To keep away enemies and evil spirits.

Lavender: This oil has many uses. You can use it for peace of mind, to promote love, attract men, for purification (when added to your bath), and to sleep well.

Lemon blossom: This is a good oil to find options for tough situations.

Marigold: This is a powerful oil used for protection.

Memory: Anoint your forehead to help remember important information.

Nervous: Use this oil when you are tense and nervous. Add it to your bath water or a white candle.

Notre Dame: Use this oil to keep sickness at bay and protect against evil.

Orris root: This oil is used to attract friendship and money.

Patchouli: This oil is used to attract love and money. It is also used to keep "lurking" people away. It is very powerful in works of magick.

Red thyme: This oil is used to give you courage in any situation.

Rose: To attract love and friendship, anoint yourself or a candle. You may also add this oil to a bath for a good affect.

Sandalwood: This oil is very powerful in magickal workings or rituals. It is a healing oil as well as an oil to heighten your psychic abilities.

Seduction: 'Nuff said.

Ti: This oil works well by sprinkling some under your bed for protection while you sleep.

Vanilla: This oil brings good luck. It is also used to attract love and lust.

Walnut: When put on your forehead, this oil prevents headaches. It also helps to increase mental clarity.

ILLUSTRATED GUIDE TO RITUAL TOOL IDENTIFICATION

*These knives have marks on hilt and blade
that shout magic! High Magic's Aid*
—Gerald Gardner aka Scire

This chapter is an illustrated field guide to commonly used ritual tools and paraphernalia. It is an easy-to-use directory and may be employed in the following manner:

- From the photos, identify as closely as possible the object in question.
- With the descriptive information given, consult the table of contents, which will lead the reader to the related text materials.

As an officer encounters a ritual scene, some questions must be answered:

Is it obvious or highly suspected that a crime has been committed?

If the answer is yes, then the scene is treated as a crime scene with appropriate crime-scene protection, the conducting of lawful searches, and the collection of evidence. Remember to treat the scene and evidence with respect because it may ultimately turn out that there was, in fact, no crime and that a religious site may have been desecrated—with the possibility of a lawsuit.

Has the scene been encountered in an ongoing non-occult-related investigation?

If so, the implements and tools should be evaluat-

ed to determine their connection to a particular group. This connection may be invaluable in furthering the investigation and tracking down a suspect or solving a crime.

Were a ritual site and/or suspicious items reported to law enforcement?

In this circumstance, the items or site should be respectfully inspected. Notes or photos may be taken, but unless there is contraband present or some other evidence of illegal activity, the site or items should remain undisturbed.

Was suspicious or mysterious activity reported to law enforcement?

In this case, the site should be approached with caution, the individuals interviewed, and the site viewed with appropriate respect. If no illegal activity is observed, officers should make a positive contact with the practitioners and leave them to continue their rituals.

The tools pictured and described here are actual tools used by practitioners of magickal belief systems. It should be noted that tools are but symbols and may hold different meanings to different groups and individuals. The meanings given to these tools come from historical documents and informant interviews.

ALTAR

Associated with:
Various
Significance:
The altar is the focal point for ceremonies and spiritual work. It may be found inside a home or outside. The altar is considered the physical world that can affect the spiritual realm.

ALTAR CLOTH

Associated with:
Wicca, Santeria, Voodoo, and Satanism
Significance:
Wicca—An altar cloth may appear above or on the altar. It may be decorated with the pentagram, moons, stars, or other planetary symbols.
Santeria—Cloth may appear on an altar or a shrine in the color of the orisha being honored.
Voodoo—Cloth may appear on altar or a shrine in the color of the loa being honored.
Satanism—Cloth may appear above or on the altar. Cloth may be decorated with an inverted pentagram, Baphomet, inverted cross, or other imagery.

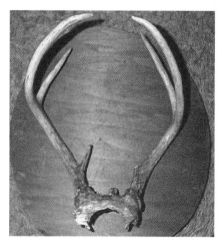

ANTLERS

Associated with:
Wicca and Santeria
Significance:
Wicca—The antlers are used to represent the Horned God.
Santeria—They represent Ochosi, the patron orisha of the hunted.

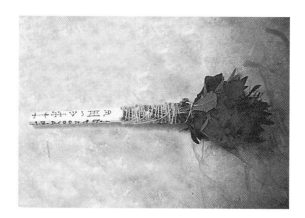

ASPERGER

Associated with:
    Satanism and ceremonial magick
Significance:
    Satanism—Practitioner may use to sprinkle desecrated water before a ritual.
    Ceremonial magick—This sprinkler was created according to the directions in the Goetia. It is also used in the creation of sacred space for rituals.

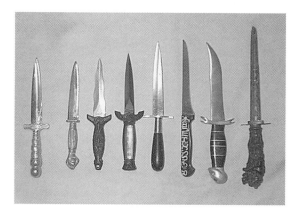

ATHAME

Associated with:
    Wicca and Satanism
Significance:
    Wicca—Practitioner may use an athame to cast a circle to create a sacred space.
    Satanism—Practitioner may use it to cast a circle to create sacred space or may use it to call upon spirits. An athame may be used by Satanists to cut animal or human flesh.

BAPHOMET

Associated with:
    Satanism and ceremonial magick
Significance:
    Satanism—The Baphomet may represent a deity or man.
    Ceremonial magick—Image may represent man or the perfect magician.

BELL

Associated with:
    Various
Significance:
    A bell may be rung to begin a ceremony. Some groups use the bell to clear the energies and spirits from the ritual area. In Afro-Caribbean religions the bell may be used to call or wake deities during rituals or at shrines.

BIBLES, DESECRATED

Associated with:
    Satanism
Significance:
    The Bible of Judeo-Christianity may be torn or spit upon, read backwards, or burned in a ritualistic rejection of the religion.

BLINDFOLD AND SCOURGE

Associated with:
    Wicca
Significance:
    These items are used in initiation ceremonies. The initiate is blindfolded and whipped with the scourge during rituals.

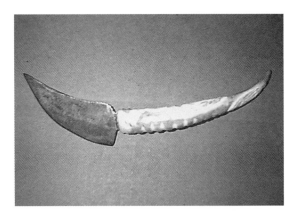

BOLIENE

Associated with:
    Wicca
Significance:
    Used to cut herbs and plants, not animal or human flesh. It is traditionally known as the "white-handled knife."

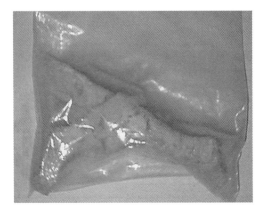

BONES, HUMAN

Associated with:
    Wicca, Satanism, Palo, and Voodoo
Significance:
    Wicca—Rarely found on Wiccan altars, a human bone may symbolize man and ancestor spirits.
    Satanism—Altars may contain human bones to represent man or spirits of the dead.
    Palo—Human bones are used to represent the nkisi, the spirit that lives in the nganga. A bone may also be used as a scepter in rituals.
    Voodoo—Bones may be used to represent ancestors and ground to be used in powders.

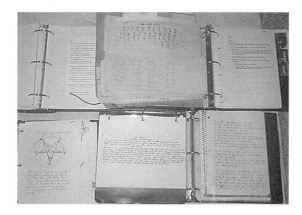

BOOK OF SHADOWS

Associated with:
 Wicca and Satanism
Significance:
 Wicca—The *Book of Shadows* (BOS) is an important tool in traditional Wicca belief. Some traditions use their BOS as a guide to worship. The Gardnerian BOS has been passed on and added to from the leaders of covens to their members. These books contain rituals, ceremonies, and personal insights into the craft.
 Satanism—The *Book of Shadows* in Satanism is usually a diary of occult activities. There is no single BOS for Satanists.

BOTTLE

Associated with:
 Voodoo
Significance:
 The bottle is found on altars to spirits. It contains herbs that will receive energy when it is placed on the altar. Some bottles may be used to give extra power to the altar itself.

CANDLE

Associated with:
 Various
Significance:
 Candles may be used simply to provide light for a ritual. They may serve as objects of spells or propellants of magickal energies to be used in a spell. There are a number of shapes, colors, and types of candles.

CANDLEHOLDER

Associated with:
 Wicca, Satanism, and ceremonial magick.
Significance:
 The candleholder is simply used to hold candles for rituals. This particular holder has several characters written on it to give it power.

CAULDRON

Associated with:
    Wicca, Santeria, Palo, and Satanism
Significance:
    Wicca—The cauldron is used to represent the Great Goddess. It may be used for herbal magick and to hold incense.
    Santeria—The cauldron represents Oggun, the orisha over iron.
    Palo—The cauldron may be used as an nganga.
    Satanism—The cauldron may be used to house herbs and incense.

CENSER (INCENSE BURNER)

Associated with:
Wicca, Satanism, and ceremonial magick
Significance:
    Wicca—The burner is found on the altar. The scent of the incense sets a ritual atmosphere and may also attract energies.
    Satanism—The burner is found on the altar. The scent of the incense sets a ritual atmosphere. The scent attracts demons.
    Ceremonial magick—The burner is used in rituals with hopes that the invoked spirits will appear in the smoke.

CHALICE

Associated with:
    Wicca and Satanism
Significance:
    Wicca—The chalice represents the female element. It is also used to hold water or wine for rituals.
    Satanism—The chalice may be used for holding wine or blood.

TOOLS OF CHANGO

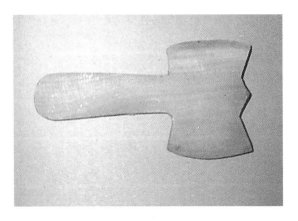

Associated with:
    Santeria
Significance:
    Wooden tools are used to represent Chango, the orisha over justice. This represents his two-sided axe of justice.

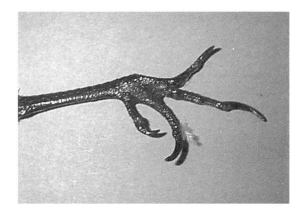

CHICKEN'S FOOT

Associated with:
    Hoodoo
Significance:
    A chicken's foot may be used to represent someone in home-opathic magick. The foot is tied in green thread and is covered with the wax from a green candle. This is used to bring financial success to a person. The foot may also be used to contain energies that can be "scratched" against someone's flesh.

CORD

Associated with:
    Wicca and Satanism
Significance:
    Wicca—Cords are used to hold a robe together or may be used to form a circle on the ground. The color of the cord may represent a degree in the coven. Cords may be used to bind members in initiations or ceremonies such as handfastings.
    Satanism—Cords may be used to hold robes together. Some groups measure the cord by the height of the member.

COWRIE SHELLS

Associated with:
    Santeria
Significance:
    These shells are used in divination. Each sopera (tureen) may have cowrie shells inside of it. The shells may be fed animal blood.

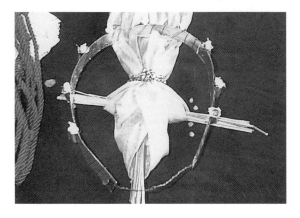

CROWN OF LIGHTS

Associated with:
    Wicca
Significance:
    May be worn during ritual celebration of Imbolc by a member representing the mother aspect of the Great Goddess.

DOLL

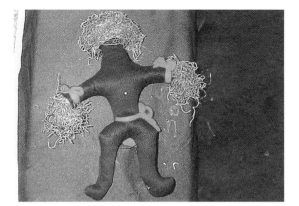

Associated with:
Various
Significance:
The doll is used in homeopathic magick. It may used to heal, bind, or curse someone. Dolls come in various sizes and can be made from various materials. They may have the name of the intended subject of the magick written on or in them.

DRUMS

Associated with:
Various
Significance:
Drums are used as tools in building power and energy. They can assist in producing the state of ecstasy. Drums can also assist in summoning down the gods of Voudon religions.

ELEKE/COLLARES

Associated with:
Santeria
Significance:
The beaded necklaces are used to identify members in the religion as well as giving the protection of the orishas that they represent. Each necklace represents a different orisha according to color and number of beads.

EL NEGRO JOSÉ

Associated with:
Santeria
Significance:
El Negro José is a statue that acts as a doorway between the orishas and the physical world. José is also the embodiment of all the spirits of the Africans who were brought over with slavery. He may be called upon to be a mediator between believers who are having a dispute.

EXU STATUE

Associated with:
Afro-Caribbean groups

Significance:
Exu is the trickster deity in many Voudon religions. He is represented by an image of the Judeo-Christian devil. He may be found with a female counterpart called the Pomba Gira, the devil woman.

FLAG

Associated with:
Voodoo

Significance:
The flag is used to represent the loa of Voodoo. The flag may hang above an altar, or it may be waved at the beginning of a ceremony.

HAMMER

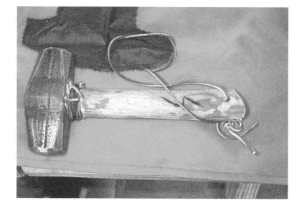

Associated with:
Neo-Pagan and Asatru

Significance:
Neo-Pagan—May be used like the athame to call the watchtowers.

Asatru and Norse religions—May represent the deity Thor and his hammer.

IRUKE

Associated with:
Santeria and Candomble

Significance:
This horsetail may be found on the shrine of a particular orisha/orixa. The iruke may be held by a priest or priestess during ceremonies.

MORTAR AND PESTLE

Associated with:
  Various
Significance:
  In most cases the mortar and pestle are used to grind herbs and powders in herbal magick. The exception is that in Santeria the tool is used to represent Chango, the orisha over thunder and magick.

OLOKUN

Associated with:
  Santeria
Significance:
  This small icon is used to represent the orisha Olokun, who is Yemaya at the bottom of the waters. She is usually found in her shrine or in her sopera.

PENTACLE

Associated with:
  Wicca
Significance:
  A pentacle may be wooden, glass, or stone. The pentacle is on the altar to represent spirit. The circle around it represents the universe. Tools may be placed on the pentacle to charge them with energy.

RATTLE/MARACA

Associated with:
  Neo-Pagan and Afro-Caribbean groups
Significance:
  Neo-Pagan—The rattle may be used to build energy by shaking it. It may also be used to build trance states.
  Afro-Caribbean—The maraca is used to call upon deities in various Voudon religions. This instrument, in Voodoo, is said to mimic the sound of Damballah, the serpent loa. Some maracas may be covered in beadwork or snake vertebrae.

ROBE

Associated with:
 Wicca and Satanism
Significance:
 Wicca—The robe may be worn during rituals. It may be decorated with planetary symbols, the pentagram, moons, or personal symbols.
 Satanism—The robe may be worn during rituals. It may be decorated with planetary symbols, the inverted pentagram, or personal symbols.

RUNES

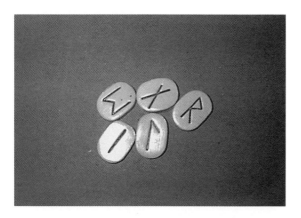

Associated with:
 Wicca, Satanism, and Asatru
Significance:
 Runes may be found made from wood, stone, or plastic. They may be found in a bag or a bowl on an altar. The runes are not necessarily used in a ritual, but may be used to perform divination.

SAINTS

Associated with:
 Santeria, Palo, and Voodoo
Significance:
 Saint statues are found in the altars and shrines of Voudon religions. These are icons that secretly represent the orishas, the mfumbe, and the loa of these religions.

SALT AND WATER

Associated with:
 Various
Significance:
 Salt and water are two common elements used in a variety of magickal traditions. Salt is typically used to represent the element of Earth and may be used to cleanse an area. Some ceremonial magick groups believe that salt can protect you from demons and spirits. Water is also used to cleanse an area.

SKULL, ANIMAL

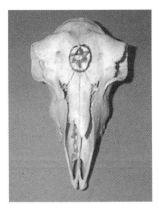

Associated with:
   Various
Significance:
   Animal skulls are used to represent various belief aspects. Some groups use them to denote death or a spirit. Some groups use them to represent a focal point for energy during a ritual.

SKULL, HUMAN

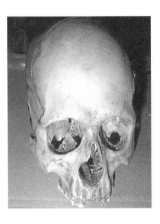

Associated with:
   Satanism, Palo, and Voodoo
Significance:
   Satanism—The skull represents man as the carnal being. The skull may be found on an altar to represent man or may be used as a chalice.
   Palo—The skull is used in the cauldron known as the nganga. The skull is known as kiyumba, or the dead.
   Voodoo—The skull is used to represent the family of spirits known as the gede that rule the dead.

SMUDGE

Associated with:
   Wicca
Significance:
   Smudge may at first appear to be contraband. Smudge is burned to cleanse areas of energies and may be rubbed onto the skin in some rituals.

SOPERA

Associated with:
   Santeria
Significance:
   This pot may be made of ceramic or wood. It contains implements that represent a particular orisha and may be fed animal blood or foods for the orisha. The insides of these pots are not to be seen by the uninitiated.

STAFF

Associated with:
Wicca, Satanism, Santeria, and Palo

Significance:
Wicca—The staff is used to create sacred space for a ritual. It may also be used to direct energy. The staff may be used to bang on the ground to build energy.

Satanism—The staff is used to create sacred space for rituals or to direct energy.

Santeria—The staff may be used as a palo to call the Eggun, the dead.

Palo—The staff may be used as the palo de muerto, the stick of the dead.

SWORD

Associated with:
Wicca, Satanism, and Voodoo

Significance:
Wicca—Used to cast a circle or to create sacred space.

Satanism—Used to cast a circle, create a sacred space, or to call upon spirits.

Voodoo—Used to represent Ogou, the loa over iron. May be used in an entrance ceremony in the temple (houmphor).

TAROT CARDS

Associated with:
Various

Significance:
Most individuals or groups that use Tarot do not use them in a religious ceremonial context. Those involved in Brujeria may use them in ceremonies.

TRIANGLE

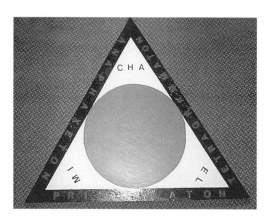

Associated with:
Ceremonial magick and Satanism

Significance:
The triangle is used in spirit invocation. The three sides represent the trinity of Christianity. The spirit or demon called upon may appear inside the triangle. The triangle may be found outside a magickal circle. Some rites have the practitioner stand inside the triangle for protection.

VEIL

Associated with:
Wicca

Significance:
The veil is used to cover the face of the high priestess during the ceremony Drawing Down the Moon.

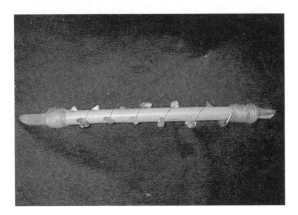

WAND

Associated with:
Wicca and Satanism

Significance:
The wand is used to create a sacred space for rituals and to call upon spirits; it may symbolize the male element.

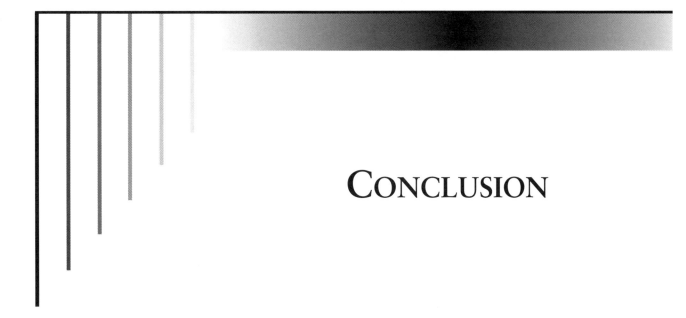

CONCLUSION

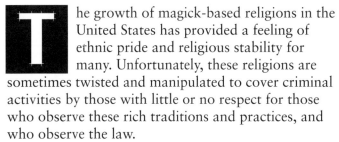

The growth of magick-based religions in the United States has provided a feeling of ethnic pride and religious stability for many. Unfortunately, these religions are sometimes twisted and manipulated to cover criminal activities by those with little or no respect for those who observe these rich traditions and practices, and who observe the law.

Law enforcement officials must continue to walk a thin line between proper respect and the protection of the constitutional right to worship and the ability to investigate groups whose activities may harm others. Officers have the responsibility to protect and serve all groups, even those that may appear strange or deviant. An officer's understanding of the worldview of these groups and individuals will greatly increase communication between cultures and assist overall in the proper detection of criminal groups.

However, it is also the responsibility of noncriminal citizens who follow their spiritual paths to cooperate with law enforcement in exposing those who misuse their belief systems and give entire communities a bad name. This cooperation need not compromise sacred traditions and religious mysteries but should assist in building a bridge of understanding between these two worlds.

In my researches I have found most members of magick-based belief systems to be noncriminal, nonviolent, and very intelligent. Unfortunately, I have also found a growing undercurrent of rage and violence that permeates those who have become fascinated with the darker religions, such as Satanism. Recently, I was given information about a criminal conviction of a man who had sexually abused his stepdaughter for two years. The sexual abuse by the "black magician" took place in a ritual context; there were others present during these rites, and the perpetrator was identified by a tattoo of a dragon on his penis.

We may wonder why individuals like this exist. An officer once told me, "Sometimes people are just mean for no reason." This may very well be true. However, criminal profilers have shown us that at the core of all violent criminals there lies a reason for their madness.

Consider the following ramblings from a member of a deviant sexual cult.

The hardest thing for me is childhood. …
I still cry. …
For example … I played my piano to escape my life
at home … I could, would and did play any song! …
This is how I found out GOD isn't real! …
Bastard raper and mother killer never would take a bath
so I could … whoopsie … toss in a radio!!!!! I prayed and
prayed to god for this prick to take a bath just once. …
Never happened!
Fuck life! My fucking piano still sits in the same place as I
left it … An old upright, though hand carved …
This mafia second husband of my mommy, nary the bath
would the bastard ever take! I hate him, yet I will have his soul!
Hail Satan! I found the way to get even! … His soul is mine!
Yet the impact of these severe things. … Things no child should
have to endure. … Prick, bastard tried to kill the demon boy at
the age of 9! … Fuck this man! I hate him … Bastard Italian,
dares to thrust the knife in the true one of Satan? Wrong!
Enjoy your disabled arm. … Oooooh, I hate this man!
Killer of my mom, the one who raped my sister and he who
shoved that fat italian dick in my boy face. … I hate you!
Mere painful seed of a lame man who in fact killed my mom. …
I will have this bastard's soul … plan on it!!!!!
Hail Satan!

BIBLIOGRAPHY

Adler, Margot. *Drawing Down the Moon*. Penguin Press, 1997.

Baddeley, Gavin. *Lucifer Rising*. Plexus Publishing, 1999.

Barton, Blanche. *The Church of Satan*. Hell's Kitchen Press, 1990.

Black, S. Jason, and Christopher Hyatt. *Pacts with the Devil*. New Falcon Publications, 1993.

Blood, Linda. *The New Satanists*. Warner Publications, 1994.

Bolayiidowu, E. Olodumare, *God in Yoruba Belief*. A&B Book Publishers, 1994.

Brandon, George. *Santeria from Africa to the New World, The Dead Sell Memories*. Indiana University Press, 1993.

Bramly, George. *Macumba*. City Lights Books, 1994.

Buckland, Raymond. *Buckland's Complete Book of Witchcraft*. Llewellyn Publishing, 1990.

_____. *Witchcraft from the Inside*. Llewellyn Publishing, 1975.

Bushart, Howard. *Soldiers of God: White Supremacists and their Holy War for America*. Pinnacle Books, 1998.

Campanelli, Dan, and Pauline Campanelli. *Circles, Groves and Sanctuaries*. Llewellyn Publishing, 1993.

Cabrera, Lydia. *El Monte*. Ediciones Universal, 1971.

Canizares, Raul. *Walking with the Night*. Inner Traditions, 1999.

Cavendish, Richard. *The Black Arts*. Capricorn Books, 1968.

Church of All Worlds, Witchcraft, Satanism and Occult Crime: Who's Who and What's What, a Manual of Reference Materials for the Professional Investigator. Phoenix Publishing, 1994.

Conway, Deanna J. *Norse Magic*. Llewellyn Publishing, 1990.

Crowley, Aleister. *Magick in Theory and Practice*. Dover Press, 1929.

Cuhulain, Kerr. *Law Enforcement Guide to Wicca*. Horned Owl Publishing, 1997.

Cunningham, Scott. *Wicca: A Guide for the Solitary Practitioner*. Llewellyn Publishing, 1990.

Deren, Maya. *Divine Horsemen: Voodoo Gods of Haiti*. Mystic Fire Video, 1953.

Dow, Carol. *Sarava: Afro-Brazillian Magick*. Llewellyn Publishing, 1998.

Elkana, Nathan. *The Master Grimoire of Magickal Rites and Ceremonies*. Finbarr Books, 1982.

Enroth, Ronald. *Churches that Abuse*. Zondervan Publishing, 1992.

Farrar, Janet and Stewart Farrar. *Eight Sabbats for Witches*. Hale Press, 1981.

_____. *A Witches Bible*. Phoenix Publishing, 1996.

Fitch, Ed. *Magical Rites from the Crystal Well*. Llewellyn Publishing, 1984.

Frazer, James George. *The Golden Bough*. Macmillan Company, 1963.

Gardner, Gerald. *High Magic's Aide*. Godolphin House, 1996.

Grimassi, Raven. *The Wiccan Mysteries*. Llewellyn Publishing, 1997.

_____. *Hereditary Witchcraft*. Llewellyn Publishing, 1999.

Haskins, Jim. *Voodoo and Hoodoo*. Scarborough House, 1978.

Hassan, Steve. *Combating Cult Mind Control*. Inner Traditions, 1990.

Humes, Edward. *Buried Secrets*. Dutton Publishing, 1991.

Hurbon, Laennec. *Voodoo: Search for the Spirit*. Harry Abrams, 1995.

Huson, Paul. *Mastering Witchcraft*. Berkley Windhover, 1970.

K., Amber. *True Magick*. Llewellyn Publishing, 1991.

Kahaner, Larry. *Cults that Kill*. Warner Books, 1988.

Lanning, Kenneth V. "Satanic, Occult, Ritualistic Crime: A Law Enforcement Perspective." *Police Chief Magazine*, 1989.

LaVey, Anton. *Satanic Bible*. Avon, 1969.

_____. *The Satanic Rituals*. Avon, 1972.

_____. *The Compleat Witch*. Dodd, Mead, 1971.

Levi, Eliphias. *Transcendental Magic*. Bracken Books, 1995.

Lifton, Robert J. "Thought Reform and the Psychology of Totalism." *Harvard Mental Health Letter* 7:8 (February 1981).

Martinez, Rafael. "Brujeria: Manifestations of Palo Mayombe in South Florida." *Journal of the Florida Medical Association*, 1983.

Martinez, Rafael. "Santeria: A Magico-Religious System of Afro-Cuban Origin." *American Journal of Social Psychiatry*, 1982.

Mather, George. *Dictionary of Cults, Religions and the Occult*. Zondervan Publishing House, 1993.

Mathers, S. Lidell MacGregor. *The Key of Solomon the King*. Samuel Weiser, 1974.

Mercer, Mick. *Hex Files: The Goth Bible*. Penguin USA, 1997.

Metraux, Alfred. *Voodoo in Haiti*. Schocken, 1972.

Montenegro, Carlos. *Palero*. Havana Publications, 1998.

Murphy, Joseph M. *Santeria: An African Religion in America*. Boston Press, 1988.

Ortiz, Fernando. *Los Negros Brujos*. Ediciones Universal, 1906.

Pardon, Robert. *Messianic Communities: Journey from Orthodoxy to Heresy*. NEIRR, 1997.

Peña, Ysamur Flores. *Santeria Garments and Altars: Speaking without a Voice*. University Press of Mississippi, 1994.

Pinckney, Roger. *Blue Roots: African American Folk Magic of the Gullah People*. Llewellyn Publications, 1999.

Ramsland, Katherine. *Piercing the Darkness: Undercover with Vampires in America Today*. Harper/Prism, 1998.

Raschke, Carl. *Painted Black*. Harper and Row, 1990.

Ravenwolf, Silver. *Teen Witch*. Llewellyn Publications, 1998.

Regardie, Israel. *The Golden Dawn*. Llewellyn Publications, 1989.

Rigaud, Milo. *Secrets of Voodoo*. 1953.

Rudgley, Richard. *The Encyclopedia of Psychoactive Substances*. St. Martin's Press, 1999.

Shah, Idries. *The Secret Lore of Magic*. Redwood Burn Limited, 1957.

Simon, Ed. *Necronomicon*. Avon, 1977.

St. Clair, David. *Drum and Candle*. Out of print.

Starhawk. *Spiral Dance*. Harper, 1999.

Swanson, Charles. *Criminal Investigation*. McGrawHill, 1992.

Terry, Maury. *The Ultimate Evil*. Doubleday, 1987.

U.S. Department of Justice. *Crime Scene Investigations: A Guide for Law Enforcement*. Technical Working Group of Crime Scene Investigators, 2000.

Valiente, Doreen. *An ABC of Witchcraft*. Bookpeople, 1988.

Waite, Arthur. *The Book of Ceremonial Magic*. Citadel Press, 1990.

Wippler, Migene Gonzalez. *The Santeria Experience*. Original Publications, 1978.

_____. *Santeria: African Magic in Latin America*. Original Publications, 1981.

_____. *The Seashells*. Original Publications, 1985.

_____. *Santeria: the Religion*. Original Publications, 1994.

ABOUT
THE AUTHOR

Tony M. Kail is director of the Center for the Study of Deviant Movements, a resource center for law enforcement agencies that assists with the problem of investigating cults, sects, and deviant movements. He has conducted ethnographic research with magico-religious groups for 13 years.

Kail has traveled the United States investigating the phenomenon of crimes related to deviant magico-religious groups. He has observed actual ceremonies and rites of passage of several groups and has conducted interviews with members and clergy of these belief systems.

As a former deputy and animal cruelty investigator, Kail has provided training for regional, state, and federal agencies, including the Federal Bureau of Investigation. Kail serves as adjunct instructor for the Police Sciences Division of Nashville State Technical College.